# Triumph and BSA Triples

# TRIUMPH and BSA TRIPLES

*Mick Duckworth*

The Crowood Press

MOTORSPORT
31757 HONEY LOCUST RD.
JONESBURG, MO 63351
636-488-3113

First published in 1997 by
The Crowood Press Ltd
Ramsbury, Marlborough
Wiltshire SN8 2HR

© Mick Duckworth 1997

**British Library Cataloguing in Publication Data**

A catalogue record for this book is available from the British Library.

ISBN 1 86126 018 0

**Picture Credits**

Illustrations supplied by Alistair Cave, Alan and Ron Barrett, Bill Crosby, Daytona Speedway, Mike Jackson, Bob Heath, Mick Hemmings, Norman Hyde, Alan Killip, Bill Milburn, John Nelson, Domenico Pettinari, Quaife Engineering, Steve Rothera, Stan Shenton, Triumph Motorcycles Ltd, Craig Vetter, Mick Walker, Jack Wilson, Les Williams. Copyright photographs by Jim Davies, Mick Duckworth, Jim Greening, Jon Gola, Ernst Leverkus, Syd Lucas, Dan Mahoney, Gordon Menzie, Mick Nicholls, Reeve Photography, Alain Rouge, Bill Bennett and Jim English.

Triumph Motorcycles Ltd has given permission for use of its trademarks, but bears no responsibility for the contents of this book, having had no part in its origination or preparation.

Typeset by Annette Findlay/Image Engineers
Printed and bound in Great Britain by The Bath Press

# Contents

# Acknowledgements

In researching material for this book I endeavoured wherever possible to talk to, or correspond directly with, those people who have been most closely involved with BSA and Triumph triples. So it follows that thanks are due to everyone who is quoted in the text for assisting me in my task.

Everyone was obliging, but some people gave more hours of their precious time than I had a right to expect. I am especially grateful to Don Brown, Alistair Cave, Bill Crosby, Don Emde, Trevor Gleadall, Doug Hele, Bill Milburn, John Nelson, Phil Pick, Stan Shenton and Les Williams.

Particular mention needs to be made of Jim Greening, a popular motorcycling photographer and writer who had a keen interest in the racing triples from the beginning. Jim had promised to provide photographs for the book when he died suddenly in January 1996. Many thanks to his brother George Greening for allowing many of Jim's photos to appear.

Thanks to the Trident & Rocket 3 Owners Club, especially club archivist Richard Darby, for assistance throughout the project and Robert Iannucci of Team Obsolete for information on ex-factory machines.

I am deeply grateful to two friends, American book author Lindsay Brooke, whose generosity and support were absolutely invaluable and English colleague Peter Watson, who, after failing to talk me out of the whole thing over a beer, subsequently offered valued encouragement.

Ostensibly a development and competition history of the Triumph Trident and BSA Rocket 3, this book also provides evidence that the British motorcycle industry did not topple and fall for lack of creativity, drive and enthusiasm at factory floor level. I hope you enjoy reading it.

# Foreword

In my role with Triumph at the Meriden factory, and later with Norton Villiers Triumph at Kitts Green in Birmingham, I was deeply involved with the development of the three-cylinder BSAs and Triumphs that Bert Hopwood and I had dreamed up in the early sixties as a fresh departure for the British motorcycle industry, then dominated by twin-cylinder designs. Mick Duckworth's book is much more than a mere list of those developments. He has interviewed almost everyone who made a contribution to the success of these fine machines. A journalist who has spent many years familiarizing himself with the British motorcycle industry, the people who worked in it and the products they made, Mick has first-hand knowledge of many of the events he describes. Born in the Isle of Man, he watched TT racing from the age of six, often in the company of his father, a special constable officiating at the event. I have been interviewed on several occasions by Mick and so I can appreciate the depth of engineering and historical detail that characterizes his work. I will be delighted to own a book that so comprehensively sums up all aspects of the story of BSA and Triumph's triples.

Doug Hele
*Chief development engineer at Triumph Engineering, the BSA Group Motorcycle Division and NVT International 1963–75*

# Introduction

Three-cylinder four-stroke motorcycle engines have a distinctive exhaust note. More musical than the coarse grunt of a twin, the sound is gruffer and more textured than the high-pitched shriek of a four. The growl of the three-cylinder 750cc BSA Rocket 3 and Triumph Trident has always made them attractive to the motorcyclist for whom a robust exhaust note conjures up ideas of effortless power and arm-tugging acceleration.

The sound of the British triples was at its most glorious when BSA and Triumph launched into international road racing in 1970. The bellow from the works racers' open megaphone exhausts had a special haunting quality, especially when a racing triple could be heard being taken to peak revs through the gears on fast sections of the Isle of Man TT Course, or screaming along the Daytona Speedway bankings at 165mph (265km/h).

For many, the sound was all the more evocative because the factory racing triples represented a glorious final stand against the world's best by the old British motorcycle industry. When the howl of the triples died away, it was replaced by the abrasive whine of Japanese two-stroke engines.

The classic BSA and Triumph triples were manufactured from 1968 to 1975. Even the most ardent admirers of the production models will admit that it was racing success that elevated these motorcycles to legendary status. The Rocket 3 and Trident roadsters broke new ground in 1968, with their shattering tyre-burning performance, mighty torque and reassuring flexibility. After the ubiquitous large-capacity twin-cylinder machines that went before, the triples felt effortlessly smooth. The seventies were to be the decade of the Superbike, and the BSA and Triumph threes can claim to have been the first of this new refined and powerful breed.

But they were not the bestsellers that their maker, the BSA Motorcycle Division had hoped – indeed prayed – that they might be. The Rocket 3 and Trident fell down on three main counts in the marketplace. The original versions were not styled attractively enough to catch the eye of the sporting motorcyclist of the late sixties, especially in the vital North American market. Some ran into unnecessary mechanical teething troubles, symptomatic of a lack of investment and poor management at the companies that produced them. And finally, they were trumped by the Japanese Honda company, when it announced its first Superbike, a 750cc luxury machine with four cylinders and electric starting, very soon after the British triples' launch.

Yet the road machines were anything but a failure, as anyone who has ridden a well-maintained example will know. When set up correctly the powerful 750cc air-cooled three-cylinder engine has a unique character. And some of the original's minor defects such as lack of cornering clearance and weak brakes can be overcome, as they were in the factories' later versions. Even when silenced, that sound is still captivating.

When BSA and Triumph started tooling up to make three-cylinder machines, the two companies belonged to a group that was riding high on export success. By the time the last classic triple rolled off the line, the British motorcycle industry was in ruins. It's a fascinating story, which unfolds in the chapters that follow.

# 1 Two Great Names

## BSA

Although BSA and Triumph were amalgamated under the same corporate umbrella from 1952, little evidence of this was apparent to the motorcycle buying public through the fifties and sixties, or indeed to staff in the companies' factories and overseas bases. The products of the two marques were quite distinct from each other in style, and their riders were often fiercely partisan in their loyalty to their chosen brand. BSA and Triumph were regarded as rivals.

The origins of the Birmingham Small Arms Co. Ltd stretch back to the nineteenth century. Then, as its name suggests, the company was predominantly engaged in gun manufacture at a factory opened in the Small Heath area of Birmingham in 1866. The first motorcycles made at the expanded works at Armoury Road, Small Heath, went into production in 1911, and by the 1920s BSA was a leader among the world's two-wheeler manufacturers. 'Beesa' motorcycles soon gained a reputation for no-nonsense practicality and value for money.

Following the Second World War, when BSA supplied hundreds of thousands of its rugged 500cc M20 side-valve singles to the armed forces, the enlarged factory busied itself making a wide range of utility and sports motorcycles. They ranged from small motors for powering pedal cycles to large-capacity machines sold in direct competition with the products of Britain's other major makers, including Triumph.

*Aerial view of the BSA works at Armoury Road, Small Heath, Birmingham. Most of the motorcycle assembly process was concentrated in the three blocks in the foreground. Even in the 1960s, this area was called the 'new building', despite having been built in 1916 and rebuilt after a direct hit by bombing in World War II.*

Exports were vital to Britain's manufacturing industry in the austere forties, and BSA took its overseas markets seriously. There it found a ready market for rugged economy mounts in developing countries, and a healthy demand for high-performance machinery from more affluent nations, including Australia, New Zealand and the United States. In 1948, BSA's output was 55,000 machines per year.

In the fifties, Small Heath had the sports machine market covered by both single- and twin-cylinder models. BSA's 350cc and 500cc ohv Gold Star singles were only available in relatively tiny numbers but they excelled in promoting the company name in competitive events from road racing to trials. More comfortable and practical for long-distance riders were twin-cylinder BSAs in the form of the 500cc A7 and its 650cc A10 derivatives. They were strong sellers both at home and in vital export markets.

While typical motorcycle factories were basically engineering and assembly plants, sourcing many materials and services from outside contractors, BSA was an industrial conglomerate with huge resources. Among the many subsidiaries it had acquired were car makers, including the Daimler limousine company, a specialist steels maker and several machine tool specialists. The expertise in metals technology at Armoury Road was respected throughout Britain's engineering industry, and a large proportion of the typical BSA motorcycle, including its drive chain, was made in-house.

The company's sturdy ohv A10 Super Rocket of the late fifties was one of the most desirable motorcycles of its time. Brisk acceleration with a top speed of 108mph (174km/h) was accompanied by engine flexibility, while BSA's duplex tubular frame with swinging arm rear suspension made it a fine roadholder.

But from the mid-fifties, there were growing problems for the once-mighty manufacturer. There were several misguided attempts to stave off foreign competition in the lightweight motorcycle and scooter markets, but despite the outlay on several projects, including the disastrous Beeza scooter of 1955, little of any serious commercial use had resulted.

Modernized 500 and 650cc twins were launched for 1962, their most obvious new feature being unit-construction of the engine and gearboxes, enveloping the lower part of their power units in common castings. Somehow, though, the A50 and A65 twins seemed to lack the rugged magic of their predecessors. Their bulbous styling was not universally appreciated, and minor contact-breaker ignition faults on early models were particularly harmful to the company's image in the USA.

Nevertheless, BSA retained a huge following in the States, and the challenge facing Small Heath in the mid-sixties was to produce a new flagship for its range with more power, better equipment and sharper styling.

# TRIUMPH

The Triumph name first appeared on a motorcycle in 1902. Products of the Triumph Cycle Co. of Coventry, founded by German immigrant Siegfried Bettman, gained an enviable reputation for exceptional reliability, especially when 30,000 single-cylinder machines of 500cc were supplied for service in the First World War. By the mid-twenties, Triumph's mass-produced Model P had become a byword for dependability, but car production took priority in 1935 when a new plant was set up and the company proposed to cease two-wheeler manufacture.

However, entrepreneur Jack Sangster, who had already saved the Ariel motorcycle factory, moved in to create the Triumph Engineering Company and continue motor-

*Production racing helped sales in the sixties. Here John Cooper competes at Brands Hatch on a 650cc BSA Spitfire Mk II twin in 1966.*

cycle production in Coventry. Edward Turner was installed as chief designer, and when his 500cc Speed Twin appeared in 1937 its twin-cylinder engine changed the course of motorcycling history, forming the basis of the marque's most popular products for half a century. Indeed, other British makers rushed to make twins with a similar 360-degree crankshaft layout as soon as the Second World War was over.

Triumph Engineering's Priory Street factory was badly damaged by bombing in the war, but the company was able to acquire an all-new plant on the main Coventry to Birmingham road, between Allesley and the village of Meriden.

In the early fifties, Triumph set an example to Britain's other makers in producing sleek and stylish machines with 100mph-plus (160km/h+) performance. Turner, who spent a portion of every year in the USA, prudently focused on the potentially huge American market.

In 1951, the Baltimore (Maryland)-based Triumph Corporation was created as a Meriden-owned distribution headquarters to serve the eastern and central states. An independent company, Johnson Motors of Pasadena, southern California, which had sold Triumphs since the thirties, continued as the West Coast agent.

British motorcyclists were still buying two-wheelers as a cheap way of commuting to work, but in the USA the accent was on the recreational aspect of riding. And, following the pattern set by North America's last surviving volume manufacturer, Harley-Davidson, Stateside buyers expected motorcycles to have engines of a larger cubic capacity than the 500cc size regarded as sufficient for a sports solo in Europe.

Meriden responded with the speedy 650cc Thunderbird of 1949, followed by the Tiger 110 with swinging arm rear suspension for 1954. These twins were not only exciting in their performance, but their sleek cosmetic styling by Turner and his assistant, Jack

# Edward Turner – three's a crowd

Edward Turner took no positive role in the creation of the 750cc triple. He dismissed the idea of a three-cylinder engine as 'potty' when it was mooted by his general manager Bert Hopwood, and it was not until the mercurial Turner had retired from the post of managing director of the BSA Group's motorcycle division in 1964 that the project really took off.

Turner does merit a role in this story, though, because the P1 triple prototype was based heavily on his immensely successful parallel twin layout, which had shaken the motorcycling world in the form of the 1937 Triumph Speed Twin. Also, Turner did much to build the Triumph name in the USA, and it was the continuing success of his enduring twin design that earned profits through the mid-sixties, enabling the triples' development costs to be met.

Turner designed his first four-cylinder motorcycle engine for Ariel in 1929, a project on which Hopwood had worked too, before moving to Triumph. After his retirement from the firm, according to *Triumph in America* by Lindsay Brooke and David Gaylin, he planned to build and market a four in America, but the planned machine never materialized.

naming its long awaited twin-carburettor 650cc model the Bonneville on its launch in 1959. Along with Triumph's other twins, the Bonneville was redesigned with unit-construction for 1963, and the 110mph (177km/h) machine enjoyed huge export sales success in the following years.

America would buy as many twins as Meriden could make. Full order books meant that the factory was fully stretched with plenty of job opportunities and highly competitive shop floor wages. To some extent, however, the high demand meant that the extremely high standards of the early fifties had to be sacrificed in the cause of productivity.

By the early sixties both BSA and Triumph's big twins were reaching the limit of development. Engine tuning to achieve greater power output had made them rougher to ride, less reliable and mechanically noisier. They were in danger of being

Wickes, made them stand out. Triumph became a predominant brand on the US market, making Harley's product look overweight, bulky and sluggish.

A Triumph-powered streamlined machine piloted by Johnny Allen set a new US motorcycle land speed record of 214mph (344km/h) at Bonneville Salt Flats in 1956. This achievement by a machine with a single unsupercharged T110 engine helped emphasize Triumph's speedy image. The company was able to exploit the publicity by

*Triumph in American sport: Bob Sholley slides a 650cc twin on a Maryland short-track in 1965.*

*Bill Johnson's 650cc T120-powered streamliner at Bonneville salt flats in 1962. His FIM world record of 224.57mph (361.33km/h) was a boost for Triumph's speedy image.*

outpaced and made to look archaic by sophisticated new products from Japan, where an enormous investment was being made in up-to-date manufacturing plants.

Although the 360-degree twin engine had been a mainstay of most British factories since the Second World War, the layout had reached its development limits. This type of engine, in which the pistons rise and fall together and the cylinders fire alternately, suffers from an inherent lack of balance, inevitably resulting in vibration.

On the earlier 90mph (145km/h) 500s some shakes had been acceptable, since the twins were still smoother and more refined than the typical high-performance single. But as capacity was increased, and engines were tweaked for higher output, the problem became more noticeable. And, as well as being uncomfortable and annoying for riders, the tremors and tingles took their toll on reliability. They caused loosening of fasten-

ers, fracturing of cycle parts and shortened the life of electrical components such as bulbs and rectifiers. Another weakness limiting development of twins with crankshafts held in only two bearings was the tendency for the shaft to flex and behave like a skipping-rope at high revs.

Triumph's brief from its influential American departments was to supersede the Bonneville with something even more exciting to see the company into the seventies – something with a capacity of 750cc and a top speed of 120mph (193km/h).

## TRIPLE THINK

The first sketches for a Triumph three-cylinder engine were made on a drawing board in the Experimental Department office at Meriden early in 1963. Development engineers Doug Hele and Bert Hopwood had

# Bert Hopwood – down-to-earth designer

It was Herbert Hopwood who persuaded a sceptical BSA Group management to back the 750cc triple concept.

Hopwood's nomadic progress around the British motorcycle industry meant that prior to the creation of the triples, he had a hand in many of the best known designs: BSA's Golden Flash and Gold Star, Norton's Dominator, Jubilee and Navigator, and Triumph's Bonneville.

Hopwood was born in Birmingham in 1908, and his industry career began at Ariel in the late twenties, under Chief Designer Edward Turner. When Turner became established at Triumph Engineering in 1935, Hopwood joined him there. After some years with the tempestuous Turner, whom he found difficult to work with, Hopwood escaped to Norton in 1947 to create the Dominator, with an ohv twin cylinder engine that the marque would still rely on twenty-five years later.

By the time the Dommie was launched, Hopwood had changed horses again, joining BSA. He became Chief Engineer and redesigned Small Heath's parallel twin in six months. Despite this haste, the 650cc Golden Flash proved to be a sturdy all-rounder.

Before leaving BSA in 1955, Hopwood had designed the Dandy, a 70cc two-speed step-through utility bike. The design was spoiled, according to Hopwood, by BSA's ineptitude, but when Honda launched its phenomenally successful Cub step-through years later, it looked remarkably similar to the Dandy.

Hopwood rejoined Norton in 1952, by which time the marque been absorbed by the Associated Motor Cycles combine. Seeing the need to widen the Norton range, he was responsible for the creation of the short-stroke 250cc Jubilee twin, and the 350cc Navigator version. He subsequently distanced himself from these models, saying that company policy had forced him to alter original designs.

Hopwood investigated four-cylinder power for road and racing Nortons, but was put off by the excessive width that a transverse engine would entail.

In 1961, unhappy with Norton's AMC parent board, Hopwood returned to Triumph to work with Turner again.

His priority was the redesign of Triumph's 650cc twins with unit-construction of the engine and gearbox. Hopwood is on record as saying that he would like to have taken the opportunity to revise the twin's lubrication system, but Turner would not allow this.

A prototype ohc 650 twin engine was built, but rejected as not being sufficiently better than the ohv design to justify its extra cost.

After seeing the three-cylinder project through, Hopwood concentrated on his vision for the seventies, a series of modular designs. He had long been a proponent of modular production, using as many common components as possible between machines of differing capacity and configuration. Manufacturing costs would thus be minimized and factory practice simplified.

Hopwood planned a basic ohc 200cc 67 x 56.6mm single with a five-speed gearbox and a crankshaft balancing device to reduce vibration. Its die-cast crankcase had no vertical joints. Based on the single, there would also be a 400cc twin, a 600cc triple and a monstrous fuel-injected 1000cc V5, all derived from the same format. Versions with four valves per cylinder were also anticipated.

Details for the modular range were prepared by Hopwood, who knew the project might cost £20 million. But then came the collapse of BSA-Triumph and when, in the autumn of 1973, the plans were presented to Dennis Poore of Norton Villiers, they were firmly rejected. Hopwood resigned almost immediately to live in retirement in Devon.

He wrote a book, *Whatever Happened to the British Motorcycle Industry?*, putting his side of the story. It sometimes gives the impression of a disgruntled and bitter man, but this is not how industry colleagues remember him. 'Hoppy', as they called him – but never in his hearing – was formal, and sometimes blunt. But those who worked closely with him remember him as a down-to-earth 'nuts and bolts' engineer who commanded respect. Bert Hopwood died in October 1996.

# Doug Hele – brain behind the triples

One man stands out as having contributed more to the triples story than anyone else: Doug Hele. He was deeply involved, from advocating the original concept to Hopwood through to the final versions, and masterminded the racing campaigns of 1970 and 1971 – among the most ambitious and successful ever mounted by a British factory team

As a boy in the West Midlands, Hele's greatest passion was horses and he spent much of his spare time at a friend's farm, where he had the opportunity to ride. Ironically, it was a horse-riding friend who introduced young Douglas to powered riding, on a 175cc Dot two-stroke.

On leaving secondary school at sixteen in 1935, Hele became an apprentice engineering draughtsman at the Austin car company, where his father was a production controller. He completed his training in 1940, and when the Second World War ended, Hele joined the Douglas motorcycle factory in Bristol as a design draughtsman. The company was developing a range of medium-capacity horizontal twins, but was always under a cloud of financial uncertainty.

Hele moved to Norton Motors at Bracebridge Street, Birmingham in 1947, by which time he had married his wife, Hazel. At Norton he came into contact with Joe Craig, the mercurial Ulster engineer behind Norton's extraordinarily successful single-cylinder racers. Norton's Chief Designer Bert Hopwood thought highly of Hele and the two men were destined to collaborate many times in subsequent years.

Soon after Hopwood moved to take the post of Chief Designer at BSA in 1949, Hele applied for a job at Small Heath, where he was put in charge of the company's first serious racing project for decades, the MC1. Aimed at matching the power output of all-conquering German 250cc NSU grand prix racers, the single-cylinder MC1 had four valves per cylinder, driven by bevel gears and radially disposed in the combustion chambers.

Hele refined Hopwood's original design until it produced 33bhp at 10,000rpm, and created a chassis around it with many futuristic features, including cantilevered rear suspension with a single shock absorber unit, an arrangement that has become almost universal on motorcycle chassis in modern times.

But BSA axed the MC1, and a promising 90mph (145km/h) 250cc roadster for which Hele had designed cycle parts. By 1955 both men had returned to Norton, now part of the Associated Motor Cycles conglomerate, which also owned the AJS, Francis-Barnett, James and Matchless marques.

In his second stint at Bracebridge Street Hele showed his true mettle as a designer and development engineer. He took over the ongoing development of Norton's Manx road racer after Craig's retirement, refining it into the form in which it is best known today.

More importantly for Norton's commercial prospects, Hele improved the Dominator roadster twin's output considerably, and the 650cc Super Sports version is still regarded as one of the most desirable British classics today.

Seeing the limitations of the dohc Manx single, which needed painstaking expert assembly to be competitive, Hele created the Domiracer. This 500cc 52bhp Dominator-based road racer caused a sensation at the 1961 Isle of Man TT, where it lapped the Mountain Course at an astonishing 100.36mph (161.48km/h) in the hands of brilliant Australian rider Tom Phillis, to finish third in the Senior race. However, financial crises at Norton, and the decision to move all production to AMC's London headquarters, meant that the Domiracer was never produced for sale as a privateer's racing machine, as Hele envisaged.

Not wishing to move to London, Hele nearly turned his back on the motorcycle industry in 1962, when he considered becoming a technical college teacher of drawing and mathematics. He also came close to taking a job in engine development at the Ford car company. However, both these options would have forced him to leave his West Midlands home for the London area, and so in the end he took up Hopwood's offer of a post at Triumph.

Developing the P1 and P2 triples was only a fraction of his workload at Meriden. Hele worked on the Triumph Tina scooter, and ploughed his Norton experience into improving Triumph's 500cc and 650cc models, undoubtedly contributing to their enormous success in the mid-sixties. He masterminded two glorious Daytona 200 wins with tuned 500cc roadster twins in 1966 and 1967, boosting Triumph's name abroad. Those who worked for him warmed to him, especially as he often rode a motorcycle himself.

When the BSA Group was merged into Norton Villiers Triumph in 1973 and Meriden closed, Hele persevered with the development of triples and other projects for a time. But in 1975 he left the motorcycle industry, taking the post of technical director at the British Seagull marine outboard motor company in Poole, Dorset.

*Doug Hele in 1995.*

Hele returned to the two-wheeled world in the early 1980s at Norton Motors, at Shenstone, Staffordshire where the Wankel rotary project initiated at Meriden had been developed for fleet use, as an exclusive roadster, and for road racing. That operation ran out of funds, and Hele retired in 1993.

Those who worked closely with him speak of his talent for problem solving, his dry humour and his readiness to listen to ideas regardless of who was voicing them. Importantly, also, he often arrived at his office by motorcycle. Hele undoubtedly had the ability to rise higher in the realms of BSA-Triumph's management but he was above all a hands-on engineer, not a bosses' man.

stayed on into the evening after other staff left for home, and their aim was to examine the feasibility of a 750cc triple.

But the concept had already been the subject of discussion between the two men for at least two years, Hele told the author in 1995. Hopwood had left Norton to join Triumph in 1961, but Hele stayed on at the Birmingham factory for a further year, where his main task at that time was the development of a 750cc version of the company's 650cc sports twin. He recalled:

Norton's American distributor Joe Berliner wanted a 750, saying that his customers were clamouring for one. We built a big engine, using the sports camshaft that had been developed for the 500cc Norton twin. The 750 was running by mid-1961, and it was fast but very rough. I remember Fred Swift [an Experimental Department fitter and tester] riding to Birmingham from the South of England on it. He reported that the performance was fantastic, but the vibration was so severe I was worried that he had damaged his hands!

The early 750cc Norton's vibration was minimized by using lightweight pistons, and 'softening' the big engine with a comparatively low 7.6:1 compression ratio. The result was a machine that went on sale in the USA as the 750 Atlas in 1962. But with pressure from America for ever better and faster 750s sure to be maintained, Hele knew that a more permanent technical solution to the vibration bogey had to be found.

He had occasional evening meetings with his former boss Hopwood, and although they were officially bound to observe confidentiality about their respective employers' plans, the two engineers inevitably discussed what they were working on.

Hopwood was finalizing Triumph's range of modernized 650cc twins with unit-construction engines and gearboxes. He was concerned that these, too, were afflicted by roughness. In this case vibration was being made noticeable because the larger unified power unit was a remarkably rigid structure. Also the market's desire for enhanced performance from the ageing Turner twin had led to the adoption of twin carburettors and hotter cam profiles, at the expense of smoothness and flexibility.

It was out of these informal talks of 1961–2 that the idea of a three-cylinder 750 arose. A more conventional route to smoothness, a four-cylinder engine, had been explored at Norton, where draughtsman Brian Jones had drawn up a transverse four engine for Hopwood. But that layout had been rejected on the grounds that it would be excessively wide, placing the rider's footrests too far apart. One of the most admired features of British-made sports motorcycles of the time was their slim build, which aided high-speed handling as well as looking attractive.

As Hele pointed out to Hopwood, a three would be narrower than a four and in theory it had obvious attractions from the balance point of view. If the crankpins were equally disposed at 120-degree intervals, dynamic forces would be in perfect balance. The only flaw would be a slight 'rocking couple' trying to tilt the crankshaft along its length, but it would still be a huge improvement on the 360-degree twin.

Whilst these informal discussions continued, Hele did not attempt to initiate plans for a radical new 750 at Bracebridge Street:

> Apart from the fact that Norton could not afford to start such a project at that time, it was evident by the middle of 1962 that AMC was going to move all Norton production to London [and Hele had no wish to move south].
>
> Bert Hopwood told me he had need of me at Triumph, and work on the three-cylinder idea was something I could look forward to doing at Meriden.

## HELE MOVES TO MERIDEN

Hele joined Triumph as Chief Development Engineer in October 1962, and although his priority work was development of the unit-construction 650s and other work including two-stroke experiments, the triple engine was uppermost in his thoughts:

> At that stage neither Hopwood or I were really sure about how evenly a three would run. I remember studying a Ford three-cylinder tractor at the Three Counties agricultural show just before I joined Triumph. I noticed that it sounded very irregular, and that gave me some doubts.

For reassurance, the Meriden engineers consulted a senior technician from the Rover car company, which had been working on three-cylinder engines, but Hele said that the Rover man was unable to offer much information on likely vibration levels in a motorcycle unit. The only way forward, therefore, was to start drawing up a prototype unit, and this is what Hele and Hopwood set about doing on that evening early in 1963.

# Other people's triples

Although the three-cylinder configuration chosen by BSA-Triumph for its 750 was unusual, it was by no means unique in the motorcycle world.

In 1932 Moto Guzzi, Italy's biggest motorcycle producer, launched a 500cc ohv 120-degree triple with its air-cooled cylinders tilted forward and almost horizontal. Intended as a luxury tourer, its 56 x 67mm engine had a low 5:1 compression ratio and breathed through a single carburettor. A three-speed gearbox with hand-change transmitted a claimed 25bhp to the rear wheel via chain final drive. An expensive and not very rapid machine, it was a victim of the depressed economic climate, and was soon discontinued. However, Guzzi used a similar layout for its 500cc dohc supercharged three-cylinder racing engine, which was raced at Genoa in May 1940 before the Second World War halted development.

In Britain, Scott unveiled a three-cylinder 750 at the 1934 Olympia Show in London. Like the Shipley, Yorkshire, factory's other products, it was powered by a two-stroke engine. Scott's 747cc unit looked like a car engine, water-cooled and set in the frame with its 120-degree crankshaft disposed along the axis of the wheels. The clutch turned at engine speed, but transmission was taken through 90 degrees to suit chain final drive. By coincidence, Scott's official tester was Allan Jefferies, father of Triumph factory triples racer Tony Jefferies. Jefferies Senior was reported to have reservations regarding the steering of the 450lb (202kg) Scott triple, which was only produced in small numbers.

A novel 350cc two-stroke racing triple, with a forward-facing central cylinder set at 75 degrees to the outer two, was campaigned by the German DKW factory from 1952 to 1956. Claimed to produce 42bhp at 9,700rpm in its ultimate form, when unreliability had been ironed out, DKW's triple had its best showing in 1956. In that year's 350cc Belgian GP a team of three 'Deeks' took second to fourth places behind John Surtees' MV Agusta four-stroke four.

When development of Triumph's 750cc triple was started at Meriden, those involved were unaware that the world famous Italian MV Agusta factory at Gallarate near Milan was working on three-cylinder engine design for racing in the 350cc road racing world championships. Former MV race team boss Arturo Magni told the author in 1990 that the choice of three cylinders had been fairly arbitrary. Count Agusta, autocratic boss of a factory where the pursuit of racing prestige was out of all proportion to a modest output of lightweight roadsters, had seen how the 350cc DKW had challenged his fours and decided that the three-cylinder format was ideal for the class.

An output of 58bhp was obtained from the 55 x 49mm 349cc dohc 120-degree MV engine, making the seven-speed machine, first raced in 1965, a convincing winner. It was soon enlarged to compete in the premier 500cc class and its advantages over the four-cylinder racer it replaced included light weight and lack of bulk.

The 170mph (274km/h) 500cc Italian triple was destined to clash with 750cc ohv BSA and Triumph triples on several occasions, most famously in the 1971 Mallory Park Race of the Year, when MV's world champion Giacomo Agostini was beaten by John Cooper's BSA.

They sketched out arrangements for a 120-degree three-cylinder engine, basing it closely on the established pattern of Triumph's twins. It even had the same 63 x 80mm bore and stroke dimensions used in Triumph's old range of 500cc twins from 1937 to 1959, giving a total capacity of 748cc.

A comparatively long stroke with relatively small diameter bores were favoured because they would help keep the width of the unit to a minimum. The pushrod-oper-

*Moto Guzzi's 500cc supercharged dohc three-cylinder racer of 1940.*

*350cc dohc MV Agusta triple in the paddock at Monza, Italy, 1965.*

ated ohv gear was based very closely on that of the existing Turner twins, with two camshafts in the upper crankcase. The shaft controlling inlet valves was placed just behind the crankcase mouth, and the exhaust camshaft just ahead of it, so both could be driven by gears from the crankshaft via an idler pinion.

To serve the extra cylinder, an additional set of cam lobes, tappets and pushrods were provided. Following twin practice, the pushrods would be enclosed by steel tubes, around which cool air could flow to reach the cylinder finning.

The designers were confident that the existing internals of the 46bhp Bonneville T120's four-speed gearbox would be suitable for a 750, too. But, inevitably, the three-cylinder engine was considerably wider than the gearbox designed for a twin. Hele recalls:

We decided that the answer would be to place the clutch inside a gap between the drive output end of the gearbox and the primary transmission line, instead of in its normal place outboard of the primary drive. That would help ensure that we had a narrow unit.

A clutch based on the T120's multi-plate item would occupy the space between the gearbox mainshaft bearing and the primary drive. The driven section of the clutch would not be carried on the mainshaft, but supported independently by the outer transmission casing, in two needle roller bearings. Clutch operation was to be by a pushrod running inside the mainshaft from a lift mechanism on the opposite side of the box, following the twins' pattern.

Advice on crankshaft design was sought from car industry engineer Donald Bastow, who had been in charge of BSA research projects when Hele and Hopwood were at Small Heath in the fifties. He prepared calculations to indicate the optimum sizes and balance factors for the crank's bobweights.

Senior Meriden designer Brian Jones had been involved in the scheme from the early sketches, and he oversaw the translation of general outlines into detailed 'sharp pencil' arrangements in Meriden's drawing office.

At this stage, the three-cylinder project was just one project among several being worked on at Triumph, with relatively low priority and with no backing from Managing Director Edward Turner.

## CUTTING METAL

It was the job of Meriden's Experimental Department to build functioning prototypes so that the practicality of future projects could be assessed and a development programme could proceed, making whatever alterations were needed.

Components were obtained from General Production, made from drawings by the Toolroom's precision engineers, or requisitioned from one of many outside suppliers serving Triumph. The first prototype 750cc

*The prototype P1 750cc triple engine as restored by the Trident & Rocket 3 Owners Club. This version has an aluminium alloy cylinder block but the first P1 engine had a cast iron block prone to distortion.*

# Alan Barrett – critical engineering

Alan Barrett and Len Udall were the Experimental Shop fitters most involved in the intensive development work required on the original 63 × 80mm P1 triple prototype.

Both had come to Triumph from the Velocette factory, where Barrett had been on experimental work and deputized as an assembly line supervisor. Udall was the younger brother of Velocette's chief designer, Charles Udall.

'The Velocette Experimental Department was only a Nissen hut, but it was a wonderful school,' Barrett told the author. He recalled a busy programme of development on the P1, constantly revising and rebuilding test engines to iron out problems:

> It started out as a quick lash-up really, based on a twin with an extra cylinder and an extra crankcase section, to see if a triple would work. That is why it had iron barrels and sand-cast crankcases. All sorts of problems arose, a big one being the bottom-end bearings which were much more loaded than on the twins. Vandervell [the plain bearings supplier] suggested the failures were caused by sand still in the castings, but as we got the horsepower up, the mains gave up faster and faster. I suggested to Doug Hele that we try lead indium bearings, and we experimented with car shells. Once we got the special high-performance shells for the triple, we never looked back.

Barrett became a foreman, and when the P2 triple was nearing production he was in the party that went to the USA for trials in 1967. When the production line was rolling, he again visited the US as a trouble shooter and was subsequently sent to Small Heath to help sort out manufacturing faults and quality control problems.

*Alan Barrett in 1996.*

triple started to take physical shape in 1964 with the factory code P1 (Project One).

Hopwood and Hele were greatly encouraged when the P1 engine was completed and tested on one of the Experimental Department's dynamometers. It gave a best figure of 59.5bhp in January 1965, representing an immediate gain of 15 per cent over the Bonneville twin. But a lot of work lay ahead in turning the crude P1 experiment into a reliable engine that could be considered suitable for production.

Carburation was arranged with three Amal Monobloc instruments. The type with 'chopped' float bowls specified for early twin-carburettor 650cc twins had to be used on the outer cylinders because of the confined space available. The middle instrument's normal float chamber was fitted with a high-flow needle valve usually supplied for use with alcohol fuel, to provide sufficient volume for three carburettors. Fuel was distributed by banjo unions of the type supplied with Amal GP racing carburettors.

A single coil ignition system was adopted, relying on one set of contact breaker points recessed in the timing cover, operated by a three-lobe cam on the end of the exhaust camshaft. A distributor unit, adapted from a

Bedford van type, was placed on the main engine casing behind the cylinders so that it could be driven by skew gears from the inlet camshaft, a system used on Triumph's 350 and 500cc unit construction twins until 1962. But on the P1, the distributor's drive shaft was set to the left of the cam lobes and it continued downwards into the crankcase, where it propelled the gear-type oil pump for the dry sump lubrication system.

## A TRIPLE TAKES TO THE ROAD

For road testing early in 1965, a functioning motorcycle was built up by Experimental Department fitter Harry Woolridge. Its cycle parts were based on the current Hele-developed single downtube 650 frame, with its bottom tubes set wider to cradle the P1's wider casings.

Various problems came to light when testing got under way, but the Experimental Department had acquired two highly proficient new engineers, Alan Barrett and Len Udall, who had arrived from the Birmingham Velocette factory. The two took over the task of developing the triple into a viable project for Hele.

Overheating of the engine was an immediate bugbear. The P1's one-piece cylinder block had been made in cast iron, mainly for speed and economy of manufacture and it tended to distort at its joint with the aluminium alloy cylinder head, due to the metals' different rates of expansion.

Wet sumping, a build up of engine oil in the crankcase, was another teething trouble. The lubrication system seemed unable to scavenge the crankcase sufficiently at high speed, and oil was tending to gather in a mass in the confined space around the crankshaft, rather than draining to the base of the crankcase where it could be scavenged by the pump. Fabricating a spacious sump onto the lower crankcase eased the problem.

*This view of the P1 engine's underside shows the makeshift oil sump welded on to original crankcase castings. The upper of the two circular apertures is the site of the oil pump, driven off the inlet camshaft.*

*Removal of inlet rocker box shows valve gear very similar to the Triumph twin's, with pushrod tubes butting up to the head casting. Mounting for the ignition distributor can be seen below the inlet stubs for the centre and left cylinders.*

Plain shell bearings, which coped perfectly well on twin cylinder crankshafts, failed with depressing regularity in the triple until better materials were specified. Oil was reaching extremely high temperatures in warm weather road tests. A large aluminium alloy oil tank with finned surfaces had been tried, but ultimately the solution was sought in the form of an oil-cooling radiator plumbed into the return side of the lubrication system.

Alloy cylinder barrels were an improvement, but brought their own distortion problems when fitted with ordinary iron liners. It was decided that the chief cause of the P1's hot running lay in the relationship of the rocker boxes to the cylinder head, the arrangement of the pushrod enclosure tubes, and the lack of air passages through the iron cylinder block. These snags would require major revisions on a subsequent prototype.

There is far more to prototyping than merely finding power and reliability. The result must be acceptable for production and sale in all respects, including a low level of mechanical noise, and this was another area in which the P1 needed revision. It had been decided to use gear-driven primary transmission from the engine to the gearbox. This had a train of three pinions which meant that the crankshaft and gearbox rotated in

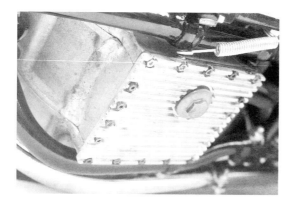

*The oil sump on the P1, with its finned alloy cover in place. It was added to overcome oil congestion in the crankcase.*

the same direction, and individual pinions were fairly small. Backlash had to be provided in the gears to allow for expansion, and there was no engine shaft shock-absorber. The drive made an unacceptably loud rattling noise, particularly on the over-run, when the gears and the clutch would chatter, and this would have to be eliminated.

From the outset, Hele's intended exhaust silencing system for the triple had large reverse-flow mufflers based on his experience at Norton. Arriving at a satisfactory

arrangement for the downpipes from the exhaust ports was more problematic.

Designing efficient pipework to conduct gas from three ports into two main pipes was made more difficult by the proximity of the frame's single front downtube to the central exhaust port. For testing purposes, the P1 had a simple arrangement with the centre cylinder's exhaust port connected to a curved cross-tube bridging the outer two downpipes.

Road mileage was also indicating that Dunlop's current K70 road tyre was inade-

*The clutch cable operates a lifting mechanism inside the gearbox end cover. The hexagonal plug on the P1 timing cover is believed to have been for crankcase ventilation experiments.*

*A simple but inefficient branch arrangement links exhausts on the P1. Rev-counter drive take-off from the exhaust camshaft can be seen to the right of the down-pipe.*

quate for transferring the triple's tremendous power to the road.

Doug Hele was among those who put road miles on a P1. On his way to Meriden one morning early in 1966 his mount caught fire, but he dismounted and leapt smartly over a farm gate, grabbed a sheet of corrugated iron and used it to scoop water from a cattle trough. With the help of a postman who arrived on the scene, the blaze was extinguished before serious damage was done. Although the ease with which the P1's fuel system could be over-flooded was an acknowledged fire hazard, it was thought to have been an electrical fault that caused trouble on this occasion.

Despite the difficulties encountered, the P1 had fulfilled its intended function of proving that the engine was powerful, and most importantly, much smoother than a twin. The project still looked viable, and the next step would be to incorporate all the necessary changes in a completely revised prototype, coded P2.

## PLANNING FOR PRODUCTION

By 1966, work had started on the second phase of the triple, the P2. It would have totally different cylinder dimensions from its predecessor, with a much shorter stroke. The new 741cc engine measured $67 \times 70$mm, and it was no coincidence that it shared this size with the single cylinder of BSA's 250cc C15 Star. Since his time as Chief Engineer at BSA in the mid-fifties, Hopwood had been an advocate of modular production, allowing engines of various capacities and with differing numbers of cylinders to share important basic components such as pistons and valves. As a result production could be simpler and less costly.

Management changes in the BSA Group were running in favour of the 750cc triple. Edward Turner had retired from the main

board of the BSA Automotive Division in 1964, and the new chief executive was Harry Sturgeon. He had come from outside the motorcycling world, having been a senior executive at the De Havilland aircraft company, and more recently Managing Director of the Churchill machine tools company, a BSA Group subsidiary. Sturgeon was determined to knock the whole BSA and Triumph organization into shape and maximize production and sales, with greater collaboration between the two main factories.

Hopwood had become Deputy Managing Director, and priority was at last being being given to long-term plans for the motorcycle companies' range of products. Sturgeon backed Hopwood's proposals for introducing the modular system where possible. A basic 250cc single, with a unit-construction engine evolved from BSA's old C15 unit was in the pipeline. Also envisaged was a 500cc twin

*A P2 engine, the second phase of 750cc triple prototyping, now with $67 \times 70$mm bore and stroke. Rocker boxes and pushrod tube layouts have been revised and cable operation of the single-plate clutch is now sited on the primary chaincase.*

with the same 67 × 70mm dimensions, so it made sense to bring a revised prototype for a projected 750 triple into line, giving it the same bore and stroke.

When the 741cc P2 took shape in the Meriden drawing office advantage was taken of the 4mm bore increase to make the valves bigger, boosting performance with more efficient gas flow. Naturally, Project Two had an aluminium alloy cylinder block, but with a completely revised pushrod tube arrangement that raised the floors of the rocker boxes away from the combustion chambers. Both changes would guarantee enhanced cooling.

The plain main bearings were made more robust, and the oiling system was redesigned with the oil pump moved from the crankcase into the primary drive case. This change had already been envisaged, with drive taken conveniently from the primary gears, but now the oil pump was driven by a slim pair of pinions inboard of the drive. The noisy three-pinion primary drive was to be abandoned, to be replaced by a triplex Renold chain.

Also dropped was the multi-plate, multi-spring clutch, in favour of a single-plate Borg & Beck item obtained from transmission specialists Automotive Products, based on a small car unit. A pull-rod mechanism was devised to make operation of the compact single-plate assembly possible from a handlebar lever and cable. Later, experiments with hydraulic clutch operation were made on triples at Meriden, but never developed for production.

Different exhaust manifolds were tried, to obtain an efficient and even flow, ultimately resulting in a fabrication of tubes that split the pipe from the centre port into two, to join the two main outer pipes.

As the P2 was developed it was now becoming a serious company project, to answer demands for bigger and faster Triumphs and BSAs. Reports that the Japanese Honda company was planning to enter the large capacity market with a four-cylinder 750cc roadster had galvanized the BSA Group into action and Hopwood had been able to reassure Sturgeon that work was already well advanced on a robust – if only

## Harry Woolridge – feeling the heat

As a member of the Experimental Shop staff in the early sixties, Harry Woolridge not only made and assembled components, but occasionally covered mileage on the road. One of his usual test routes was to ride eastwards to the M1 motorway (motorway speeds were completely unrestricted in those days), and cruise southwards along it to Stony Stratford before turning round for the return journey.

The prototype triple was definitely the fastest thing I'd ever ridden,' he told the author. 'But I remember coming back from one summertime run and the engine oil was so hot we thought the bearings would melt.

Woolridge recalled how the first oil-cooling radiator was tried:

I had a mate who worked in a local Volkswagen garage, and we scrounged a secondhand oil-cooler from him. We stood it vertically on top of the gearbox, plumbed it in and it worked. From then on, all triples have had oil-coolers.

temporary – response to Honda in the form of the three-cylinder 750.

Sturgeon looked on the triple project much more favourably than Turner had.

According to Meriden sales boss Neale Shilton's autobiography, *A Million Miles Ago*, the new chief had even insisted on displaying a prototype triple to police fleet buy-

## Percy Tait – the ultimate tester

Riding 200 miles (320km) a day on Triumphs during the week and racing them at weekends was Percy Tait's lifestyle for many years, and he is estimated to have notched up a million miles of road testing on Meriden products. The irrepressible Tait also found time to keep livestock as a sideline.

The tough but ever-genial Percy played a vital role in the triple story, from putting miles on the P1 prototype as Meriden's senior road tester, to development riding and racing – with an impressive tally of wins – aboard works racers. He was a veteran of the tracks by the time the Trident came along, having road raced Triumphs and other machines since 1950.

When completing the compulsory military service demanded of young men in the postwar years, Tait became a member of the Royal Signals motorcycle display team, the White Helmets. Back in civilian life he joined Triumph as an assembly worker, but was soon recruited to Experimental, and encouraged to go road racing by department boss Frank Baker.

Tait's gift for fast travel on two wheels meant that he became Doug Hele's right hand man during the programme of highly effective chassis development instituted at Triumph in the early sixties. When triples development got under way, his high speed experience stood him in good stead.

'The only big problem I had with a triple was when I tried to ride one home in the snow. The power characteristics made it a real handful,' Percy told the author. His job was often far from glamorous, with road mileage to be covered in all weathers, and gruelling sessions to be endured at the MIRA proving grounds or in a chilly wind tunnel.

But Percy was always cheerful, and an inveterate practical joker both around the factory and in race paddocks. Because he often fetched and carried urgent packages on his tester's travels, his nickname at Meriden was Sam the Transport Man, giving rise to the Slippery Sam production racing legend.

Being a Triumph employee was a mixed blessing when it came to racing. Tait had the glory of finishing second to Giacomo Agostini's works MV Agusta four in the 1969 Belgian Grand Prix on Meriden's 500cc twin racer, but he had also been flung off the Triumph when its half-developed gearbox locked up at the previous year's Isle of Man TT, and broke his collarbone.

Although he scored many triple-mounted successes, Percy had firm orders to make sure that racers he tested for other works riders were as fast as, or faster than, his own. 'When John Cooper wanted a bike, the one we had wasn't very good, but we spent two weeks on it and it ended up being one of the best,' he recalled.

Tait sometimes had to give up bikes or engines when they were needed for star riders who earned much more than his Meriden wage. 'I was being elbowed out by BSA's marketing people in 1971, because they didn't think I should be a team rider,' he told the author. Because triples racing was primarily for publicity, marketing chiefs had a major say in campaign organization.

Percy set up on his own successfully in the motor trade after the Meriden closure, but continued racing two-strokes – and sometimes Slippery Sam – in his late forties. He broke five ribs, punctured a lung and smashed a knee when he crashed on the T160 Son of Sam production racer in the 1976 Production TT. That ended his racing, but since then he has become one of Britain's top sheep breeders, winning England's Royal Show, the Royal Welsh and Scotland's Royal Highland with his Blue Demaine ewes. 'I think I've now won more cups with my sheep than I ever did in racing,' he said.

ers at a demonstration day, despite the embarrassingly noisy primary drive.

Three P2s were on the road by mid-1966 and Dunlop's development engineers had been called in to design a rear tyre capable of coping with the substantial power increase over the Bonneville. The two testers who put most miles on the triples, Percy Tait and Tony Lomax, were hard riders.

'They used to say that if a bike could stand up to me, it could stand up to anything', Tait told the author in 1995.

Distortion occurring in the outer cylinders' bores was cured by using an austenitic steel material for cylinder liners, and after many experiments with various oil-coolers, a sophisticated, and relatively expensive, type made by Coventry Radiator Co. for the Mini Cooper car was specified.

Warning had been served to manufacturers that motorcycle noise levels were soon to become subject to minimum requirements on the US market, and the development of efficient air filters that would silence intake roar was part of the preparations.

One experimental air filter tried at the triple's P2 stage was a type with a plastic foam element. Alan Barrett recalled an incident when this was on test:

> Fred Swift [the former Norton experimental technician now at Triumph] took the machine out on test with the foam filter, and didn't return. Eventually he arrived with a policeman, holding the trade plate. The bike had caught fire and burned out on the Meriden Mile [a stretch of straight road often used by testers].

The cause had been that blown-back petrol had accumulated in the foam filter, and then been ignited by a carburettor backfire.

*Percy Tait enjoys a victory drink with US racer Gary Nixon (left) at the 1971 Anglo-American match races.*

# Harry Sturgeon – a mission to unify

An exciting new motorcycle with sales potential was exactly what Harry Sturgeon was looking for when he became Chief Executive of the BSA Motorcycle Division in 1964. He immediately embraced Hopwood and Hele's proposals for a new 750 which would be more potent than anything previously offered in large volume production.

Sturgeon came from outside the world of motorcycling, having been Managing Director of the Churchill Machine Tool Company, owned by the BSA Group. Before that he was a senior executive of the De Havilland aircraft company. His main concern was to maximize production and boost sales, whilst trying to turn the fiercely partisan Ariel, BSA and Triumph sections of the group into a cohesive, collaborative organization. Rationalization of the factions in the Group had been at the core of recommendations made by McKinsey and Company, the management consultancy commissioned to advise BSA in 1964.

Tackling the unpopular task of modernizing an ageing industry preoccupied with tradition, Sturgeon closed the Ariel factory, but spent £750,000 on much needed equipment for Small Heath. And his reorganization of operations in America, which forced BSA and Triumph factions to work together, was contentious. But despite the disruption, the motorcycle companies' production and turnover increased markedly during Sturgeon's regime.

Unlike his successor, Lionel Jofeh, Sturgeon did not remain aloof from the factories he ran. Les Williams recalls that when he was a chargehand in the Experimental Department, Sturgeon would sometimes call in at eight o'clock in the morning to enquire how things were going.

When Sturgeon became seriously ill in 1966, his absence probably contributed to the confusion surrounding the planning of the triples, especially with regard to styling. He finally died in April 1967, the month in which BSA and Triumph were conferred with the Queen's Award to Industry for export achievement.

## TRIPLES UNDER TWO FLAGS

Sturgeon wanted to unify the BSA Group's disjointed operations as far as possible, and to this end it was decided at top level that the new 750 was to be made in two forms. Both BSA and Triumph variants of the triple would be sold, emphasizing the companies' links. The Triumph was to be the T150 Trident, a neat name encapsulating the triple theme, and the BSA was originally to be the A75 Tri Star. The BSA's name was subse-

*Harry Sturgeon (right) congratulates Buddy Elmore on winning the Daytona 200 on a Triumph twin in 1966.*

quently changed to the Rocket 3, perhaps because aircraft manufacturer Lockheed was collaborating with Rolls-Royce at the time to build a three-engined airliner called the Tri Star. Also BSA's Super Rocket and Rocket Gold Star models had been successful models in the US, so Rocket was an established buzz-word.

Commercially, much would be demanded of the new 750s, which would be expected to sell in substantial numbers in major markets, especially in North America. Judging by the performance of Meriden's P2, the triples would have all the speed that customers craved, but hard work still lay ahead.

Although BSA/Triumph was enjoying escalating export success under Sturgeon, there were warning signs apparent for those prepared to see them. The rumoured Honda four-cylinder 750 had now been confirmed as a reality, and on past form there was no reason to suppose that the Japanese company would not make a first class job of it.

The vulnerability of even the biggest British motorcycle manufacturers was to be demonstrated by the collapse of Associated Motor Cycles, maker of AJS, Francis-Barnett, James, Matchless and Norton in 1966. Now more than ever, the BSA Group's future fortunes were pinned on it making a success of the new 750cc models.

# 2 The Triples Take Shape

## STYLE COUNCIL

Styling can make or break a new vehicle. If it looks too different or radical, buyers will take fright. Yet too conservative an approach will present a dull and dated image, also bad for sales.

Motorcycles present a particular challenge to stylists since, unlike cars, they do not have clearly defined exteriors and interiors. The whole aspect of a two-wheeler must look inviting to potential riders, who will place their bodies on and around a motorcycle, rather than in it.

Everyone involved in development of the three-cylinder 750 at Meriden had assumed that the final product would look very much like the fast-selling 650cc Triumph Bonneville, but with an extra cylinder. And at Small Heath, it was reasonable to expect the new model to follow the lines of the more sporting versions of BSA's 650cc A65 Lightning.

Meriden's P2 prototype triple married the new engine unit with a slightly altered version of the Bonneville chassis, and had the makings of a handsome motorcycle. Styling was something that Triumph regarded with pride. Ever since the late forties the company's products had been lovingly shaped by Edward Turner, assisted by his in-house team with senior designer Jack Wickes playing a major role in producing sleek and pleasing shapes.

But the triple was no longer a purely Triumph project, and setting two companies' design teams to work on styling would have been complicated and costly. Also, it appears that some senior BSA Group managers felt that Turner's departure presented the ideal opportunity for Triumph to move on and strike out with a bold new look. Wickes told the author in 1995 that he felt 'pushed to one side' when the triples' styling was on the agenda. It was decided at BSA board level to break with tradition and give the the job of styling the new models to an outside consultancy.

The company chosen was Ogle Design of Letchworth, Hertfordshire. Founded by David Ogle in the fifties, Ogle Design had become one of Britain's most successful independent industrial design houses. It had excellent facilities and was considered a style leader in the design-conscious sixties. Ogle's best known road vehicle work had been demonstrated in the styling of the glass-fibre bodied Reliant Scimitar car.

Such companies were used to creating new designs from scratch, but Ogle were to be presented by the BSA Group with basic rolling motorcycles, around which they would be asked to wrap the important visible components such as fuel tanks, panels and mudguards.

Styling of the triples' engines had already been finalized in development, based on the P2 prototype but in two distinct forms. To distinguish it from the Triumph, the 750cc BSA had its cylinders tilted forward at 15 degrees from the vertical. This was achieved by changes to the main crankcase castings but the internals, and engine components from the crankcase mouth up, were identical. Further marque differentiation came from the shaping and badging of outer covers on the power units. Sloping the cylinders was a throw-back to pre-war years. Postwar

*A prototype Triumph triple prior to Ogle's styling input – basically, a three-cylinder engine with 1966 cycle parts. Note that this machine's engine and gearbox unit has twin-style clutch operation in the gearbox end cover. The object attached to the frame downtube ahead of the exhaust manifold is believed to be an experimental oil cooler.*

*Rear view of the pre-Ogle prototype, with enclosed carburettor throttle linkage mechanism visible below seat nose. The rev-counter drive from the end of the exhaust camshaft can be seen on the crankcase. A triple produced in this form would have appealed to Triumph fans more than the Ogle designed one.*

four-stroke BSA motorcycles invariably had upright cylinders, but one of the best loved Small Heath products in the thirties had been its Sloper models, with inclined single cylinders.

Late in the summer of 1966, Ogle was supplied with a Triumph triple, in the form of a three-cylinder engine minus its internals and fitted to a version of the T120 frame, complete with other current Bonneville cycle parts. A BSA rolling chassis, based on the A65 twin type, was also taken to Letchworth, installed with the essentials of an inclined engine.

Two of Ogle's designers were assigned to the company's first motorcycle project: Jim English, allocated to the job because he was a keen motorcyclist and Bryon Fitzpatrick,

an Australian who specialized in industrial design. English had joined Ogle in 1965 after training in vehicle design at the Ford Motor Co and he had worked on the Scimitar project. Having recently bought himself a 650cc Triumph Trophy twin, he was excited when he first set eyes on the triple at Letchworth. He told the author in 1996:

Tom Karen [head of Ogle Design then and now] took me to the back of a workshop and pulled the cover off a bike. It looked like a Triumph Bonneville, but I noticed three exhausts coming from the engine and realized that it must be something a bit special. I was told that this was our next project.

To design a car we would lay out four wheels, seats and an engine, then create a

*A BSA rolling chassis with engine as supplied to Ogle Design. The all-welded frame is based on the contemporary 650cc A65 twin. Obsolete model wheel hubs on this chassis were not used in production.*

body around them. But the bikes were a purely cosmetic job, because the frames and engines had already been designed and supplied to us.

If I had been able to have my way, we would have gone for a café racer look, because that was the 'in thing' with British bikers at the time. But as we understood that job, BSA wanted a very flashy American look, like a Cadillac car. We really let our hair down doing futuristic stuff. I sketched out a shape for a silencer, with a few flowing lines and three tailpipes coming out of the end.

To English's surprise, his flamboyant silencer shape was one of the elements a BSA committee liked best when presented with early ideas. 'When I drew out a more

dctailed version, I toned it down a bit. But I still didn't really expect it to go into production like that,' he said.

Those huge silencers were probably to attract more comment, and little of it favourable, than any other feature on early Tridents and Rocket 3s. They were soon nicknamed 'ray-guns', because they looked as though they belonged in a dated science fiction film, or the Dan Dare space adventure comic strip known to most British schoolboys in the fifties.

English told the author that as this look was what he had strived to achieve, he has never been offended by negative comments. And his silencers certainly did fulfil a requirement laid down in BSA's brief by Doug Hele that they should be of large volume, suitable for containing reverse-flow internals to mute the three-cylinder growl.

Various renderings, the sketches showing the designers' ideas, were provided for BSA to study and make choices about preferred features. It was normal for design houses' clients to pick and choose a blend of elements from the various proposals. Mock-up components were made from drawings in the workshops of Ogle Design's sister company Ogle Models.

Other distinctive features of the Ogle designs were the squared-off shapes given to the fuel tanks, seats and side panels. Box-like shapes were considered ultra modern at the time, and they were also to be an Ogle

hallmark on products ranging from record players to refuse trucks. They also echoed the square cylinder head finning used to give a narrow profile to the engines.

Although each of the two versions was given its own identity, they shared the ray gun silencers and other components and were broadly similar in their angular appearance.

Fitzpatrick applied his experience of designing household appliances to produce push-button handlebar lighting and horn controls set in the front brake and clutch lever housings. Flashing direction indicators, clearly set to become compulsory in some markets, were also part of the Ogle

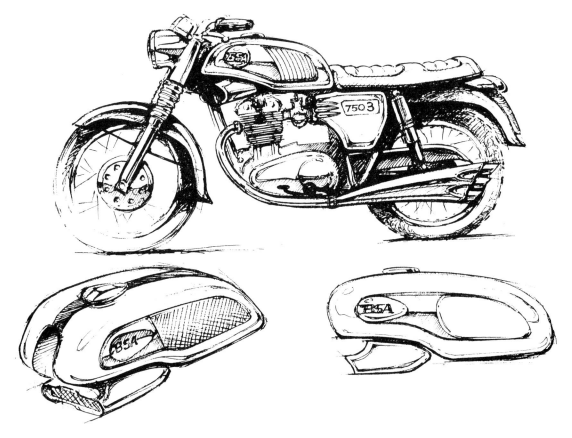

*Sketches by Ogle designer Jim English, including early ideas for silencers with three outlets. Italian Gilera marque's 'double bubble' logo inspired some of the shapes.*

package. A single pair of winkers, intended to be seen from both front and rear, were mounted on either side of the headlamp.

Looking back at the project, Tom Karen told the author that his team had never achieved as close a working relationship with BSA as it had with Reliant:

> It was not a classic example of working together. I felt that their management was groping its way, without the clear leadership we might have hoped for. Our sketches were much better than the end results, partly because of restrictions on the amount of spending available for tooling, and constraints on the design of lighting equipment. Also, we didn't get the chance to style the engine, which is something the Japanese did so well.

In February 1967, when Ogle was finalizing its designs, the story took a new turn. Harry Sturgeon left his post because of ill health, and two months later finally succumbed to the brain tumour that had been the cause of his frequent absences from work. Hopwood apparently believed that he would now be made Managing Director of BSA's Motorcycle Division, but in the event the main board, guided by Chairman Eric Turner, appointed Lionel Jofeh.

A newcomer to the motorcycle industry, Jofeh arrived from an aerospace instruments and controls company. Hopwood's first reaction was to resign, but he was ultimately persuaded to stay with the company. He and others got the impression, however, that the new man had come to teach the old guard of the motorcycle industry how to run a modern business.

## FACTORY REACTION

Perhaps not surprisingly, when Ogle's designs were seen by Meriden staff they

*Lionel Jofeh in 1967.*

were greeted with disdain. 'We fell about laughing,' ex-Triumph man Harry Woolridge told the author. 'It looked so Japanese – we thought they must have copied a Honda Dream.' Hele said that he too was disappointed by the Trident's cosmetics:

> When I got back from racing with 500cc twins at Daytona in March 1967 there were all sorts of bits scattered around Jack Wickes' office and I was horrified, particularly by the square tank. I never liked that shape and have to admit I still don't to this day.

There were those at BSA with reservations, too. Among them was Peter Glover, Assistant Export Manager at the time, who would have responsibilty for selling the Rocket 3 abroad. He remembered being called over to

# Lionel Jofeh – a mission that failed

It would be easy to blame the demise of the BSA Group Motorcycle Division on Lionel Jofeh. His appointment as Managing Director in February 1967 appears to coincide with the point at which both BSA and Triumph started their tumble into decline from world leaders to lame ducks.

Jofeh, who had been managing director of the aerospace company Sperry Gyroscope, did not endear himself to the motorcycle industry men he came to manage. They found him unapproachable and disliked his methods. He had no affection for motorcycles and did not understand motorcyclists. According to Don Brown, who met Jofeh in his role as vice president of BSA's US East Coast division, he openly said as much at social occasions.

'That meant he had no way of knowing which of the people under him was talking sense,' Brown said in 1996, adding that he found Jofeh to be extremely astute with figures. 'He could read columns upside down on your desk and add them up correctly in his head in no time,' Brown recalled. And race team fitter Arthur Jakeman told of an episode at the 1970 Daytona race meeting: 'Mr Jofeh took us all to lunch at the Holiday Inn, and then put the bill down to my room!'

And yet this picture of parsimony contrasts with Jofeh's apparent corporate extravagance in the way he ran the BSA Group. Many well-paid senior posts were created by him, to be filled by former employees of the British aircraft industry. And it was Jofeh's idea to set up the Umberslade Hall research centre in a spacious country mansion where money was spent on the leisurely redesigning of BSA and Triumph motorcycles with apparently no thought as to whether their sales would bring in enough to pay the R & D bills.

Jofeh was very rarely seen in either the BSA or Triumph factories and is said to have called Armoury Road a 'muck heap' – the archaic BSA plant must have come as a shock to an aerospace executive. He wanted to set the British motorcycle industry on the right lines for the future, making it modern and highly productive. But, because he didn't give motorcyclists around him a sympathetic ear, his policies had the opposite effect.

Former Meriden service chief John Nelson summed up the bad effect Jofeh and his aircraft industry associates had on staff: 'They came in saying that they would show us how to run a business. After that, I'm afraid the attitude at both factories was: " – them, let them find out for themselves!"'

However, Jofeh cannot take all the blame for the collapse that followed. Cracks in the industry's structure had started to spread before he arrived at BSA. But he was in a position to pull things together, and he failed, with catastrophic consequences. One of his many mistakes was to bank on earning significant revenue from the Ogle-designed Trident and Rocket 3.

Bert Hopwood's Meriden office to see Ogle's renderings:

As the most senior member of the sales side available at that moment I was asked to select what I thought was the best of three designs which he had hung on the wall. I didn't really like any of them, but I did what I was asked, and chose the one I disliked least.

He added that he believed that his choice was the version which was accepted, although he cannot be certain that the final decision was his.

BSA's general works manager Alistair Cave, who attended several meetings at which there were protracted discussions about the styling of the 750s, recalled dissension over the square shapes and the flared silencer, 'but there were those who approved of them. The criticism was to come later, especially from America'. BSA's East Coast Vice President Don Brown never concealed his misgivings about the new look

*These Ogle renderings show the Triumph Trident designs preferred by BSA/Triumph.*

from his English colleagues, but he told the author that Ted Hodgdon, an older, more senior executive from BSA's New Jersey base was full of enthusiasm for the ray guns. They appealed to him because they evoked the prominent 'fishtail' silencers on pre-war machines such as the BSA Sloper.

Ogle's original mock-ups were finished by March 1967, but they did not survive unaltered into production and changes were made at both BSA and Triumph. For purely industrial reasons, the handlebar switchgear was rejected and replaced with

relatively archaic Lucas equipment. The BSA Group was restricted to what components ancillary companies were prepared to supply in large quantities, and its influence with a company such as Lucas was weak

*Finished Ogle BSA design, with wire-type front mudguard supports and star-type tank badges not used in production.*

*Complete mock up for the Trident, at Ogle Design in March 1967. The headlamp shrouding, oil cooler scoops and seat would be changed by Triumph.*

compared with that of the free-spending car manufacturers. Also, equipment had to be approved for fitment to machines being sold in the USA and Lucas usually obtained approval for its products directly, saving its customers trouble and expense.

Other details that were dropped before production included tubular handlebar braces containing electrical wiring, which bridged the combined control lever and switch units. Mudguard stays made from chrome-plated steel wire were discarded on the BSA, although something similar was to re-emerge on later triples. The side panels were made slightly less flat-sided and the detailing of them was revised, and on the Rocket 3 the tank badges and rear grab rail were changed.

Alan Barrett told the author that the air scoops Ogle designed for the oil coolers proved inefficient on test. The cowlings were removed, and on the Trident the outer ends of the small oil radiator were concealed by rectangular side reflectors. Orange reflector discs were placed on fluted alloy trims placed over the ends of the Rocket 3's cooler. From 1968, all of BSA and Triumph's US-export machines carried front and rear side-reflectors to comply with US regulations.

Perhaps alone among industry men, former Triumph draughtsman Brian Jones thought that Ogle's efforts were not fully appreciated. 'After bringing them in to do the work, to then water down the designs seemed a bit unfair,' he said in 1996. After all, the wish to break with traditional BSA and Triumph styling on the triples was understandable. It was all very well laughing at Hondas, but advances in Japanese motorcycle design were in danger of making British products look as old fashioned as the plants they were made in.

Where the BSA Group had gone wrong with the Rocket 3 and Trident styling was in not thinking deeply about what its potential customers liked and disliked in the looks

and handling of a motorcycle. And in losing time through indecision: an original plan to launch the triples at the UK's 1967 Motor Cycle Show had to be shelved.

## TOOLING UP

Although the three-cylinder machine had been conceived and developed at Meriden, the bulk of its manufacture was to be carried out at Small Heath. There were several reasons for this. Triumph's plant was fully stretched in meeting the huge overseas demand for its twin-cylinder models, particularly the 650cc Bonneville. And, while Meriden relied a great deal on outside contractors for metal pressings and plating processes, the bigger Armoury Road site had traditionally produced almost every metal component used in a motorcycle. Also, it had been part of Sturgeon's strategy to maximize Meriden's productivity by making nothing but the Triumph range of twins there. Singles, scooters, and anything else that wasn't a Triumph twin would be dealt with at BSA.

However, Meriden was to make certain common engine components for triples of

*Rear view of cutaway engine shows the clutch sited between the primary and final drive sprockets. The selector camplate can be seen in the gearbox compartment.*

both makes. They included the camshafts, for which the Triumph factory had specially purchased modern cam-grinding equipment, and the cam-follower tappets, as well as cylinder heads and cylinder barrels, which were machined at Meriden after raw castings were supplied from outside foundries. Gearbox parts were made at both sites.

Complete Rocket 3 machines would be built at the BSA plant, whilst assembly of rolling Tridents would be Triumph's responsibility, using power units trucked in consignments of 200–250 for a distance of approximately 12 miles.

Alistair Cave, who was the general manager in charge of motorcycle production at BSA and was responsible for setting up tools and training staff to produce the new engines, maintained that while BSA's fac-

tory was better able to cope with the additional burden of making triple power units than Meriden, manufacture of the new 750s served to aggravate an increasingly difficult situation at Armoury Road:

The fun really started when three-cylinder manufacture went ahead. As much as 20 per cent of our plant was fifteen to twenty years old. Some of the machinery to be used for three-cylinder production was the same as had been used to make the M-series BSA side-valve singles and C-series lightweights back in the fifties.

Furthermore, the Armoury Road shop floor was still reeling from a series of tumultuous morale-sapping episodes. For example, a series of major engine revisions had been

*A pre-production Rocket 3 after BSA had revised some Ogle details. The front mudguard is now secured direct to the front fork sliders, and alloy covers with reflectors enclose the oil cooler. The tank badge has been redesigned, but the side panel badge and silencer with long tail pipes were to be further changed for production models.*

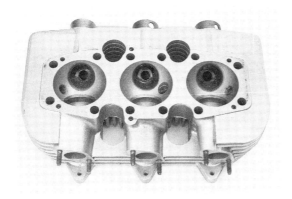

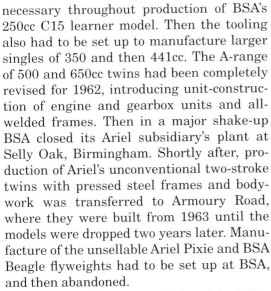

*The cylinder head casting. Four apertures are provided for the pushrod tubes, which mate up to the separate rocker box castings*

*The head casting from above, showing the six cast-in recesses for valve springs. It can be seen that the centre spark plug is offset to one side.*

necessary throughout production of BSA's 250cc C15 learner model. Then the tooling also had to be set up to manufacture larger singles of 350 and then 441cc. The A-range of 500 and 650cc twins had been completely revised for 1962, introducing unit-construction of engine and gearbox units and all-welded frames. Then in a major shake-up BSA closed its Ariel subsidiary's plant at Selly Oak, Birmingham. Shortly after, production of Ariel's unconventional two-stroke twins with pressed steel frames and bodywork was transferred to Armoury Road, where they were built from 1963 until the models were dropped two years later. Manufacture of the unsellable Ariel Pixie and BSA Beagle flyweights had to be set up at BSA, and then abandoned.

Following that came Triumph's 200cc Tiger Cub single, formerly made at Meriden. Switching Cub production to Birmingham in 1965 was in line with Sturgeon's rationalization plan, but it proved unpopular at both plants: Triumph staff were sorry to lose it and BSA were unhappy to accept it. In fact, switching work between plants often stirred up an undercurrent of dissatisfaction, largely because considerably higher rates of pay were earned at Triumph.

Over a period of ten years there had also been a series of catastrophic new models for which the Small Heath factory had spent time and money gearing up. They included the 70cc Dandy, one of BSA's most dismal failures.

Cave recalled that while there was excellent co-operation between Small Heath and Meriden at works level, discord in the upper echelons of the BSA Group tended to filter downwards, making life difficult for the production department. According to Cave, Lionel Jofeh's management methods also contributed to the difficult situation. 'The last person in the world who should have been put in charge of a motorcycle factory,' is Cave's scathing assessment of Jofeh.

At the outset, it had been understood that the 750cc triples were to be a short-term measure to combat Japanese competition until something else could be developed. For that reason, it had been stated in management meetings that production costs should be kept to a minimum. But as the project progressed, it began to consume large amounts of money, apparently regardless of any thought about what the new models could eventually earn back in revenue. Cave estimated that each triple cost the company

39

# Alistair Cave – managing in chaos

Others thought up the concept of the triple, but it fell to Alistair Cave to organize and supervise much of its volume manufacture, and ultimately help make it a viable high performance product.

Born in Leicester in 1918, Cave joined BSA as a time-served apprentice in 1940, when the company was heavily engaged in war work.

After the Second World War he worked on pedal cycle production, despite his enthusiasm for powered two-wheelers, firstly at Small Heath and then as a Superintendent at the company's Waverley works. There he introduced compressed air-powered tools to improve productivity, and when he returned to Small Heath, he took charge of the enamelling and plating department.

He took responsibility for procurement of spares for obsolete models, and learned much about how chaotic BSA's organization was becoming. As he progressed through the company, his common-sense grasp of the complex business of manufacture and assembly was apparent to his seniors and in 1964, as soon as Harry Sturgeon became Chief Executive, Cave was made Works Manager at Small Heath.

A tall and slim man, who went everywhere in the plant at running pace, Cave had to maximize productivity despite having a disjointed management above him. In his book *The Giants of Small Heath*, Barry Ryerson suggested that Cave would have been a better choice of Managing Director for the BSA Motorcycle Division in 1967 than Lionel Jofeh.

To this day, Cave defends the Armoury Road workforce against allegations that they were primarily responsible for deficiencies in the triples:

Triumph had brilliant concept designers and engineers, but I don't think they tested and improved the product enough at the pre-production stage. Perhaps machines should have been given to non-experts for evaluation. And quality control needed to be improved at both Small Heath and Meriden.

In the successive crises of the mid-seventies, Cave made strenuous personal efforts to save the triple and keep it in production, but they were in vain. Even after retirement, he maintained a keen interest in BSA history and is a leading authority on the chronicles of Small Heath.

*Alistair Cave (middle) with Lionel Jofeh (right) and grinding department foreman H. Jenson at Small Heath in the late sixties.*

£400–£500 to make, while the retail price had to be in the region of £600 to be competitive.

## Two of Everything

Producing the new 750 in both BSA and Triumph guises was an expensive scheme. It may have started out as an attempt at group rationalization, but in fact it created a multitude of additional – and unnecessary – production headaches. Far from being a matter of superficial 'badge engineering' involving cycle parts screwed on at a late stage, the triples' branding ran deep, mainly because of the decision to tilt the cylinders of the BSA version's engine forward.

The result of this apparently minor variation between the BSA A75 and the Triumph T150 power unit was that several of the major engine castings, including large and elaborate crankcase components, the timing covers and the gearbox end covers, had to be made in distinct versions for each marque. Supplied by outside contractors as raw gravity and die-castings in aluminium alloy, these components required a large number of machining operations to provide bores, threads, and precision-finished surfaces. Working with two sets of castings doubled the complexity of the work, from the point where the foundry had to be supplied with two alternative sets of patterns, through to final assembly.

'We had to involve ourselves in making sixteen castings instead of eight,' Cave recalled. He was also appalled at the prospect of having to assemble precisely aligned and oil-tight engines based on the elaborate 'sandwich' of vertically joined castings that constituted the main engine structure. Pressure die-casting, as used by Japanese motorcycle manufacturers, had been considered too expensive a process for BSA at this point.

*Amal Concentric carburettors rubber mount to upright Triumph cylinders.*

*The Trident side panel is shaped to enclose a single air filter serving all three carburettors.*

*The Trident grabrail and rear lamp unit, carrying side reflectors.*

*Cylinder barrel with three austenitic steel liners. Four alloy tappet blocks are pressed in.*

*Engine details are clearly shown by this cutaway BSA A75 engine prepared for display at shows and now owned by triples specialist L.P. Williams. The centre spark plug can be seen to tilt for accessibility.*

*This view of cutaway engine shows the inlet camshaft with two lobes for the left and one for the right cylinder. The pressed steel pushrod enclosure tubes have neoprene oil sealing rings at their ends. Blanked drillings on the cylinder base flange show where internal oilways were made.*

## Missed Opportunity

For some years prior to the triples' arrival Cave had been among those who advocated switching from the vertical crankcase joint traditionally used on British motorcycle engines, to a horizontal engine split, as used by the Japanese. The latter system would, in his view, have simplified production and have made it easier to produce oiltight units.

Such a complete re-think on engine production methods would have been timely. It can be argued that by the sixties, the British motorcycle industry should have been prepared to abandon its adherence to engine designs based on traditional capstan lathe machining techniques originally set up to make simple crankcases for the earliest single-cylinder internal combustion engines. In America, and most significantly in Japan, automotive manufacturers were already investing heavily in numerically controlled machining technology, which allowed them to break free of age-old procedures. Throughout much of British industry, however, investment was a lower priority than short-term gain for shareholders.

As Cave had noted, bold new designs from Honda and other Japanese motorcycle makers were mostly based on main engine castings that were pressure die-cast and horizontally split. They were structurally strong, and having the main joint on the axes of the crankshaft and gearbox shafts, they were simple to assemble with speed and accuracy. Former Meriden Experimental Foreman Alan Barrett told the author that senior engineering and design staff

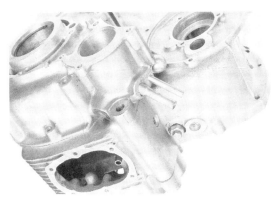

*Left: Three-piece crankcase, showing the two inner main bearing housings supported by the centre section.*

*Below left: View from below the crankcase, showing the main feed and return oil pipes projecting from behind the oil pump housing. The oil scavenge tube can be seen in the lower opening, where the removable cover for oil-changing contains a gauze filter.*

*Below: Finished one-piece crankshaft forging, made with journals in a flat plane and then heated and twisted.*

*Cutaways on primary drive casings show the triplex chain on cast iron shock absorber wheel and the clutch adjuster under the side cover. The lug at the bottom right was for a left-foot gearchange shaft, abandoned before production started.*

favoured the more modern layout, but the BSA Group insisted that production methods dictated the retention of the traditional vertical engine joints.

Problems arising from the use of vertical crankcase joints were to be particularly acute on the three-cylinder engine, which has two main crankcase joints, rather than the single joint found on two-bore BSA and Triumphs. 'Making sure that every joint face was flat, and that they were all true with each other was not easy,' Cave recalled. 'The latest jointing compounds were helpful, but we eventually had to buy special lapping machines to clean up the faces.'

In those days before computer controlled machining centres, setting up the numerous operations to mill, drill, ream and tap engine castings was a major undertaking on any engine. On the three-cylinder engines, it was to involve horrendously complex procedures. As Cave said:

> Nearly sixty individual operations were required to machine the central set of crankcase castings alone. As you can imagine, whenever we switched from making A75s to Tridents, all the setting changes made to the machinery increased the possiblity of errors. And setting time increased our production costs.

There was a particular problem with the camshaft bearing bores in the outer crankcase castings. They were blind, and could only be machined from one end. Machinists were expected to achieve tolerances down to 0.001in (0.025mm) in a place

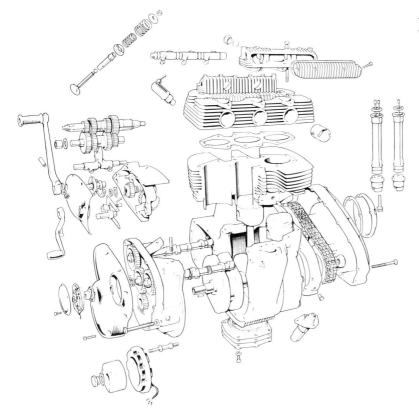

they could not see. Centre and side portions had to be assembled together, turned upside-down to be bored, and then separated again.

BSA had never had to deal with a crank-shaft as big as the three-cylinder component. In the absence of forging equipment capable of making the one-piece 120-degree crankshaft 'in the round', a special technique was devised. The basic shaft was produced 'flat' with all three of its crankpins in the same plane by the existing drop-forging plant at Armoury Road.

Then it had to be part-machined, ready for clamping in a press. The outer ends were cropped and centred before returning the shaft to the forge. After being heated up again it was fixed in a hydraulic press. One end was twisted to the left and the other to the right, until the crankpins were set equally at 120 degrees. Cranks made this way proved strong, but the process, whilst ingenious, was long-winded and consequently expensive.

## Keeping up the Pace

On top of all these complications, BSA's production team was set an ambitious output target when engine manufacture commenced following the plant's annual summer holiday in 1968. After a preliminary output at the modest rate of fifty units a week, Armoury Road was expected to work up to building 150 engines of both the BSA and the Triumph type every working week.

On completion, each engine unit was motored on a Heenan and Froude static test

*Complete clutch assembly.*

rig to circulate lubricant, and run briefly. Oil was flushed through, drained out and the filters changed. Every twentieth engine was dynamometer tested and its output recorded. When production was fully under way, samples of completed machines were taken at random for comprehensive testing at the Motor Industry Research Association (MIRA) proving ground near Nuneaton. Triumph had a similar method of monitoring the performance and settings of completed triples.

In comparison with power unit manufacture, making the triples' cycle parts was relatively straightforward. But the decision to make two different frames at two factories was another example of needless high expenditure. At both factories frame, telescopic fork and spoked wheel construction followed procedures already set up for twin-cylinder manufacture. Like that of the 500 and 650cc BSA twins, the Rocket III chassis was MIG-welded together from steel tube.

At Triumph, the Trident frame was made by a traditional process of hearth brazing lengths of tube and forged lugs together, and assembled in two main bolt-together sections. There was no tube bending equipment at Meriden, so curved lengths of A-grade mild steel tubing were supplied ready shaped by Reynolds Tube of Birmingham.

## Cycle Part Production

A 600-ton flat-bed press was bought purely for the purpose of making the 'ray gun' silencers at Small Heath. But, despite their unusual appearance, Cave says making them was the least of his worries, as their seamed top and bottom longitudinal joins were much easier to cope with than the traditional cigar-shaped silencers, from which joins had to be made invisible by laborious polishing prior to chromium plating. Unlike Meriden, Armoury Road still had its own plating shop, but no auto polishing

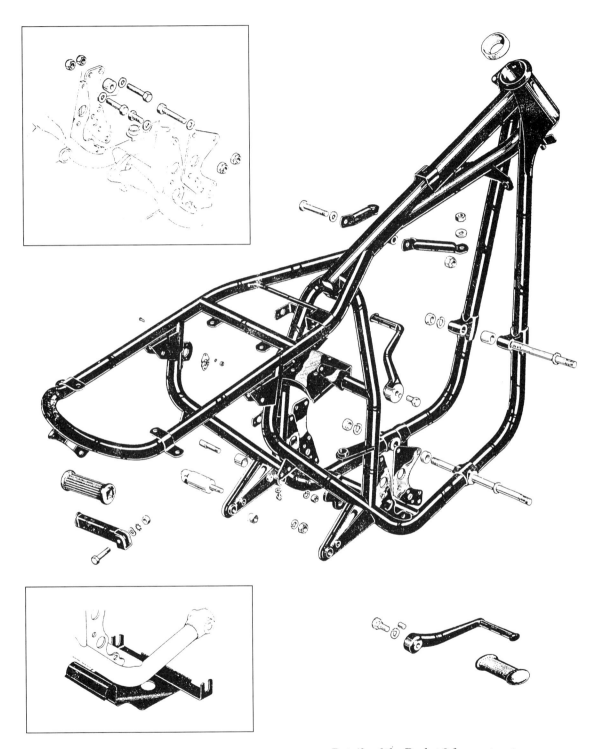

*Details of the Rocket 3 frame structure.*

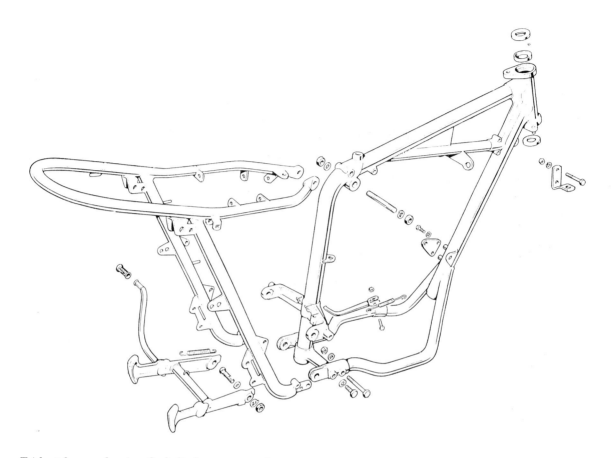

*Trident frame, showing the bolted-up construction.*

*Set of three carburettors, with mounting bar and
alloy throttle operating linkage above the bodies.*

machines. One hazard with the ray guns
was that their large surface areas were easily damaged by rough handling: even one
small dent would show up clearly.

When it came to production line assembly, extra supports for the heavy silencers
had to be added. Also, the three-into-two
exhaust manifold assembly proved awkward to make accurately. Cut tubing had to
be fixed into place by clamping and tack-
welding but the heat applied when finally
welding the fabrication together was apt to
throw the pipes out of alignment. Attaching
the manifolds to the machine on the assembly line was a fiddly job.

*Small Heath acquired a modern assembly system, costing £250,000, but not until the end of 1969, when triples had been in production for a year. This view shows 1971 single cylinder BSAs being built: Rocket 3s were assembled on one of the three tracks fed by overhead conveyors and leading to the rolling roads. The plant was to be scrapped early in 1971, when 3,000 workers were made redundant.*

However, the Homer company in Birmingham, which usually made petrol tanks for the BSA Group, adapted to Ogle's boxy shapes type without complaint.

When triple production was being set up in the spring of 1968, BSA and Triumph was in the throes of changing the thread forms used on its products from traditional British threads to the American Unified system. The change was instigated by Umberslade Hall, the remote design facility set up in a large country house by Lionel Jofeh. In the long term it was intended to cut the cost of buying-in fasteners, since Unified was being adopted across the UK automotive industry, temporarily as it turned out, for metric fasteners were to be adopted eventually.

In reality, the change caused disruption through the manufacturing process, as all taps, dies, and thread gauges had to be changed. At Small Heath, it became usual for the assembly area to be littered with trays of fasteners which looked alike, but had different thread forms. The triples incorporated many UNF (fine) and UNC (coarse) threads from the outset.

At Meriden, machining of triples parts was fitted into the hectic twins programme, and a special track was laid for Trident assembly, intended to turn out twenty-five machines per day. Volume assembly of complete BSA Rocket III and Triumph Trident motorcycles began after the works' holidays in August 1968.

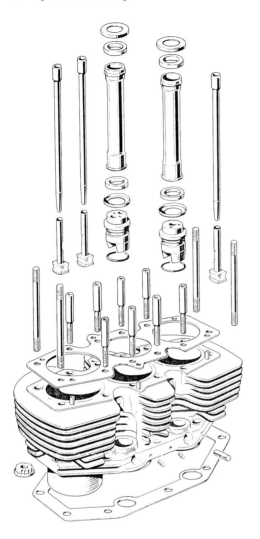

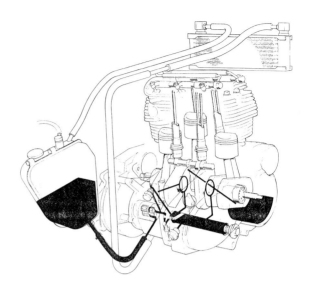

*Left: Cylinder barrel details. The cam follower
blocks and steel pushrod tubes with oil seals
follow Triumph twin practice. The eight inner
head studs are a sleeve type with internal threads
to receive bolts through the head.*

*Above: Diagram showing how oil circulates
through the engine. The pump is below and to the
left of the crankshaft; access to the changeable
filter is by the threaded cap on the right.*

*Below: Exploded drawing of the clutch assembly.
The splined shaft on the left carries the
chainwheel and shock absorber.*

*Below left: Diagram showing location of primary
transmission support bearings in the inner and
outer chaincases.*

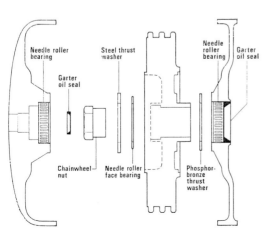

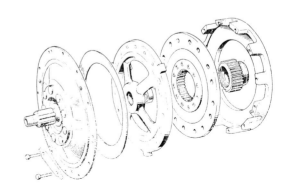

# A75 and T150 (1969)

## Engine

### Crankshaft

One-piece steel forging with big-end journals disposed at 120 degrees, supported in four main bearings. Inner mains: two plain shell Vandervell VP bearings supported on clamp mounts in the central crankcase casting. Outer mains: ballrace on drive side, roller bearing on timing side. Lateral crankshaft location at drive-side main bearing.

Alloy I-section connecting-rods with steel end caps, on Vandervell VP 6 shell big-end bearings. At small ends, gudgeon pins bear directly in rod metal. Hepolite pistons have raised crowns with flat areas facing valves. Three rings per piston: two iron compression rings, one oil control ring.

### Valve Operation

Two camshafts, inlet and exhaust, located in upper crankcase ahead of and behind bores, each supported on three bearings directly on crankcase metal. Camshafts driven by steel gears, via idler pinion, from pinion at timing-side end of crankshaft.

Cam lobes align with Stellite-faced tappets in alloy blocks located in base flange of cylinder block. Lobes and tappets for cylinders 2 and 3 grouped together.

Alloy pushrods transmit tappet motion to valve rockers via steel cups at their upper ends. Rods enclosed by steel tubes, two inlet, two exhaust, sealed by compressible neoprene rings. Upper ends of tubes pass through apertures in cylinder head casting to locate into the two cast alloy rocker boxes.

Two valves per cylinder. Included angle between inlet and exhaust: 75 degrees. Inlet valve diameter: $1^{17}/_{32}$in, exhaust: $1^{5}/_{16}$in, seats cast in head. Phosphor bronze valve guides. Two springs per valve supported on steel cups, outer spring variable rate type.

Rocker spindles supported in alloy inlet and exhaust rocker boxes. Three rockers located endwise on each spindle by Thackeray spring washers.

### Cylinder and Cylinder Head

One-piece aluminium alloy cylinder block secured to crankcase by ten studs through base flange. Three bores with austenitic steel liners extending into crankcase mouth. Corgasyl steel cylinder head gasket, replaced by copper early in production.

One-piece die-cast aluminium alloy cylinder head, with spark plug apertures for outer cylinders angled outwards at 20 degrees from vertical. Centre plug location angled at 40 degrees and tilted to left for accessibility. Exhaust ports threaded to accept screw-in steel stubs for mounting exhaust manifold.

### Lubrication

Dry sump system with remote oil tank. Steel-bodied oil pump with two pairs of pumping gears for feed and scavenge, driven from pinion on drive side mainshaft inboard of main engine output sprocket via intermediate pinion .

Oil from feed side of the pump passes via cartridge filter to feed holes at crankshaft centre mains. Internal drillings in crank convey oil to big-end bearings. Pressure relief valve threaded into the rear face of drive-side crankcase connects to filter chamber: oil released by valve returned to scavenge line.

Circulated oil drains down through mesh filter recessed in base of crankcase, where scavenge tube draws it through return side of pump. Return line to tank passes oil through cooling radiator, and to rockers via auxiliary take-off line. Oil from rocker boxes drains to crankcase via six oil drains running through head and barrel, dwelled at cylinder head joint, and also down pushrod tubes and drillings in tappet blocks.

Pressure oil feeds to exhaust tappets and cams from centre mains via oilways in cylinder barrel. Tappet blocks sealed with O-rings (feeds later blanked off and seals discontinued).

| Engine type | air-cooled ohv transverse triple |
| --- | --- |
| Bore and stroke | $67 \times 70$mm |
| Cubic capacity | 741cc |
| Compression ratio | 9.5:1 |
| Claimed output | 58bhp @ 7250rpm (60bhp also claimed) |

## Ignition

Coil ignition system with contact breaker points housed in outer timing chest cover, driven by exhaust camshaft. Three independently adjustable points on backplates, fixed to common backplate with Lucas centrifugal auto-advance mechanism. Three Siba ignition coils sited under seat.

Lucas 120-watt alternator mounted on timing-side mainshaft outboard of camshaft drive gears.

| Ignition timing | 38 degrees fully advanced |
| --- | --- |
| Contact breakers | Lucas 7CA |
| Spark plugs | Champion N3 14mm, gap 0.020in (0.5mm) |
| Firing order | $1 - 2 - 3$ (counting from left cylinder) |

## Carburation

Three Amal A626 Concentric instruments with chokes of 27mm diameter. Bolted to a cast-alloy beam supporting rod and linkage throttle operating mechanism, and connected to inlet stubs by flexible hose. Single external slide return spring. Standard jetting: 150 main, needle jet .106in, needle position 2, throttle slide cutaway no. 3.

## Air Filtration

Single filter unit with wired felt element.

## Exhaust System

Fabricated tubular manifold from three exhaust ports in head connects to two main exhaust pipes of 1⅛in outside diameter. Centre cylinder's outlet bifurcated into two tubes meeting outer manifold tubes. Down-pipes fixed to the manifold by pinch bolts terminate in two reverse-flow silencers, each with three small-diameter outlets.

## Rev-Counter Drive

Drive unit in front section of centre crankcase section contains skew gear meshing with teeth cut on exhaust camshaft.

# Transmission

## Primary Drive

Endless triplex chain in oilbath. Tension maintained by rubber-faced blade, externally adjustable.

Driving sprocket located on splines at drive end of crankshaft. Driven iron sprocket wheel mounted on cush-drive shock absorber, with six vanes and rubber inserts, supported in two needle roller bearings.

## Clutch

Borg and Beck single-plate, dry, inboard of primary chain oil bath supported in needle roller bearings. Operated by three-ball ramp mechanism in outer chaincase acting on a pull rod. Driving plate disengaged against pressure from single dished diaphragm spring. Driven plate carried on splined boss keyed and secured to gearbox mainshaft.

## Gearbox

Four-speed constant mesh. Housed in centre and left crankcase castings. The mainshaft and layshaft supported at drive side by ball-races in left crankcase. Shafts' other ends located in bearings in gearbox inner cover bolted to centre crankcase. Main shaft extends through roller bearing in cover to carry kick-starter ratchet pinion.

Selection of ratios by two forks on spindle ahead of layshaft, engaging with sliding dogs. Forks controlled by camplate and positive stop footchange mechanism within outer cover.

## Final Drive

Single row chain on left side from sprocket inboard of clutch on gearbox mainshaft to sprocket on rear wheel hub.

| | |
|---|---|
| Primary chain | ⅜in pitch triplex, 82 links |
| Primary chaincase capacity (nominal) | 0.5 pint (290cc) |
| Engine sprocket | 28 teeth |
| Clutch sprocket | 50 teeth |
| Gearbox sprocket | 19 teeth |
| Gearbox ratios (overall) | |
| first: | 11.95:1 |
| second: | 8.3:1 |
| third: | 5.83:1 |
| fourth: | 4.87:1 |
| Gearbox oil capacity | 1⅓ pints (750cc) |
| Secondary chain links | ⅝ × ⅜in, 106 |
| Rear wheel sprocket | 52 teeth |

## Cycle parts

### Frame, BSA A75

Duplex cradle, all-welded tubular structure. Twin front downtubes continue under power unit and up to rear suspension upper mounts. Single main top tube from upper steering head to two mid-section bracing tubes, welded to main loops near swinging arm supports. Additional top tube braces main tube to lower steering head.

Rear subframe loop to support seat welded to main top tube and welded to main duplex tubes ahead of rear suspension unit top mounts.

Rear suspension's swinging arm constructed of braced tubes, pivoting on plain bushes. Fixed spindle secured in gusset plates welded to main frame.

### Frame, Triumph T150

Tubular structure of tube and lugs in front and rear sections, bolted together. Front section: single front downtube from steering head divided into two to form engine cradle. Single top tube continued downwards behind power unit, connected to cradle tubes via forged member.

Rear section: two main tubes bolted to forged section at their lower ends and brazed to seat loop at their upper ends. Seat loop bolted to main top tube where it curves downwards.

Swinging arm spindle supported in forging on main vertical tube, carrying arm on plain bushes. Spindle also supported in outer plates on main subframe tubes.

## Suspension

### Front

Triumph-type telescopic front fork with steel sliders and stanchions. Springing by external coil springs. Two-way damping by shuttle valves controlling flow of oil within each leg.

Weather proofing of upper stanchions by compressible synthetic rubber gaiters.

At steering head, stanchions clamped in malleable cast iron yokes, with cup, cone and ball steering head bearings. Friction damper for steering, adjustable by hand knob.

| | |
|---|---|
| Fork spring rate | 32.5lb/in |
| Fork oil capacity | 190cc |

### Rear

Springing and damping for swinging arm rear suspension by detachable Girling shock absorber struts, with three-position spring adjustment.

| | |
|---|---|
| Shock absorber spring rate | 110lb/in |

## Wheels and tyres

Spoked wheels with chromium plated steel rims.

| | |
|---|---|
| Spokes | 40 per wheel |
| Rims | front, WM2 × 19in, rear WM3 × 19in |
| Tyres | front, 3.25 × 19in Dunlop K70, rear 4.10 × 19in Dunlop K81 |

## Brakes

Front drum brake of twin-leading-shoe type in full-width hub. Two cams linked by adjustable rod operated by cable from handlebar lever.

Single-leading-shoe rear drum brake bolted to full-width hub, operated by rigid rod from foot pedal on left side.

| | |
|---|---|
| Front | 8in diameter, shoe width 1⅜in |
| Rear | 7in diameter, shoe width 1¼in |

## Other cycle parts

Steel blade-type mudguards front and rear. On T150 front guard held on tubular stays. On A75 guard attached to front fork sliders. Adjustable friction steering damper.

Steel oil tank placed on right, shrouded by moulded side panel also forming an air filter housing at forward end. Matching panel on left conceals battery and vertically mounted ignition coils and a toolkit.

Pressed steel fuel tank with longitudinal tunnel to clear frame top tube, cushioned on rubbers. On A75 secured to top tube by single bolt, embellishment strip over top. Badges and knee grips carried on side panels. On T150, secured by studs at front, bolt at rear, embellishment strip over top, badges and knee-grips on side panels.

*Tank Capacities*

| | |
|---|---|
| Fuel | 4.25 gallons (5 US gallons, 19 litres) |
| Oil | 5 pints (6 US pints, 3 litres) |

Dual seat: foam-filled and vinyl covered, on steel pan. Hump at rear on A75. Seat is hinged for access to battery, other electrical equipment and tools storage space in frame.

Chromium plated ⅞in tubular handlebar with single-pull throttle twistgrip, clutch and brake operating levers, choke lever. High rise 'Western' bar on US export A75 and all T150s.

## Electrical equipment

Positive earth wiring. Lucas 7in headlamp with chromed flat-backed shell. Lucas cast-alloy rear lamp unit with side reflectors. Twin Windtone horns. Switch for stop lamp operated by rear brake rod.

Battery charging control by Lucas rectifier and Zener diode.

| | |
|---|---|
| Battery | 12 volt, 8 amp hour |
| Alternator | Lucas 20 watt |
| Headlamp bulb | 50/40 watt |
| Pilot bulb | 6 watt |
| Stop/tail bulb | 21/5 watt |

## Instruments

Smith 150mph speedometer and 10,000rpm rev counter, both magnetic type, embedded in rubber in moulded instrument binnacle with ignition and oil indicator lights, and Lucas ammeter. Ignition switch in right-side headlamp bracket on front fork top shroud.

## Dimensions (in/mm)

| | *BSA* | *Triumph* |
|---|---|---|
| Wheelbase | 56.25/1,429 | 58/1,473 |
| Ground clearance | 7/178 | 6.5/165 |
| Seat height | 32/813 | 31/787 |
| Dry weight | 470lb (213kg) | 468lb (212kg) |

## Colour schemes

*BSA*

Fuel tank, side panels, mudguards: Flamboyant Red or Flamboyant Blue. Frame: Black.

*Triumph*

Fuel tank, side panels, mudguards: Aquamarine. Frame: Black.

# WESTERN TESTING

BSA's American subsidiaries would be expected to sell large numbers of triples. To sound out distributors' reactions to the 750s and to discover how the machines would fare in typical transatlantic conditions, a team from the UK went to the USA in November 1967. It comprised Doug Hele and Alan Barrett representing Triumph, while BSA sent senior engineer Clive Bennett (formerly of Ariel) and Graham Saunders from Small Heath's Experimental Department. Four pre-production machines were shipped to California: two BSAs and a pair of Tridents, plus a stock of spares.

Key staff from BSA's two main headquarters, and Triumph's East and West bases, were invited on a three-week testing session.

Pete Colman, a Vice President and General Manager of the recently-merged BSA and Triumph operation on the West Coast, set up a base at his home in Claremont, from where the secret tests could be carried out. A 2,500-mile (4,000km) itinerary was planned to take in every type of terrain from snowy mountain roads to blistering desert conditions. It traversed northern and southern California to Arizona, where the riders encountered colossal rain storms, finishing at the Mexican border. Along the way, speed tests were laid on at the Orange County Raceway drag strip near Los Angeles, with top Triumph racers Gary Nixon and Gene Romero.

Hele told the author that on the whole he thought the triples coped well with conditions varying from torrential rain to scorching desert weather. Colman's recollections were much more negative. 'Unfortunately, the road tests were considered to be less than satisfactory,' he told the author in 1996, recalling daily electrical and other problems.

According to Alan Barrett, most electrical troubles had stemmed from the ignition points, because Lucas had recently changed the material used for the points' cam-following heel from Tufnol to a nylon substance, which wore rapidly. But, he said, that fault had been cured by applying small amounts

*Unbadged pre-production BSA and Triumph triples during American tests in October 1967.*

*Graham Saunders of BSA overhauls a Rocket 3 on a makeshift bench in Pete Colman's garden.*

# American reorganization

Under Harry Sturgeon, BSA and Triumph operations in the US were rationalized. Johnson Motors (Jomo) of Pasadena, California, a Triumph dealer since pre-war days, came under the direct control of the BSA group early in 1965. Hap Alzina, BSA's traditional West Coast outlet based in Oakland, California, was acquired by Jomo.

The two operations were brought together in the BSA-Triumph Western Distribution Center, a single 60,000sq. ft complex at Duarte, 10 miles from Pasadena, during 1966. In the east, separate BSA and Triumph entities continued at their traditional bases, the Triumph Corporation in Baltimore and BSA Inc. (East), formerly the Rich Child Cycle Co, in Nutley, New Jersey.

Former Johnson Motors manager E. W. 'Pete' Colman was given the unenviable task of heading up an organization comprised of hitherto rival teams.

Lionel Jofeh installed Peter Thornton as President of a new parent company, BSA Co. Incorporated, in 1969, his base being at Verona, New Jersey. Baltimore then became the eastern distribution centre for both BSA and Triumph, and Duarte continued as a the western HQ for both makes, but under Thornton's ultimate direction. The Nutley centre was closed. Colman became Vice President of Engineering and National Director of Racing, with Duarte Service chief Bob Tryon becoming Technical Center Manager under him, overseeing both Baltimore and Duarte.

*The Duarte, California, western base opened in 1966, with BSA occupying the half of the building furthest from the camera, and Triumph the rest.*

of graphited grease. There had also been trouble with a machine because one of its ignition coils had turned out to have a manufacturing defect.

Interestingly, the pre-production machines taken to America were equipped with left-foot gearchange. The change mechanism was supported by a lug on the inner primary chaincase casting, which remained redundantly in place on production machines. To suit rightfoot brake pedals, old production BSA hubs with right-side brake backplates were used.

There was growing pressure for standardization on the American market, and the left-side change was preferred as a standard, even by importers of British machines invariably equipped with right foot gearchanging. This was because of the growing numbers of customers who traded up from lightweight Japanese starter machines to larger capacity British products who had

already become accustomed to the left-foot change on oriental motorcycles. Another argument for standardization was that placing the brake pedal under the right foot related to the controls of a car.

Making the switch with the new triples might have been a useful marketing move for BSA on the US market, but UK and some European customers may have reacted against the change. Eventually the American view was to prevail, when the left foot change pattern was imposed on British manufacturers in the mid-seventies.

Following the 1967 American trials of the triples, questionnaires were issued for US personnel to make their observations about the new machines, which both Barrett and Hele recalled as being very useful. But whatever else was to be altered in the light of the research, the Ogle tanks and silencers were to stay firmly in place on production models.

# 3   The Triples are Launched

## FIRST UK IMPRESSIONS

Not surprisingly, given the long development period, rumours had circulated for some time about new three-cylinder machines from BSA/Triumph. But when the Rocket 3 and Trident were officially revealed to the British public in September 1968, the impact was blunted by the news that machines would not be available on the home market for several months.

Full details and test machines were released to UK motorcycling publications,

but as the weekly *Motor Cycle* warned, the A75 and T150 were 'essentially export jobs' and even if they reached British dealers' showrooms in the spring of 1969, numbers were expected to be limited.

Early road tests were complimentary about performance and roadholding of the 750s, with reservations about the styling and some practical aspects.

In his Rocket 3 report, *Motor Cycle's* veteran tester, former road racer Vic Willoughby, was enthusiastic about the triple's acceleration, reporting that even

*Model poses with an early T150 at a UK show. White pants would not be recommended Trident riding gear, as early machines tended to leak oil.*

with the rider sitting bolt upright and a pillion passenger behind him, 105mph (169km/h) was reached 'in a breathtakingly short time'. Using 7,250rpm for maximum power, he found he was making gear changes into second, third and top gears at 45, 65 and 95mph (72, 105 and 153km/h). The throttle's light action was commended, especially as it had to operate three carburettors.

Praise was also given to the engine's flexibility and smooth power delivery, although a period of noticeable vibration was reported, peaking from 5,500-6,000rpm. The clutch, whilst found to be drag-free, was criticized for being heavy and upward gearchanges were not slick.

Willoughby liked the Rocket's handling, writing of 'flip-flop cornering at speeds of up to 80mph' and, rather surprisingly, he did not report that limited ground clearance was a problem. Braking on both wet and dry roads was found to adequate, considering the machine's considerable 485lb (220kg) weight, thanks to the Triumph-designed 8in (200mm) twin-leading-shoe front brake already fitted to BSA and Triumph 650 twins for 1968.

Negative findings included difficulty in using the centre stand despite the lifting rail provided, leakage of engine oil, and awkwardly placed electrical switchgear.

Gavin Trippe of *Motor Cycle News* was similarly impressed by the Trident's acceleration, and in speed tests at MIRA it was timed at 130mph (209km/h) on a one-way run. A mean two-way speed was calculated at 126.45mph (203.46km/h), a touch faster than *Motor Cycle's* figure for the slightly heavier A75.

Prophetically, Trippe said that the triple's distinctive exhaust note would go down in history, 'along with the Scott "yowl" and the Vincent "burble"'.

Criticizing the untidy and archaic handlebar layout, and being less than enthusiastic about the fishtail silencers, *MCN's* tester nevertheless concluded that the T150 was the best two-wheeler he had ridden. If he was to buy a new motorcycle, he said, this would be it.

'What a fantastic machine,' enthused Charles Deane, editor of the UK monthly *Motorcycle Mechanics* in the magazine's test of the same Trident, a press model carrying the registration SAC341G. Caught out by the deceptive speed of the 750cc triple, he had crashed it at a roundabout near Rugby, but despite having to visit hospital was not seriously injured.

*MM's* test suggested that the brakes were only just up to the T150's speed, and vibration between 5,500rpm and 6,400rpm again attracted comment. A thirst for fuel, which saw consumption at the rate of 32–4mpg (8–9l/100km) during speed testing, was frowned upon. Docility for town riding was commended, but a high-speed weave 'at full bore in a straight line' was mentioned. Deane also remarked that the proposed price of £550 was expensive for the average UK motorcyclist.

The price was not the only sales deterrent. Many bikers found the styling and bulk of the new models off-putting. In the UK, the prevailing fashion was to customize second-hand, and even new, machines. Following a trend set by a hard core of performance-mad 'café racers', stripping machines down to make them into pseudo racers was all the rage. Any removable mudguarding, panels and plated embellishments were being torn off, and an industry had grown up to provide aftermarket 'goodies' like clip-on racing handlebars, rear-set footrests and racing seats. Manufacturers were aware of the trend: BSA had adopted café racer style with the 250cc C25 Barracuda and the 441cc B44 Victor Roadster of 1967, and the later 250cc Starfire.

In that climate, the almost car-like style of the Trident and Rocket 3 was out of place,

# Bahn stormer

In Germany, the critical test of a 750cc motorcycle was its ability to withstand the long periods of ultra-high speed cruising which that country's de-restricted autobahns allowed. To show that the 750cc triple was up to the job, Triumph sent SAC341G, a press test Trident, to Germany in April 1969 for the magazine *Motorrad* to test.

It was accompanied by Meriden's press officer David Lloyd, advisor and test rider Percy Tait and experimental fitter Ron Barrett, who subsequently worked together in a department at Meriden where press and publicity machines were fettled. Barrett recalls that the T150's engine was almost entirely standard, except for S & W racing valve springs. He put them in for safety after spotting a broken standard inner spring during UK tests. Overall gearing was raised by changing the stock 52-tooth rear wheel sprocket for a 50-tooth item.

*Motorrad's* Ernst Leverkus organised a 1,235km (767 mile) run on autobahns from Hamburg in northern Germany to Vienna in Austria, to which the magazine had previously submitted a Yamaha two-stroke. Speeds of 90–110mph (145–177km/h) were maintained by rider Hans Ehlert, despite extreme cold, but approaching Nürnburg snow was encountered. South of Munich, the Trident rode into a blizzard, and the run was abandoned. *Motorrad* reported that after 800km (500 miles) the rear chain was worn out, and the rear K81 tyre showed signs of cracking. 'I had left the tyre pressure normal because of the bad weather. Otherwise I would have upped the pressure and it would have lasted better at speed,' Barrett explained.

A second successful attempt with Peter Karlau riding started from Vienna to run northwards to Hamburg at 4.45am on 2 May. With stops, including one for drive chain replacement, the average speed was 130km/h (81mph). The actual riding time was 8 hours 43 minutes, making an average of 143.3km/h (88.85mph). It bettered the Yamaha's run by 18km/h.

On the following day, the Trident was ridden from Hamburg to Stuttgart by an indirect route, and after three days it had covered 2,800km (1,740 miles) most of it at high autobahn speeds. Another tyre had been worn out, half of the Duckhams Q oil in the tank had been used and some small fasteners had dropped off.

Average speeds had been reduced, said *Motorrad*, because of the frequent need to fill the fuel tank, which it felt was too small. At the higher speeds, fuel consumption had been as heavy as 25mpg (11l/100km).

*Peter Karlau cruises towards Vienna on the autobahn to make a successful high-speed run in May 1969.*

even though the pricy triples were aimed more at the mature and experienced rider, rather than the less affluent café racing generation. The exhilarating power that buyers craved was there, but the ability to use it was curbed by meagre cornering clearance. Even if the 750s had been available in large numbers in the UK from their launch, it is doubtful that they would have been strong sellers.

## THE SEARCH FOR US SALES

More effort was expended on publicizing the new models in America, the principal target market for them. Attractive brochures were distributed, and a press release put out by BSA Inc. in October 1968 tried hard to sell the Rocket 3's looks, boasting of its 'unprecedented beauty'. It also claimed that 'sleek styling … provides less wind drag and easier handling.' A valiant attempt was made to hype the 'ray gun' silencer, which was described in US publicity as 'the futuristic TriPak muffler'.

*Test rider Hans Ehlert and German Triumph importer Detter Louis with Trident SAC341G in Hamburg before the first abortive run in April 1969.*

*Plastic accessories: BSA-made Motoplas touring screen for the Rocket 3 and pvc boots for the promotion girls.*

*Models Alice Stobbs and Caron Gardner smile for the cameras with a Trident at a Photo-Cine fair in London*

But despite this, the all-important American motorcycling public did not take to slabby fuel tanks and weird-looking silencers. Whoever had briefed Ogle to design 750s with the brashness of that nation's saloon cars had been ignorant of Triumph's experience in the late fifties.

When Meriden had launched the Bonneville with a headlamp enclosed in a pressed-steel nacelle and heavy mudguarding in 1959, US buyers reacted against this staid appearance. The lesson learned, and acted upon then, was that sporting American riders, particularly in the wide-open spaces of the Western States, were attracted most by the lean profile of semi-off-road machines like the Triumph's 650 Trophy.

The leading US monthly *Cycle World* seemed unsure how to categorize the Trident, comparing it with the defunct 1,000cc Ariel Square Four, a luxurious eye-catching machine with a smooth engine but strictly tourer performance. The magazine only managed to push its T150 to 117.03mph (188.3km/h) and the brakes were criticized as not being up to their task of stopping a 500lb (225kg) projectile. The tester found that a lack of torque below 3,000rpm made town riding tricky, and noticed high-frequency vibration at high engine speeds. Oil leaks from beneath the crankcase were noted.

When *Cycle World* got its hands on a Rocket 3, it called the BSA a two-wheeled Cadillac in a double-edged phrase that could have referred either to comfort and stability, or excess weight and brash styling.

Considering that the 750 had been conceived as a motorcycle expressly aimed at the US market, sales were very slow. It is estimated that fewer than 7,000 triples were sold in 1969, which was not in any case a strong selling season for larger capacity machines in North America.

American managers had warned that the triples' look was wrong. Pete Colman told

the author that although Ted Hodgdon, outgoing President of BSA Inc., had been keen on the silencers, there were strong protests over what Colman called 'ugly' machines from him and Earl Miller, general manager of Triumph Eastern.

BSA had also been warned about the new models' less-than-rosy prospects by Don Brown, sales chief of BSA Inc. A former sales manager at Californian Triumph distributor Johnson Motors, Brown had joined BSA after a stint with Suzuki's US operation. During 1967 he had submitted a report to Small Heath expressing strong reservations about the 750s.

Brown told the author in 1996 that when he had originally seen drawings of the fishtail silencers he had not believed that they would survive into production. He had also advocated electric starting, a feature of Honda's 750cc four. But his biggest misgiving had been the high sales price of $1,750, 30 per cent higher than that of BSA's 650cc Lightning. Colman had also made it known that he thought the 750 overpriced.

At a pre-launch meeting in England in 1968 Brown had forecast that BSA Inc, would sell fewer than 2,000 Rocket 3s in the first year. This projection had been received badly, as the BSA Group were banking on rapidly recouping the massive tooling outlay for triples production. Brown believes that some BSA Group executives were expecting a return inside one year.

Nevertheless, Brown was determined to maximize sales as best he could, and hit on a theme:

> I remembered being told in England that the Rocket 3 could reach and sustain speeds of at least 125mph. I thought it might be time to thumb our noses at Harley-Davidson and some others, and go for some records. I wanted a plan that would have national, even international, press coverage.

*A Johnson Motors triples service school at Duarte, California. General Manager Pete Colman stands on the right. On Colman's right are instructor Dick Lytell, Service Manager Pat Owens (wearing tie) and Foreman Bob Ellison (in white coat, middle).*

Without telling BSA in England, he organized an AMA-sanctioned record breaking session at the Daytona International Speedway's high-speed banked circuit, with four riders, including a press man, aboard Rocket 3s in near-standard trim.

Brown broke the news of his plans, to be implemented in April 1969, to a final pre-launch meeting in England. He recalled that Miller and Colman seemed displeased by the surprise announcement. 'But, finally, Jofeh approved the plan as it had been presented, and that was that,' Brown said.

The Daytona enterprise was a success, setting a string of records over 120mph (193km/h), and a 5-mile (8km) flying start figure of 131.723mph (211.218km/h). Brown made sure that this speed, astonishing for a standard roadster of the day, was quoted in BSA's advertisements, which appeared on both sides of the Atlantic.

As a result the Rocket 3 outsold the Trident in the US for some months. The venture also gave rise to a contentious theory that has been argued over ever since – that the A75R was always a shade faster than the T150 out of the crate.

Triples were eventually launched in Britain at the Easter-time Brighton Show in April 1969, now priced at £614. Honda managed to steal some of the thunder by rushing an early example of its four-cylinder 750 to Brighton. The machine that had spurred the BSA board into action four years earlier had arrived, and it offered buyers several attractive modern features in addition to an overhead camshaft engine of a type hitherto only seen on grand prix racers. It was equipped with an electric self-starter, a disc front brake and a five-speed gearbox. When the price was announced at the show, it was £35 more than the British

---

# Hatching the Rocket 3 records plot

Before his records assault at Daytona International Speedway in April 1969, Don J. Brown secured the co-operation of Bill Berry, executive director of the American Motorcyclist Association, the governing body of two-wheeled sport in the USA:

> I approached him privately and convinced him to sanction the records and to do it in secrecy. Then I rented the Speedway for several days. Actually I didn't know what records we were going after. All I wanted was to put the AMA's stamp of approval on the events and certify the speeds achieved, and to ensure that the machines were absolutely standard.
>
> That was important, because I knew that if we were successful there would be a hue and cry that the machines weren't standard, or that the deal was somehow rigged.

The aim was to gun Rocket 3s round the banked circuit at specified distances of up to 200 miles (320km), at 130mph (209km/h) or as near that speed as possible. Four A75s were taken from BSA's stock in New Jersey, carefully stripped and reassembled. Any suspect parts were replaced, but only with standard BSA spares.

Minimal modifications were made for Daytona. The handlebars were dropped for rider comfort at speed, the front mudguards removed and the front wheel rims shod with Dunlop K81 tyres in place of ribbed Dunlops. Lighting and other road equipment was left in place and no engine, air filtration or exhaust alterations were made. Overall gearing was raised slightly.

The riders hired for the session were racers Dick Mann, Yvon DuHamel and Ray Hempstead. Experienced record breaker and journalist Gordon Jennings of *Cycle* magazine was also given a machine, but like Berry of the AMA, he agreed that should the attempts fail, not a word would be said or printed.

In the event, there was plenty to shout about. French Canadian rider DuHamel set a clutch of records for various distances covered around the banked circuit. As well as his 131.723mph (211.942km/h) 5-mile figure, he clocked a one-hour average at over 127mph (204km/h), and covered 200 miles (320km) at 123.40mph (198.55km/h). Mann hammered his BSA round at over 125mph (201km/h) to set figures for the 100-mile and 150-mile distances. They were classified by the AMA as 750cc Stock Machine records, although Brown says that some members of the organization, notably industry representative William Harley of Harley-Davidson, were displeased when they heard of the almost-secret session.

Jennings got his story, which made the cover of *Cycle*'s May 1969 issue. Brown suggests that this useful publicity could have accounted for BSA triples outselling Triumph triples in their first full year on the US market.

Brown knew that by creating a record class for street Superbikes he was encouraging other makers to respond by bettering the Rocket 3s' achievement. But a rumoured Harley-Davidson counter attempt did not materialize, and the BSA speeds stood for several years until 900cc Kawasaki Z1 fours bettered them in an FIM-sanctioned session at Daytona.

---

750s. 'We are very gratified,' a relieved Lionel Jofeh told an *MCN* reporter when he heard the news.

In America, however, the news wasn't so reassuring, for there Honda's four managed to undercut the Rocket 3 and Trident on price. Brown recalled:

Honda's first price was $1,295, but when they realized they had the best game in town, they actually increased the price to $1,495, compared with ours of $1,750. It didn't matter, their model was a first rate design and the 750cc Honda, more than any other single model, spelled the end for the BSA Group.

*All smiles at Daytona Speedway in April 1969. From left: William Berry, AMA President, Yvon DuHamel (rider), Paul Shattuck (AMA timekeeper) and the man whose idea it was, Don Brown of BSA Inc. The Rocket 3 can be seen to be standard, except for its missing front mudguard.*

*Refuelling DuHamel's machine during the record-setting runs in front of an empty Speedway grandstand.*

*John Nelson explains the workings of a T150 engine to an attentive audience at his New Zealand dealer school, one of many he conducted around the world.*

# Honda four – a sophisticated rival

Although it was a shade slower 'out of the crate' Honda's four cylinder CB750 appealed to American motorcyclists more than the Rocket 3 and Trident. The Honda had chain drive to a single overhead camshaft and could be constantly revved to a vibration-free 7,000rpm without shedding a drop of oil. Reliable electric starting, a five-speed gearbox and the first disc brake to be fitted to a mass-produced motorcycle were all features that made life easy for Honda sales staff and tough for British triple vendors. When launched in the spring of 1969, the CB750's 61 x 63mm engine produced a claimed 67bhp at 8,000rpm. Weighing a substantial 530lb (240kg), top speed was in the region of 120mph (193km/h). One of motorcycling's most influential designs, the Honda paved the way for a mind-boggling array of fours and even sixes in the late seventies.

To American eyes, the CB750 looked more like a traditional British machine than the triples did, and its modern specification was a strong selling point.

Many BSA and Triumph dealers in the US were also Honda agents, and ironically it had been Johnson Motors' policy to team up with Honda to benefit from the company's generous advertising budgets.

'I guess we always knew that a day of reckoning would come if they ever started selling big bikes,' Brown told the author.

## TROUBLE ON THE ROAD

If it had been possible to assemble the triples' power units with the care and precision lavished on factory racers and some press test machines, superbly powerful and reliable high-performance Superbike engines could have been the outcome. But when produced in the high volume demanded by commercial realities, early Tridents and Rocket 3s suffered from several

*Honda's 750cc four, launched against the triples in 1969.*

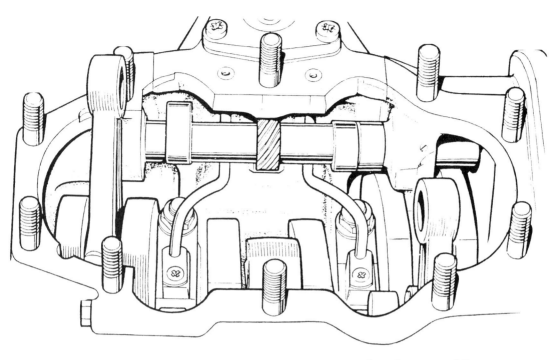

*Drawing showing the oil feed pipes from the inner main bearings to the exhaust cam followers, discontinued in 1970.*

faults that only came to light when machines were in customers' hands. There were both assembly and design faults.

Alan Barrett told the author he found a horrendous catalogue of errors in the engine and gearbox units of some of the earliest machines to be shipped to the US.

> We had a series of inexplicable blow-ups when testing Tridents at MIRA. Apparently this was due to a bottom-end fault, and we were told that similar engines had already been shipped abroad. I was dispatched to America with Mick Crowther, a young engineer from the Meriden Experimental Department and told to report back.
>
> When we started stripping engines over there we discovered all sorts of other things, and I found it incredible that machines in that condition could have been sitting in Los Angeles ready to be sold to the public.

Barrett's notes recorded faults in hundreds of engines. One entry alone, on Trident 00274, listed the following observations:

- swarf in carburettor, jet holder loose
- corroded rocker box feed pipe
- face of pressure relief valve not square in thread
- face of high gear nut not square in thread
- three pistons seized in bores
- loose alloy, from assembly of timing wheel spindle
- alternator rotor nut threads out of true
- layshaft third gear and selector fork blued
- layshaft second gear not meshing correctly
- cam timing not at optimum settings

Among errors Barrett said he found in other units were an oil pump gasket where an opening had not been fully punched out, resulting in blockage of the engine feed, and sludge in some crankcases, found to be residues of sand in the oil, thought to be left from the casting process. 'I took photographs, so that they could compile a 'Black Museum' of all the horrors at Small Heath,' he recalled. He then set to with teams of American technicians to rectify the problems.

Other flaws afflicted early production. One was misalignment of the rows of triplex teeth on the primary transmission, which sometimes resulted in chain breakages, in some cases accompanied by crankshaft damage. One cause was that the original chain tensioner design was weak. Another problem was caused by incorrect machining of teeth on the driven sprocket and shock

*John Nelson in the 1960s.*

## John Nelson – Triumph's world service

As Triumph's Service Manager, John Nelson had the responsibility of familiarizing sales and repair staff with the three-cylinder machine. Armed with yards of stapled-together airline tickets and a Trident engine, he toured the world to conduct Dealer Schools.

'I prepared a special engine with free-running bearings, so that it would be easy to turn over and would dismantle quickly. I had to do without special tools,' Nelson told the author.

His tour took in Australia, New Zealand, Canada and the United States, running through service procedures and answering questions.

The Service Department also had to bear the brunt of warranty claims when things went wrong. 'About 150 of the early Tridents came back to the factory for a free overhaul. Every one had its engine rebuilt with the crankshaft ground all over to prevent vibration,' Nelson recalled. Vibration problems were sufficiently widespread for his department to issue a Service Bulletin (number 341) on the subject in February 1970.

Nelson had joined Triumph after gaining a degree in Engineering at Cambridge University. He had to do his time in engine assembly, but then moved to design and development directly under Edward Turner. In 1960, he took charge of the Service Department with his long-time assistant Stan Truslove.

Although he admired Harry Sturgeon, Nelson faced some tough tasks during his regime in the mid-sixties, including being sent to the USA to pacify staff who were up in arms over the merging of BSA and Triumph operations.

The triples' launch brought many service snags, and the Umberslade Hall fiasco with the 1971 Group range was the last straw for Nelson, who left for Norton. He returned to Meriden to manage the co-operative until 1979, and since then has built a business, JR Technical Publications, specializing in reprinting workshop literature for obsolete Triumphs, including of course the T150 and T160.

absorber unit, which occurred when castings were machined in stacks of several at a time, and the scrolling action of the tooth-cutting machine tended to rotate the job. 'I remember preparing a Service Bulletin on that one and thinking to myself: "Mr Honda is going to enjoy this!" ' John Nelson told the author. As Triumph's UK-based World Service Manager, he had overall responsibilty for sorting out post-launch glitches. He recalled:

> Another problem came about because the three sets of contact breakers were quite tricky to adjust properly. Poor adjustment sometimes caused a holed piston. In some parts of America that caused the Trident to be called the 'cripple' instead of the triple.

*The triple as sidecar tug. Stan Shenton (left) of Boyer of Bromley outside his London shop with customers John and Maureen Cullen with their new Trident outfit.*

Altogether, the three-cylinder machines' relative complexity compared with traditional twins did not endear them to workshop staff.

Crankshaft balancing was also hit or miss in the early days of production. This was particularly unfortunate, as a poorly balanced shaft promoted engine vibration, and smoothness was meant to be one of the triple's biggest selling points.

'I remember that a brochure of the time used a shimmer effect in its design. I thought it rather appropriate, because that was the way the scenery looked when you sat on some triples,' Nelson said. His Service Bulletin 341 issued early in 1970 was headed 'Trident 150 Vibration Problems.'

Meriden's Mick Crowther had detected the source of vibration: because of inadequate machining, some crankshafts had wildly varing balance factors on each of the cylinder's webs.

On his return to Britain, Barrett was among Triumph engineers who were seconded by Hopwood to Small Heath, to ensure that the various faults occurring in power unit manufacture could be eliminated. And Nelson's assistant Stan Truslove spent a considerable amount of time in the USA.

Triumph loyalists have often laid the shortcomings in triple manufacture at BSA's door, but Meriden had to shoulder its share of blame too, for it had provided troublesome transmission parts as well as drawings which had later to be revised. Twenty-four modifications to 1969 models included stronger connecting rods, gearbox design revisions and several changes to the primary chain tensioner.

## TAKING STOCK

At the end of July 1969, 1,200 staff were laid off at BSA, the cuts being blamed on falling sales. Stocks of triples were beginning to

# The Utah gold rush

To try to kick-start sluggish sales – and counter BSA's Daytona records propaganda – Triumph's US West Coast subsidiary staged the $25,000 Bonneville Speed Contest in 1969. Prize money would be dished out to anyone setting a new record with a Trident, or Trident powered machine, during the AMA-run Bonneville Speed Week records meeting at the Utah Salt Lake venue.

Tridents took fifteen out of sixteen possible records in the 750cc categories for machines without full enclosure. Most of the new records were set by machines entered by Big D of Dallas, Texas, and Bob Leppan's Triumph-Detroit. But the fastest two-way aggregate run by any T150 was by Jeff Gough at 169.331mph (272.454km/h), netting him $3,750 (then about £1,800) including bonuses. His partially streamlined machine with a 750cc engine running on alchohol fuel was prepared by fellow Californian Bud Hare.

The best one-way speed was a run at 169.891mph (273.355km/h), set by Big D's rider Rusty Bradley on his Jack Wilson-tuned, partially streamlined, gasoline-fuelled 750, running in the stock engine class.

Even some of the more standard T150s comfortably exceeded 130mph (209km/h) in the Salt Lake spree, confirming the stock Trident's awesome speed potential and giving dealers useful sales ammunition.

A newsletter dispatched to dealers after the event said: 'Now it's time for you to crow! Be sure to get your full share of the free publicity value of Bonneville Speed Week.' It was not enough, however, to make the Trident a best seller like the 650cc Bonneville.

*Art Houston gets a tow from a truck to start his supercharged Trident, which has a standard tank and seat. Running in the altered frame class, Houston's best Bonneville run was 151.407mph (243.614km/h).*

*Rusty Bradley accelerates down the Bonneville strip on Big D Cycle's Jack Wilson-tuned rigid framed T150, minus its half-fairing. His best speed was 148.323mph (238.652km/h).*

*Triumph-Detroit rider Joe Baker at speed on a Trident with standard frame and engine. He set the 750cc stock record of 137.407mph (221.088km/h) unfaired, and 147.723mph (237.686km/h) with partial streamlining fitted.*

build up at BSA and Triumph. This at least gave Armoury Road a breathing space for some rearrangement of production processes and the introduction of specification changes at both factories for the 1970 model year. 'Over 100 major engineering changes had to be made to components following the reports from America,' Alistair Cave recalled.

It was then that new precision joint-lapping machines were installed at Small Heath, and they were to make an improvement to the truth of crankcase joint faces. Combined with new gaskets, this resulted in improved oil tightness. Porous and contaminated castings were dealt with by a shellac coating process.

*Staff attending a Triumph service school line up behind a Trident at Bill White's shop in Auckland, New Zealand, in June 1969.*

# 1970 Model Changes

### Engine

Cylinder head gasket: Klingerite compound fibre material. Lubrication: pressure feeds to tappet blocks blanked off. Ignition: three Lucas 12 volt coils

### Tyres

Front           4.10 × 19in Dunlop TT100

### Cycle parts

Horns           Two Clearhooters

### Gearbox

Revised overall ratios (third gear lowered slightly):

| | |
|---|---|
| first | 12.15:1 |
| second | 8.42:1 |
| third | 6.17:1 |
| fourth | 4.98:1 |
| rear wheel sprocket | 53 teeth |

### Colour scheme

*T150*
Fuel tank: Olympic Flame/Silver. Mudguards, side panels: black

Complaints about vibration were addressed by attention to the crankshaft manufacturing method. At first, the three-cylinder shaft had been treated in much the same way as BSA's twin-cylinder type, in that non-bearing areas on the forging were not finished with precision. To remedy the fault, full precision machining of the crank webs was introduced.

During the first year of production, a German crankshaft grinding machine was procured for £80,000, making it the single most expensive piece of equipment bought expressly for triple manufacture. All areas of the shafts were then machined, after which balancing was carried out electronically.

Small Heath's forge, which had been engaged in general contract work as well as motorcycle manufacture, was closed during 1970. Crankshafts for the triples were subsequently produced by the specialist company Garringtons Ltd, then in Bromsgrove, Worcestershire, which supplied forgings to the car industry. The contractor's superior plant was able to turn shafts out more quickly than had been possible at Armoury Road. Final machining and balancing of the shafts was still done at BSA, however.

Huge improvements in Rocket 3 production came with the building of a new 50,000sq. ft assembly area at Armoury Road, completed in the winter of 1969–70. There were four main tracks for machines to travel along as they were built up. Overhead hanging racks supplied components from various manufacturing areas disposed conveniently around the plant. Rolling road test stations were placed to receive motorcycles, which could then go straight to the warehouse for despatch, or to the rectification team if snags showed up. Meriden also had rolling roads to obviate the need for outdoor test riding.

Triumph responded to American criticisms of its triples' styling by putting together a 'retro' makeover kit with which

*A police rider astride a white Trident supplied through Swiss importer Jacques Berlioz. Triples did not appeal to UK police forces, who mainly stuck with BSA and Triumph twins.*

## The Trident beauty kit

Desperate to move slow-selling Tridents from American showrooms, Triumph implemented an idea that had occurred to many members of its UK and US organizations: make the triple look like a twin.

A restyled T150 without the 'breadbin' fuel tank and raygun silencers was displayed at Southern California's annual Anaheim Show in February 1970. Consignments of parts were despatched to America from Meriden, so that dealers could update unsold Tridents in their showrooms to the new look. The kits of cycle parts enabled rapid conversions to the Bonneville or Trophy look preferred by customers, creating a machine close, but not identical to, the 1970 US model which arrived in April of that year. Quickly dubbed the 'beauty kit', the set of makeover components comprised the following:

3.5 gallon fuel tank based on 650cc Trophy type

Twin-style tank badges and knee grips

Bonneville-style dualseat

Replacement main exhaust pipes

Barrel-shaped silencers

Side panels without air filter shrouds

Replacement air filter

Replacement mudguards

Combined fuel tank/oil cooler bracket

Miscellaneous brackets and fasteners

The kit, which was listed in full in the 1970 Trident parts book under the heading 'North American variant 1970 Trident' paved the way for the shape of subsequent triples, which were better sellers than the original Ogle-styled machines.

*Replacement fuel tank is a 3 ½ gallon type similar to the Triumph 650cc twin type.*

dealers could change the look of the Trident. The 'beauty kit' as it has become known, transformed the T150 into something looking more like the Bonneville. A traditional rounded fuel tank, plainer side covers, and barrel-shaped silencers were included in the package, which appeared in the Trident parts list under the heading: 1970 North American Variant.

Several internal changes were made to home and export models for the 1970 season. The positive feeds taking oil from the centre main bearings to the cams were discontinued as they were found to be unnecessary, and lubricant had tended to leak at the tappet blocks. Also, to reduce an over-large step between second and third gears, the third ratio was lowered slightly.

## DIMINISHING RETURNS

Early problems afflicting the triples were gradually being overcome, but tribulations affecting BSA and Triumph as a whole were coming to a head. Full redesigns of the entire BSA and Triumph range for 1971 had been set in progress, but a series of errors

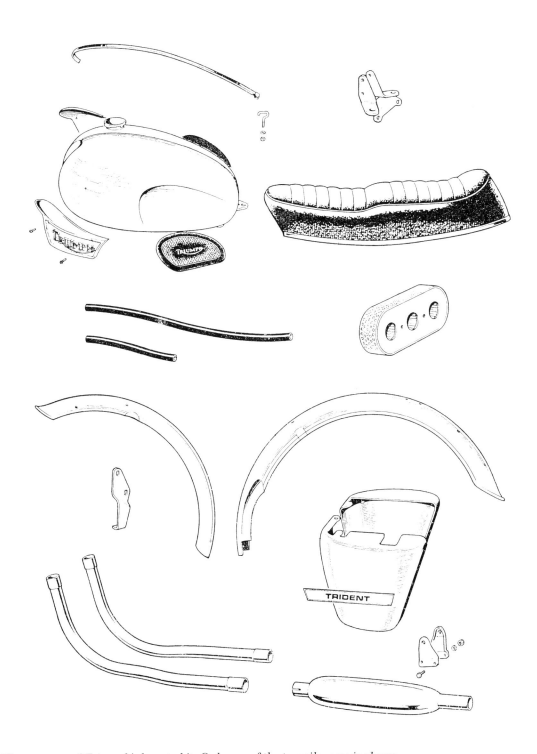

*The contents of Triumph's beauty kit. Only one of the two silencers is shown.*

and delays had put everything several months behind schedule. Spending had been lavish, but revenue was not coming in from sales to justify it. To complicate matters, labour relations throughout the West Midlands were deteriorating and disputes, sometimes leading to stoppages, were becoming more frequent.

Calamitous hold-ups were caused by the introduction of the new-look BSA and Triumph 650 twins, with a common frame and other cycle parts designed by the non-motorcycling boffins of Umberslade Hall. The new twins' frame, which carried engine oil in a large diameter main spine, caused produc-

tion havoc that took months to sort out, creating problems at both the Small Heath and Meriden plants.

The oil-bearing chassis, which was to be roundly criticized for its excessive seat height, was not adopted for the triples. However, like the rest of the BSA and Triumph range, both the Rocket 3 and Trident were the subject of significant cosmetic changes for the 1971 selling season.

A new sturdy and more modern-looking telescopic fork was shared with the 650 twins. Devoid of gaiters to protect its stanchions, it is easily identified by its unpainted alloy sliders, which have four studs to secure

## Hele's baby triple

Encouraging results with the prototype 750cc spurred Bert Hopwood and Doug Hele to crack on with another three-cylinder project.

Triumph needed a 250cc engine with better performance than the 199cc Tiger Cub. The old Turner-designed ohv single had served as an entry-level Triumph for UK learner riders restricted to 250cc, and had performed well in off-road competition both in British trials and on American dirt tracks. But faced with the powerful and exciting quarter-litre products arriving from Italy and Japan, something with more zip than the ohv single was sorely needed.

In 1965, Hele drew up a unit with crankpins set at 120 degrees as on the 750, and short-stroke internal dimensions of $50 \times 42mm$ giving a total capacity of 249cc. Unlike the bigger unit, the baby three was to have valve operation by overhead camshafts driven by a combination of a chain and gears from the crankshaft.

A dohc layout made high revs possible and Hele anticipated engine speeds of up to 14,000rpm with a power output of 40bhp, a considerable improvement on the measly 17bhp available from the best Cubs. The high-revving triple was intended to have a six-speed gearbox. With a horizontally split crankcase, the Hopwood-Hele 250 could have been the most significant British machine of the seventies.

Hele's arrangements progressed to the drawing office for detailing, but then a company decision forced a redesign to boost the engine to 350cc capacity, and it was in that form that one engine was completed. On taking over BSA, Sturgeon toured America with Turner, and both had returned convinced of the need for a new 350, considered an entry-level motorcycle in the USA.

Unfortunately this triple, which promised some solid opposition to the latest Japanese products and would have given the British industry a boost, was dropped. In an act of corporate lunacy it was condemned to one of many bomb shelters under the Meriden factory. Not just any cellar, but the one kept under lock and key.

A 350cc dohc twin-cylinder design was commissioned from Edward Turner following his retirement but the BSA Fury and Triumph Bandit, as the models were to be designated, were scuppered almost as soon as they had been announced in 1971.

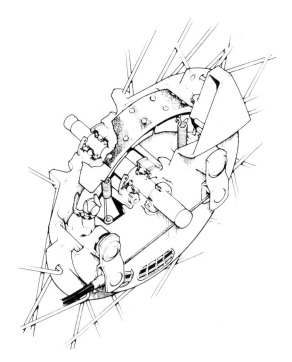

*Sectioned drawing showing details of the twin-leading-shoe front brake and conical hub introduced on the Rocket 3 and Trident for 1971.*

their wheel spindle retaining caps. Umberslade Hall-designed conical hubs and redesigned drum brakes introduced on the triples for 1971 were further examples of how the BSA Group was losing its grip on reality.

While the 1968 twin-leading-shoe drum front brake had been just about adequate for the 750s, something more powerful was really needed for the fast and weighty machines. Adopting disc brakes, as seen on the Honda 750 and even BSA-Triumph's own racers, seemed an obvious development. Instead, the 1971 triples were given a front brake that tried hard to look like a racing drum, but was less effective than its predecessor.

Instead of having a rigid linkage that pulled the brake shoes' operating cams together in the same direction, the new 8in

front drum used an operating system seen on BMW and Gilera drum brakes of the fifties. The inner brake cable pulled on the front operating arm, and the outer butted up against the rear arm, so that squeezing the handlebar lever pulled the two arms towards each other, turning the cams in opposite directions. Apparently designed as a cheap-to-make component by a car industry brake specialist, the prototype version was particularly ineffectual because it had steel shoes, which expanded at a slower rate than the alloy drum when heat was generated by braking.

Factory testers reported that the brake was poor but, according to former Experimental Department man Bill Fannon, staff were told that 'everything would be all right when it went into production'. Final versions had alloy shoes, but the brake was still not up to its job. Not surprisingly, the conical hubs are often called 'comical hubs'.

The ray guns disappeared at last, replaced by tapered megaphone-style silencers. But a less popular move was the introduction of unattractive wire stays for the front mudguard and the headlamp, which was still of the flat-backed design but carrying warning lights. There was one ben-

*New-look Trident for 1971 with traditionally styled fuel tank, front fork with alloy sliders and megaphone-style silencers.*

efit from the restyling exercise, however – the machines' weight was trimmed by several pounds.

On the 1971 A75, which has become known as the Rocket 3 MkII, new moulded side panels with flatter flanks were introduced. The majority of that years' BSA triples were shipped to overseas markets with small chromium-plated 2.5 gallon fuel tanks, but 100 home market MkIIs were made with the usual 4.25 gallon tank. Five-speed gearboxes were fitted to 200 machines.

The new gearbox was one of the clear benefits of the combined BSA/Triumph racing programme, which had been underway at Meriden for two years. Close-ratio racing

---

# 1971 Model Changes

## Engine

*Carburation*
Throttle valve cutaway number 3½.

Exhaust system. Tapered 'megaphone' silencers.

## Transmission

Five speed gearbox optional.

## Brakes

| | |
|---|---|
| Front brake | 8in diameter, twin leading-shoe, conical hub |
| Rear brake | 7in diameter single-leading-shoe, conical hub |

## Suspension

Front telescopic fork with alloy lower sliders, internal coil springs, no gaiters. Fork oil capacity 210cc. Rear Girling units with fully exposed springs

## Electrical

Flashing direction indicators, updated handlebar switchgear.

## Cycle parts

Side panels reshaped (as restyled 1970 US T150) on Trident. Wire-type front mudguard stays and headlamp holders, pressed steel rear lamp bracket T150 only.

Fuel tank: round-shaped 2.75 gallons (3.3 US gallons, 12.5 litres) for US, combined tank/oil cooler mount

A75 only: 2.75 gallon (3.3 US gallons, 12.5 litres) fuel tank with chromed panels on export models. Moulded side panels, part of oil tank exposed on right.

## Dimensions (in/mm)

| | BSA | Triumph |
|---|---|---|
| Wheelbase | 58.5/1,486 | 57/1,448 |
| Seat height | 33/838 | 31/787 |
| Ground clearance | 8.75/222 | 6.5/165 |
| Dry weight | 450lb (204kg) | 460lb (209kg) |

## Colour schemes

*T150*

Fuel tank: Spring Gold and Black. Side-panels: black. Mudguards: chromed.

*A75*

Fuel tank and side panels: Flamboyant Red/Flamboyant Blue/Firecracker Red. Frame: Dove Grey. Mudguards: chromed. Export fuel tank had chromium panels.

*Front end of a 1972 Rocket 3, showing wire mounts for the headlamp and plated front mudguard.*

clusters had been bought from Kent engineering company RT Quaife, but after the rights to Quaife's design were bought in 1970, the transmission was adapted for production at Meriden's drawing office. It was a difficult process, exacerbated by industry changes from imperial to metric bearing sizes, and snags were to arise with early five-speed boxes on triples, which were not detected until machines had been shipped across the Atlantic and then necessitated an expensive rectification programme.

Pete Colman told the author that failures of early five-speed gearboxes were so common in the US that 'rework' lines were set up to remedy the faults, mainly concerning

metal hardness, on machines as they arrived for distribution.

Also unsatisfactory was the A75's new colour scheme. Someone at Umberslade Hall had hit on the bold idea of finishing the frames of BSA's 1971 range in Dove Grey, a poor choice as it made them look as if they had been cellulose primed, but not given a top coat. Old hands at Small Heath recalled sales resistance to a green-framed 500cc BSA twin of the fifties.

Even in countries where they were not mandatory, Superbike customers expected flashing direction indicators as a standard fitment, and they appeared on the triples for 1971 along with modernized, but not particularly ergonomic, handlebar switch clusters. The speedometer and rev-counter were no longer set in a binnacle but mounted separately in rubber cups and held in brackets secured by the front fork's top nuts.

During 1971, BSA's Small Heath factory took over manufacture of some engine parts, such as cylinder heads, which had previously been produced at Meriden. Towards the end of the year, production of a restyled 1972 Rocket 3 commenced. It can be identified by a black frame and also black finish on the front brake backplate. UK models had the 'breadbin' fuel tank, whilst export machines kept the small plated tank, but the paintwork was now Burgundy, rather than Flamboyant Red.

## DEEPENING CRISIS

In June 1971 Peter Thornton quit as chief of BSA-Triumph in America, and the parent company announced that it expected to report a 'substantial loss' that year. The blame for production delays was put on a string of difficulties, including pre-production problems, shortages of parts from outside suppliers, labour shortages and strikes. Ever optimistic, however, the official

## 1972 Model Changes (T150/T150V)

### Engine

Shrunk-in valve seats in cylinder head.

### Transmission

Gearbox with five-speed internals standard on T150V from July 1972. Overall ratios:

| | |
|---|---|
| first | 13.59:1 |
| second | 9.66:1 |
| third | 7.36:1 |
| fourth | 6.26:1 |
| fifth | 5.26:1 (4.98 for 1975) |
| Gearbox sprocket | 18 teeth |
| Rear wheel sprocket | 50 or 53 teeth |

### Brakes

Front brakes   10in disc, hydraulic operation, master cylinder on handlebar

### Cycle Parts

No steering damper.

### Colour schemes

Fuel tank, side-panels: Regal Purple. Frame and side-panels: black. Decals on side-panels.

UK fuel tank similar shape to 1969 model. Export fuel tank: Regal Purple with Cold White panels.

## 1972 Model Changes (A75)

### Transmission

Gearbox with five-speed internals as T150 (some machines only).

### Colour schemes

Fuel tank painted panels: Burgundy. Frame, front brake, backplate: black. Export fuel tank Burgundy/chrome. Sticker on side panel changed from Rocket 3 to Rocket Three.

### Seat

Flat top with moulded ribbing (UK), humped type (US).

announcement quoted by *MCN* in that month stated that following the massive reorganization at Small Heath, output of 100,000 machines was envisaged for 1973.

Then BSA announced losses of nearly £3m in July and Lionel Jofeh agreed to resign. He received a generous £35,000 golden handshake and took a post with the aircraft hydraulics company Dowty. Corporate consultants Coopers & Lybrand were called in to draw up a survival plan, and it was reported that an estimated £15m was needed to ensure sufficient liquidity to prepare for the 1972 selling season. In October Brian Eustace, formerly of GKN, took over as chief executive of BSA Group. and Lord Shawcross became chairman to replace the outgoing Eric Turner.

The effect on morale at Armoury Road was devastating. Orders were received to clear the assembly area, which had been totally modernized at great cost in the winter of 1969–70, and prepare that part of the building for demolition.

The plan was to sell off most of the Small Heath site along with several of BSA's smaller ancillaries, and transfer all motorcycle assembly to Meriden. Engines for the Trident, however, and some other components for Triumphs, would continue to be made in the scaled-down Amoury Road premises. It fell to Alistair Cave to sack 3,000 employees at a stroke. There was no major dispute, although a clerical union did make its protest by refusing to issue staff with redundancy notices. Cave remarked:

> I was proud of the co-operation I received from the workforce, many of whose families had worked at Small Heath for years. They took into consideration that the future of the 1,500 remaining staff depended on them.

Most of the factory and office premises was evacuated and sold. Motorcycle-related production was concentrated in the newest part of the factory, and surplus machinery was auctioned off.

Meanwhile, Kawasaki had announced a four-stroke Superbike. The Japanese company had made its name with rapid two-stroke triples, but now revealed plans to produce the 900cc four-cylinder Z1 in September 1971. Weeks later at Italy's annual Milan Show, Laverda unveiled its response to the British triples, the 180-degree three-cylinder 1,000cc 3C; at the same time Ducati promised to start shipping its 750cc ohc V-twin sportster to Britain for 1972.

*A UK market Trident for 1972, identifiable by its decorative side panel decals, used for that year only. Those on five-speed T150V models included the letter V.*

## 1973 Model Changes (T150V)

### Engine

| | |
|---|---|
| Carburation | return springs on slides. |
| Exhaust system | longer 'cigar' silencers. |

### Electrical

Full-shell chrome plated headlamp. Ignition switch on left of lamp, headlamp brackets changed back to sheet metal type.

### Cycle parts

Revised alloy rear lamp unit.

### Colour scheme

Fuel tank: Jet Black with Red panels. Top embellishment strap anodised alloy. Side panels: black with screw-on badges, silver lettering on red ground. Frame: black.

## FAREWELL TO THE ROCKET 3

The Rocket 3 was discontinued in January 1972 and the final example, a five-speeder, was shipped out of Small Heath for Germany in May. However, manufacture of A75-type engines with inclined cylinder units was not entirely finished, as very similar units would be required for the radical American-styled X75 Hurricane version of the triple assembled at Meriden later in the year as a Triumph-badged machine.

Engine units and other parts for the Trident continued to be made at Small Heath, for assembly into machines at Meriden, where increasingly frequent industrial disputes were causing production delays. The Triumph triples started being fitted with five-speed gearboxes from mid-1972, models so equipped being coded T150V.

Another useful spin-off from the expensive racing campaigns came when the T150V finally got a hydraulically operated 10in disc front brake for the 1973 model year. It was also equipped with a new elongated silencers, necessary to keep pace with ever more stringent American emission restrictions. Minor changes included moving the ignition switch to the left of the headlamp and screwed-on side panel badges to replace the short-lived transfers used on the previous year's models.

When early five-speed gearbox troubles had been cured, the extra ratio was found to be a welcome improvement to the triple, increasing rider enjoyment. Along with the disc brake and the direction indicators, it makes the T150V a practical and pleasurable proposition even on today's over-populated roads.

# 4 Born in Troubled Times – The Trident T160

The early seventies were not just a difficult time for the British motorcycle industry, but for Britain as a whole. Upheavals on the wider scene included rising inflation in the economy and changes of government. There was a sudden increase in oil prices, creating an energy crisis and industrial strife was spreading. Most of the UK's manufacturing industry worked a three-day week for a period during the dark winter of 1973–4.

## MERGER WITH NORTON

Barclays Bank issued an ultimatum to the Department of Trade and Industry in the autumn of 1972: if Britain's important exporter BSA did not receive government assistance, it would have no choice but to call in a receiver. The matter was passed to the Department's Industrial Development Unit, which was empowered to allocate public funds for the purpose of protecting employment or promoting an industry where it was deemed to be in the national interest.

Dennis Poore, whose Manganese Bronze company had run the Norton Villiers motorcycle enterprise following the collapse of AMC, was asked by DoT officials to form a merger in the interests of saving BSA/Triumph. A plank of the Conservative government's economic policy was to achieve growth through exports, and BSA's past record was seen to qualify it as a national asset worth rescuing with taxpayers' money.

After much deliberation a plan was thrashed out. It was announced in March 1973 that Norton Villiers would take over BSA. A few days before this was made public, a fall in the BSA share price had seen £2 million wiped off the company's value. By July 1973 new Norton Villiers Triumph companies had been formed with Poore as chairman and chief executive: NVT Manufacturing Ltd was at Small Heath and Norton Villiers Triumph Ltd at Wolverhampton where the Norton Commando was manufactured. The optimistic target was for NVT to make 60,000 large-capacity motorcycles in its first year, including 10,000 Tridents. Meriden was not included in the plans. Poore believed that the plant should be closed because in his view it had become uneconomic through high wages and over-staffing.

Poore announced his intention to shut the Triumph factory to a canteen convention of union officials and others on 14 September 1973. He told them that he envisaged an orderly run-down of the plant with full production being maintained until the following February.

There was no chance of that: the workforce decided to fight the measure. This was hardly surprising, given the intense loyalty to Triumph traditionally felt among Meriden staff, and the relatively strong union organization in the factory. Poore was denounced as an asset-stripper. A sit-in occupation of the Meriden factory was accompanied by a blockade of the gates, and motorcycle production ceased.

*Dennis Poore takes a spin on an NVT-built export Trident T150V.*

## Dennis Poore

Variously seen as a well-intentioned industry saviour and a cynical asset-stripper, Poore was a wealthy and astute businessman. An engineering graduate, he served in the RAF in WWII and had been a sucessful racer on four wheels, being RAC hill-climb champion in 1950, fourth in the British Grand Prix of 1952 and winner of a 9-hour race in a works Aston Martin at Goodwood in 1955. His Manganese Bronze Holdings company acquired Norton and the Villiers engine company to launch the 750cc Norton Commando in 1967. Poore regarded the triples as being almost as outmoded as the Norton's twin-cylinder engine, but envisaged keeping the Trident on the market, preferably in 900cc form, until the rotary Wankel-engined machine initiated at Meriden could be developed into a commercially viable Superbike. In 1977 he relinquished rights to the Triumph name to the Meriden Co-operative. NVT went into liquidation soon afterwards, but the Rotary project continued under the Norton Motors name, eventually enjoying remarkable racing success in the early nineties, thanks to input by Norton technician Brian Crighton.

At Small Heath, where the output of three-cylinder engines had been running at up to 300 a week, Trident units that couldn't be delivered to Meriden for assembly into complete machines began to stack up. And there was growing resentment towards the Triumph plant among BSA staff, some of whom were already bitter that the mass sackings of 1971 had not affected Meriden workers.

NVT's planned manufacture of complete T150s at Small Heath was stymied by the fact that jigs and tooling for the frame and some other parts were locked in at Meriden, along with Trident drawings. Alistair Cave told the author that to avoid further lay offs, he set engine assembly staff to work on painting the factory.

By November, NVT had given the go-ahead for all the unavailable Trident production tools to be made afresh at Small Heath. Although a high proportion of parts were already sourced at BSA, it was a major task to complete in short time. Brian Jones, who played a large part in this exercise, remembers instituting a massive search for any drawings that could be recovered from outside contractors and having his draughtsmen create drawings referenced from completed components. With government approval, an estimated £500,000 was spent on the process, and perhaps millions more were lost in a winter when no Triumphs of any sort were being made.

## TRIDENTS ROLL AGAIN

In the spring of 1974, complete Tridents rolled off the line again. NVT, which felt that the media, particularly television, had shown the Meriden workers in a sympathetic light, needed some positive publicity for itself. With motorcycles back in production it was able to stage a grand opening for its hand-pushed production track, and announce in publicity that 'Tridents are Rolling Again'.

Most of the Experimental Department at Meriden accepted redundancy terms – Les Williams, then a foreman, recalled that he received about £700 – but they were also approached with offers of employment with NVT International at former BSA premises in Mackadown Lane, Kitts Green, in south-east Birmingham. A team of twenty designers and draughtsmen was assembled under chief designer Brian Jones, and Doug Hele's Development Department re-engaged most of the key Meriden Experimental staff.

At Kitts Green, work resumed on the long-awaited electric start version of the Trident, which was well advanced at Meriden but had fallen behind schedule. The project had been around for several years, since electric starters were experimentally rigged on BSA and Triumph triples as early as in 1969. As a self-starter was a feature of the Honda 750, customers could expect it on the British equivalent, but a stumbling block for Triumph had been a lack of room on the

---

# 1974 Model Changes (T150V)

## Engine
Revised air filter housing with two flexible intake hoses.

## Transmission
Rear wheel sprocket 50 teeth (UK).

## Cycle parts
Fuel tank (UK market): increased cutaway area in base (Small Heath build)

## Colour scheme
Fuel tank: black with Sundance Yellow panels. Frame and side-panels: black. Side-panel badges: gold lettering on black ground.

*Delivery of the biggest UK dealer order ever placed with NVT. South London dealer Elite Motors took a hundred machines in one delivery, worth £75,000, in 1974. They were T150Vs and Norton Commando Mk IIIs. NVT's sales chief Mike Jackson stands on the left, with Elite boss Wally Young (middle) and shop sales director Ron Welling. Jackson told the author that the consignment reached Elite several months overdue.*

*Left: Alistair Cave shows a T150 crankshaft to Dennis Howell MP, a government minister visiting Small Heath to inspect resumed triple manufacture in 1974.*

*Below: Small Heath technician Sid Kay sets a Trident engine up for static testing in 1974.*

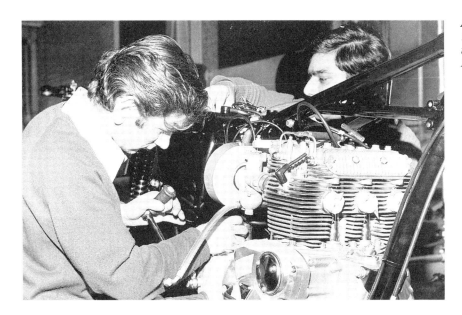

*Assembling a T150 in 1974, with cycle parts now made at Small Heath.*

*Checking valve timing on a partially assembled engine. Even factory staff found the triples' tappets fiddly to adjust.*

machine for adding a motor tidily. The BSA's inclined cylinder design left plenty of room for installation on top of the gearbox, and once the BSA-engined X75 had been marketed as a Triumph, the old marque distinction had become irrelevant. Because it blended the Rocket and Trident, the model was affectionately known among some factory staff as the 'Rodent'.

Experimental Department staff at Meriden had been building and testing prototypes for the second-generation electric start T160 Trident since racing activity was curtailed carly in 1972. It had been intended to

# Brian Jones – quick on the draw

As a draughtsman and designer, Brian Jones had involvement with the triples from the earliest P1 days through to the T160. He had joined Triumph in 1961, having followed Bert Hopwood from Norton. Jones's association with Hopwood dated from the early 1950s, when he had worked under him at BSA.

Born in Cheltenham, Jones had entered the motorcycle industry through an appenticeship at the Douglas factory in Bristol, where he had met Doug Hele.

Jones had started work on planning the electric-start triple when he was based at Umberslade Hall, the research centre set up by Lionel Jofeh in 1967. He told the author in 1995 how a frame he had drawn up for the electric start machine got embroiled in the 1971 debacle:

> One of our problems at the outset was that the high capacity battery to be supplied by Lucas weighed a ton. So, I sketched out a frame which would have its battery platform as strongly supported as possible. I came up with a large-diameter central tube to hold it, and carried it on as a spine up to the steering head. Having been a Vincent owner in the past [the fifties V-twins carried oil in a chassis member], it seemed a good idea to me keep the engine oil in the big frame tube.
>
> I was working on the triple design when Dr Stefan Bauer [a scientist employed by BSA who had earlier been involved in designing an anti-vibration frame for Norton] came into my office. I knew he had got in a terrible mess trying to design a monocoque chassis on computers. He was running out of time to come up with the new frame that would be common to the BSA and Triumph range. He saw my drawings and said: 'That looks good, can I borrow them?'

Jones believed that his design was adopted as the basis of the botched 1971 oil-bearing frame for twins, quoting its uneccessarily widely-spaced bottom tubes as proof.

When the new Trident became a reality, it was to able to use a compact and light Yuasa battery and its frame was closely based on the T150-type.

Following the NVT merger, Jones was in charge of drawing offices at both Meriden and Wolverhampton simultaneously, and then moved to Kitts Green after the Meriden shut-down. A short spell at Automotive Products in Leamington Spa followed before he joined the Meriden Co-operative to work on twin cylinder engine design, and later some experiments with triple engines in Meriden chassis. Jones subsequently worked on Devon company LF Harris's revived Bonneville in the eighties, and later on the Norton Rotary at Shenstone before he retired in 1993.

name the new Triumph the Thunderbird III, but although the name harked back to one of Meriden's most loved touring twins, Triumph's American staff warned against using it. They feared that Ford, who had originally obtained blessing from Triumph Engineering to put the traditional Meriden name on a sports car in the fifties, might take legal action.

So the model became the Trident T160, although a quantity of Thunderbird III side-panel badges were manufactured, which eventually reached the open market, and they are sometimes seen attached to T160s. One variant of the Thunderbird III prototype, first road-registered by Meriden in 1973, survives in private ownership, fitted with a T150-type fuel tank and experimental chain driven camshafts.

More than one design of frame, including a duplex type, was experimented with for the T160. In the end, however, the develop-

*Brian Jones in 1995.*

ment team settled on a chassis based on the high ground clearance version of the standard T150 Trident frame devised for production class racers.

To make room for the battery, the new frame's swinging arm was made 1in (25mm) longer than the T150's and the rear sub-frame was also changed. The front fork was shortened to keep the wheelbase at 58in (147mm).

To install the inclined engine in the single downtube Triumph frame the exhaust manifold had to be redesigned to clear the frame downtube. Early T160 prototypes had three-header pipes that swept to the right to merge under the engine, and terminated in a 'double-decker' silencer. This Hele-designed system was a derivative of both the racing triples' exhaust and a Triumph police silencer designed to meet stringent US regulations. The whole of the upper deck was a reverse element with the the outlet on the lower barrel. It looked radical, but it did the job well, muffling noise efficiently whilst maintaining power output.

*Triumph designer Jack Wickes works on the T160 prototype at Meriden: seat and tank are clay dummies.*

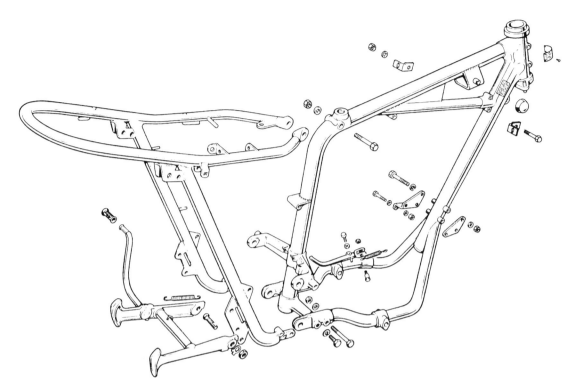

*T160 frame: similar to the original Trident type with some dimensional change to give more ground clearance and make room for a bigger battery under the seat.*

For production, however, NVT ruled that a large silencer similar to a device developed for Norton twins should be used. The annular-discharge silencer developed for Norton Villiers by university academic Dr Geoffrey Roe was known as the 'black cap' because of its distinctive black end pieces. After a programme of dynamometer testing, a Triumph version was arrived at for the T160. A new symmetrical manifold quite different from the T150's was used, with two down pipes from a Y-piece on the centre port, which splayed to either side, to join the outer cylinder's pipes into the two main pipes. The cast alloy manifold was bolted to the centre exhaust port.

Intake noise was subjected to increased muffling, too, with a large moulded airbox containing a paper filter element. To accommodate these changes, the carburettor slides and needles were changed. On the T160's cylinder head casting, the carburettor mounting stubs were now spigoted into the ports.

The Lucas electric starter was fitted unobtrusively on top of the gearbox, so that it could turn the engine via a pre-engaged gear mechanism, which transmitted drive to a toothed ring on the clutch drum. A trio of ignition contact breakers was retained, but with three six-volt coils powered via a ballast resistor. This was shorted out during starting, when a higher than normal current was thus available to the coils.

Left-foot gearchange, which had been under development at Meriden, was permanently arranged using a crossover shaft

*The airbox above the starter motor on the T160 was introduced to reduce intake noise.*

*A 1975 Trident T160 with electric starter mounted behind the inclined cylinders and annular discharge silencers. The new fuel tank shape makes it look quite different from earlier triples.*

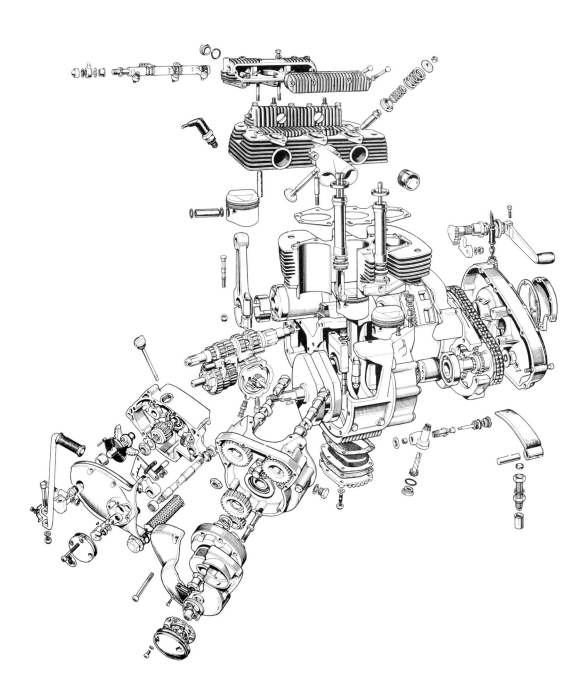

*Exploded drawing of the T160 power unit with left-side gearchange and duplex primary chain.*

mechanism designed by Brian Jones. He incorporated a gear and quadrant mechanism in order to avoid having to move the footrests forward to be nearer the foot pedal, as was done on Meriden's twins. The gearchange shaft was arranged to pass through a bushed and sealed opening in the primary chaincase, where a duplex chain replaced the triplex type, but the clutch remained the same.

Another development carried over from Meriden planning was the replacement of the rear drum brake by a disc, with its operating caliper slung below the swinging arm on the right side of the machine. The Vetter-influenced teardrop-style fuel tank and tilted-up instrument binnacle helped give the T160 a fresh look, as did a plain oil tank with no side panel to cover it. A small engine modification, which would make life easier for owners and service staff, was the new type of tappet adjuster on the rockers. Copied from a Ducati design, it incorporated a captive ball and obviated the need for a bent feeler gauge to check clearances on earlier Tridents. Many T150 and A75 owners have fitted this modification.

## LAUNCH

Production of the Trident T160V got rolling at Small Heath in November 1974, and in the following March a joint press and trade launch was organized at Ragley Hall, Warwickshire, with NVT's other new model, the electric starter-equipped 850cc Norton Commando Mk III. Export machines were a priority, but batches for the home market were being supplied to UK dealers by the summer.

In 1975, the new 750cc Triumph triple was entering a Superbike arena changed beyond recognition since 1969. There was now intense competition on both specification and price. Competitors included BMW's luxurious 900cc twin, Ducati's sporting 750cc V-twin, fours from Honda and Kawasaki (including Honda's liquid-cooled Gold Wing flat-four), Laverda's 1,000cc triple, and Suzuki's RE5 Rotary.

British motorcycles were already coming to be seen as occupying a niche in the market, rather than being mainstream contenders, a situation that was accentuated by NVT with its patriotic sales slogan: 'Bike

*Hot pants in March. The joint launch of NVT's Norton Commando and Trident electric-start 750s early in 1975.*

# Trident T160V (1975–7)

## Engine

Crankcase casting changed to accept electric starter, with pre-engage drive to clutch drum. Cylinders tilted as A75. Minor changes to cylinder head casting, copper head gasket, captive-ball tappet adjusters. Enlarged main oilways. Rev-counter drive from left end of exhaust camshaft. Kickstart lever pivots at lower end.

| | |
|---|---|
| Engine type | ohv transverse triple |
| Bore and stroke | $67 \times 70$mm |
| Cubic capacity | 741cc |
| Compression ratio | 9.5:1 |
| Ignition timing | 38 degrees fully advanced |
| Claimed output | 58bhp @ 7,250rpm |

*Carburation*
$3 \times 27$mm Amal Concentrics. Revised throttle lever action, internal slide return spring only. Extension lever for centre tickler.

Standard jetting: 150 main, needle jet .106in, needle economy position 2, throttle valve cut-away number, 4.

*Air Filtration*
Replaceable paper element

*Exhaust System*
Cast alloy branched manifold at centre port. Four into two arrangement of down pipes, with collector box linking all pipes under gearbox. Annular discharge silencers.

## Transmission

Primary drive. Endless duplex chain in oil bath, ⅜in pitch. Primary chaincase oil capacity ⅝pint (350cc). Engine sprocket: 23 teeth; clutch sprocket: 43 teeth.

*Gearbox*
Left foot gearchange.

Overall ratios:

| | |
|---|---|
| first | 12.71:1 |
| second | 9.04:1 |
| third | 6.89:1 |
| fourth | 5.85:1 |
| fifth | 4.92:1 |
| Gearbox sprocket | 19 teeth |
| Gearbox oil capacity | 1.75 pints (850cc) |
| Rear wheel sprocket | 50 teeth |

## Frame

Similar to T150, with altered dimensions. Raised bottom tubes, lengthened rear sub-frame and swinging arm. Steering head bearings: tapered rollers.

## Tyres

| | |
|---|---|
| Front and rear | $4.10 \times 19$in Dunlop TT100 |

## Brakes

| | |
|---|---|
| Front and rear | 10in disc, hydraulic operation |

## Cycle parts

Pressed steel fuel tank, painted finish, on rubbers at front, bolted at rear.

*Capacities*
Fuel tank   4.5 gallons (5.25 US gallons, 20 litres) or 2.5 gallons (3 US gallons, 11 litres)
Oil tank   5 pints (6 US pints, 3 litres)

## Electrical

| | |
|---|---|
| Battery | 12 volt |
| Alternator | Lucas 120 watt |
| Coils | $3 \times$ Lucas 6 volt with ballast resistor |
| Contact breaker | Lucas 7CA |
| Starter motor | Lucas M3 |
| Horn | Lucas |
| Headlamp bulb | 45/40 watt |

| | | | | |
|---|---|---|---|---|
| Pilot light bulb | 6 watt | | Ground clearance | 5.5/140 |
| Stop/tail bulb | 21/5 watt | | Kerb weight | 552lb (250kg) |
| Indicator bulbs | 21 watt | | | |

### Dimensions (in/mm)

| | |
|---|---|
| Wheelbase | 58/1,473 |
| Seat height | 30/762 |

### Colour schemes

Sunflower Yellow/Ice White or Cherokee Red/Ice White.

---

British'. In a *Motor Cycle Mechanics* T160 road test, John Robinson wrote: 'I'd forgotten what it was like to ride a British bike.'

## Press Reactions

Hard-riding Robinson approved of the T160's steady handling, especially on a race circuit, where he ground chunks of rubber off the footrests. Braking from the two discs was praised as being powerful and controllable, and the gearchange as being smoother than of old.

But vibration felt through the footrests on acceleration was criticized, and the curtailing of top-end performance by the latest silencers was mourned, with top speed said to be 110mph (177km/h) with the rider flat on the tank. NVT's own testers reported a best one-way speed of 118mph (190km/h) from a wet pre-launch MIRA session.

And Robinson commented wryly that the British industry had nearly caught up with the Japanese when it came to high fuel consumption. The test Trident drank fuel at the rate of 35mpg (8l/100km) at high speeds.

Worse, it burned oil at an alarming rate. *MCM* were told by NVT that this was due to the first versions of the T160 having been fitted with unsuitable piston rings. Unfortunately it wasn't just press machines that were affected and it was susequently discovered that early machines had cylinder manufacturing faults.

*MCN* approvingly dubbed the new Trident a 'satisfying mile eater' but one of its two test triples broke down with electrical failure caused by a chafed wire, and suffered oil leaks from a porous casting. 'A bit naughty on a £1,215 motorcycle with under 1,000 miles on the clock,' was the comment in its report.

Obviously, the new silencers and air filtration had cut performance, but power was still claimed at 58bhp, as for the original Trident. *Bike* magazine got a very respectable maximum speed figure of 126.05mph (202.81km/h) from its T160, running it against the Norton Mk III, which only managed 111.11mph (178.78km/h).

In an early test of a T160 in January, John Nutting of *Motor Cycle Weekly* said that despite the extra weight of the starter, the new Trident 'feels smaller, lighter and more responsive to seat-of-the-pants reflexes.'

## Launch in America

A nimble five-speed Trident with disc brakes, electric starting and a teardrop tank might have done big things for Triumph in America if it had been launched in 1970. In 1975, however, it proved to be as sluggish a showroom performer as its predecessor.

But Mike Jackson, NVT's sales director at the time, recalled how he did his bit to help T160 sales when the British government

# Other people's triples, from Italy and Japan

The transverse three-cylinder layout may have been novel for motorcycles when the Triumph triple was conceived, but during the seventies it became the choice of several manufacturers.

Kawasaki of Japan marketed a range of two-stroke triples from 250 to 750cc. These machines offered sensational straight line performance at the cost of fuel economy, an important consideration during the mid-seventies' fuel crisis. Suzuki went triple, too, first with its adventurous water-cooled 750cc two-stroke, and then lively air-cooled two-stroke threes of 380 and 550cc. Racing derivatives from both makes were overtaking the ageing British triples in Formula 750 road racing by 1972.

More akin to the Trident and Rocket 3 were the triples sold by Laverda and Yamaha. Laverda had broken into the large capacity market in 1968 with an ohc 750cc parallel twin. To minimize vibration the Italian factory used a 180-degree crankshaft layout, in an extremely robust horizontally split crankcase. A prototype 1,000cc triple on similar lines appeared in 1969, which was developed into the dohc 75 × 74mm five-speed 1000 3C launched for 1974. Its engine used a 180-degree 'two-up, one down' crankshaft arrangement. The 90bhp, 136mph (219km/h) tuned version, with cams and pistons based on Endurance racing experience, was sold in the UK as the Jota, but it did not meet US road regulations. A handsome but high-built Superbike, the Jota was raced heroically on British circuits for importers Slater Brothers by Pete Davies. Laverda changed to a Triumph-like 120-degree crankshaft layout in 1982, but by then the company was in decline.

Yamaha drew inspiration from both BMW and Triumph in designing the XS750 launched for 1977. The 68 × 68.6mm 750cc Japanese triple employed chain drive for its dohc valve gear and a HyVo inverted-tooth primary chain drive, a method considered by Meriden for its triple at the prototype stage. From the Yamaha's five-speed gearbox, drive was taken through 90 degrees to suit shaft final drive. The latter system meant that power at the rear wheel was only a modest 57.5bhp, but clean, maintenance-free shaft drive was in demand from high mileage riders, as BMW had proved.

Highly praised on its launch by the press, and selling for a fraction of BMW twin prices, the Yamaha looked set to cause trouble for the German company. In the long term, however, it failed to achieve great popularity despite being uprated to 850cc for 1980 and was discontinued after 1979.

*Pete Davies racing a 1,000cc Laverda in the UK.*

*Yamaha's dohc shaft-drive 750cc triple of 1977.*

withdrew the company's export credit guarantees:

> I rushed out to Duarte, got on the phone and contacted Norton and Triumph dealers all over America. I managed to move 1,000 T160s in a week, some at prices as low as $995 each, to dealers in minimum batches of fifty. Until then the recommended price to customers had been between $1,250 and $1,350. One dealer took 100 of them.

## CARDINAL SINS

The final phase of the Trident production story concerns the special fleet version of the T160. Neil Shilton, a former Triumph employee who had taken charge of Norton Villiers police fleet sales, had successfully negotiated a deal for NVT with the Saudi Arabian Defence Force. The Middle Eastern state had originally agreed to take a significant number of NVT's 750cc Norton Commando-based Interpol police machines.

But NVT's Wolverhampton plant closed in July 1975, when the company's debts forced it into liquidation. Shilton failed in an attempt to persuade the receiver to sanction the production of the Nortons he had promised to Saudi Arabia. However, as he related in his autobiography *A Million Miles Ago*, Shilton was determined not to let his client down, and he hit on the idea of using Small Heath-built Tridents to fulfil the order. Satisfied that the T160, with its oil-cooler, would perform satisfactorily in a hot climate, he persuaded the Saudis to take triples, at an increased price.

A first consignment of 175 specially-equipped Tridents finished in white were due to be shipped in the autumn of 1975, with more batches promised. But a complication arose when a packing case supplier took Norton Villiers Manufacturing to court to recover of a debt amounting to more than £20,000.

At Shilton's request, Alistair Cave arranged for production to resume. This was made possible by creating another company. The Receiver at the Small Heath-based NVT Manufacturing Co. would first sell the machines to NVT Motorcycles, the marketing arm of NVT based at Shenstone in Staffordshire, for subsequent distribution. Production of T160s proceeded at Armoury Road right up until a small band of workers assembled the very last one in February 1976, when the receiver closed the factory in order to sell the property. The final output of T160s, an estimated 500 machines, were in Saudi trim.

Les Williams was involved in the project, working as a freelancer for Poore. He remembers that the first batch of machines he had to uncrate came with loose Norton badges, in case a quick change of marque was required to placate the client. Williams thinks that the Saudi authorities were anticipating thousands more T160s to follow the first consignment of 350, unaware of NVT's predicament.

Some 130 surplus machines built to the Saudi specification, which included pistons machined to give an 8.25:1 compression ratio, were stored in the UK and eventually dispersed by Shenstone to be sold to the public through specialist Triumph dealers during 1977. Costing £1,523, and named the Triumph Cardinal, the white T160 with windscreen and spotlights was a bargain for anyone seeking a well-equipped tourer, as *Bike* magazine pointed out in its May 1977 test.

In October an Official Receiver was appointed who oversaw all activity at Small Heath. In a bid to preserve the Trident, Alistair Cave formed a further subsidiary company, NVT Engineering, with the blessing of Poore and funding from a bank, NVT and the government. He bought all the existing jigs, stock and 'work in progress' amounting to 900 finished machines, and moved them

## T160V Cardinal (1976)

As T160 Trident except for:

### Engine

Compression ratio: 8.25:1 (standard pistons machined). Modified exhaust system.

### Cycle parts

Collector box revised to accommodate luggage panniers. Solid mounted handlebars. Silencers lower for panniers. Fuel tank capacity: 4.5 gallons. Single seat.

### Colour scheme

Fuel tank, mudguards, side panels, luggage panniers: white.

### Accessories

Usually include: windscreen, crash bars, spot lamps, air horns, panniers.

to a former BSA plant in Montgomery Street, Birmingham. Completed machines were to be put on the market via NVT's sales operation.

## BACK TO MERIDEN?

With government backing, the co-operative that had been set up at Meriden following the 1973 blockade had succeeded in maintaining production of the 750cc T140 Bonneville five-speed disc-braked twin, for which there was significant demand, especially from Triumph twin diehards in America. In 1976, Poore proposed that Meriden could benefit by also making three-cylinder Triumphs as a more modern alternative.

Apparently he envisaged that Meriden should adopt the 830cc version, taking over its development from Kitts Green, which had been closed.

In May 1977, rights to the Triumph name were sold by NVT to the Meriden Co-operative, and Cave received instructions to sell all tools and drawings pertaining to the triples to the Co-op. Much of it was taken from Birmingham to Meriden, but special Trident manufacturing equipment, including the crankshaft manufacturing machinery, was sold off at auction.

## PROTOTYPES

### Cams Upstairs

A version of the 750cc triple with overhead camshaft valve operation, the layout employed by Honda on its CB750 four and smaller twins, was sketched out by Doug Hele soon after the launch of the ohv production machines and prototyped at Meriden. The engine had a new casting placed on the cylinder head, in which a camshaft with one inlet lobe and one exhaust lobe per cylinder ran directly on bearing surfaces in the aluminium alloy. The lobes operated the valves via rockers, with pusher blocks interspersed between lobe and rocker.

Drive to the camshaft was by a toothed belt. At its lower end it engaged with a pulley on a countershaft placed where the exhaust camshaft had been on a pushrod operated engine, and at the upper end it turned a pulley on the timing side end of the camshaft. A number of the special castings were made and a complete machine, built with a BSA Rocket 3 chassis, was road tested.

'It went well enough, but never actually gave more power than the standard engine. The valve gear was a bit heavy,' Hele told the author. After thorough bench testing the

*Prototype overhead camshaft 750cc triple engine made at Meriden, restored and installed in a BSA A75 Mk II chassis by Triumph dealer Bill Crosby. Camshaft drive is via a countershaft, replacing the exhaust camshaft, and ignition points are on the inlet camshaft. The inscription referring to Kitts Green, 1974, on upper drive cover is now known to be inaccurate.*

project, for which a heavy-duty oil pump was specially made, was put to one side.

**Bored for Power**

Later, Hele got an electric start 'jumbo' triple to the prototype and road testing stage during his stay at Kitts Green, which lasted until the facility was closed by NVT in 1975.

Designated the T180, its capacity had been boosted to 870cc by taking the bores to 68mm, the T160's maximum oversize, and lengthening the stroke of the crankshaft by welding and re-grinding to 80mm. The main aim was to boost horsepower in the face of ever bigger and more powerful machines arriving on the market. Like some Trident and Rocket 3 racers, the T180 prototype had revised valve gear with clearance adjustment at the tops of the pushrods and line-contact rockers. Inspection caps for access were added to the rocker box castings. A new clutch for road machines, based on the lightweight primary transmission fitted to some works racers in 1971, was also envisaged for the T180.

Norman Hyde, one of Hele's right-hand men on the Experimental Design team, had successes with oversize T150 engines he built for his own record-breaking activities. He ran an 850cc engine in 1972 and a 1,000cc version in 1973, using barrel castings of his design made by RT Quaife, the company which made five-speed racing gearboxes for Triumph, to accept 71mm Bonneville pistons. A stroke lengthened to 82mm created the biggest unit. Since 1970, Hyde and Quaife had been planning an ultra short-stroke 500cc three-cylinder racing engine using a mix of Triumph and Quaife parts, including the barrel casting.

Hele's thoughts had also turned to changing the triple's crankshaft layout from 120 degrees to a 180-degree one-up, two-down layout of crankpins, which Laverda had favoured on its 1,000cc triple when it was launched in the mid-seventies. A 180-degree triple was built and running during 1974, but Hele concluded that its benefits were limited. A planned chassis development was to prove prophetic: Hele told the author he had laid out a single-sided swinging arm rear suspension system in 1972. This layout is widely used on motorcycles today.

## The Quadrant

Another fascinating Kitts Green prototype is the four-cylinder 1,000cc Triumph Quadrant, built in the summer of 1974 as an evaluation exercise rather than a pre-production machine.

Hele executed the experiment in secrecy. Technicians Alan Barrett and Jack Shemans built an engine from T160 parts. They took two standard barrels and cut a bore off each and built a bottom end with two centre sections. A special crankshaft was manufactured by adding a section to one of Hele's experimental 180-degree triple shafts.

Two T160 cylinder heads were sawn up to serve two cylinders each, and camshafts were made to measure by an outside contractor so as not to give the game away. Four short rocker boxes were made by cutting standard items down, and blanking their ends off using Devcon epoxy metal putty.

'We finally showed it to Poore, and he was amazed, and seemed quite keen for it to go into production,' Hele told the author. Poore had suggested that a four-cylinder engine was needed during an early meeting with Hele and Hopwood, when the latter's modular scheme had been rejected.

The Quadrant engine was placed in a Rocket 3 frame, previously employed as the mobile testbed for the ohc triple engine prototyped at Meriden, and it took to the road equipped with left foot gearchange early in 1975.

Hele recalled that the four was smoother than a triple. It handled well despite its width, the engine being offset half an inch to the right to prevent it from protruding too far on the left. With mild cams, and the fragile built-up crankshaft, it reached 119mph (192km/h) on test at MIRA.

NVT took the venture seriously enough to assess likely production costs, reckoned to be roughly 15 per cent higher than those of the T160 triple. Two rival NVT projects, the Wankel rotary, and the water-cooled twin commissioned from racing car engine specialist Cosworth, would both be more economical to manufacture according to NVT's calculations.

## Rubber Triple

Merging with NVT had introduced the possibility of mounting the T160 engine in the Norton Commando chassis. Norton's frame, designed by NVT technicians Bernard

*The Quadrant in restored condition in 1995. The four is displayed at the National Motorcycle Museum.*

*NVT tester Neil Coombes on the road aboard the experimental 1,000cc four-cylinder Quadrant. Its frame started life as a BSA Rocket 3.*

*This Norton-badged Trisolastic triple of 1975 houses an 870cc engine in NVT's Norton isolastic anti-vibration frame.*

*Meriden Co-operative T160 prototype uses Bonneville twin's oil-bearing frame but with normal oil tank added. Wheels are cast alloy.*

Hooper and Bob Trigg, featured the Isolastic system of cushioning the rider against engine vibration. The engine, and the transmission unit including the swinging arm, were all suspended in the main frame on large rubber mountings.

As an experiment, the 'Trisolastic' prototype was built at Kitts Green in 1975. According to Hele, it was not a success, as the form of vibration that the three-cylinder engine triple produced was so different from that of the Norton twin.

Both the Quadrant and the Trisolastic have survived, and are now owned by the National Motorcycle Museum.

Another interesting prototype from that period survives in the NMM. At Meriden in the late seventies, Brian Jones blended a T160 engine with the duplex frame of the current 750cc T140 Bonneville twin, which had descended from his early T160 ideas at Umberslade Hall. Although an oil-carrying chassis, it was equipped with a normal oil tank under the right side panel, and was built with cast alloy wheels.

## THE X75 HURRICANE

Even before the triples' launch in 1968, American BSA executive Don Brown had doubts about the Rocket 3 styling's suitability for the market he knew inside out.

On his flight back to America from a pre-launch meeting in England he had a lot on his mind.

'I honestly couldn't believe they were serious,' he told the author in 1996. 'I was disgusted with the 'rocket ship' mufflers and I also thought the overall appearance was of bulk and weight.'

Brown kept thinking about a motorcycle that had caught his eye when he had been on military service in 1950. It was a customized 650cc Triumph Thunderbird he'd seen at a shop in Oakland, Northern California. 'It had alloy sport fenders, a small James petrol tank, tachometer and speedo, a single big chrome headlamp, a solo saddle and a pillion pad. It was beautiful,' recalled Brown, who had bought the modified Triumph on sight.

Back at his office in Nutley, New Jersey, Brown decided to look for a design engineer who could capture what he was thinking and produce a mockup for restyling the A75 on those lines. He knew that his scheme was unlikely to be supported by anyone else at BSA, and that eventual production was most unlikely. But he nursed the idea of a slimline triple, styled rather like a fifties Triumph.

In May 1969, Brown asked his sales manager Harry Chaplin if he knew of a motorcycle design specialist. Chaplin said that he had met the creator of a neat 500cc Suzuki twin with a shapely combined tank and seat unit at that year's Daytona Cycle Week. It was an example of the growing interest in customized machines among young American motorcyclists. Brown was given Craig Vetter's card.

## Meeting of Minds

A keen motorcyclist since his childhood, Vetter had graduated in 1965 with a BFA qualification in Industrial Design. One of his heroes was the mathematician and radical designer Buckminster Fuller and his philosophy of 'doing more with less.' Vetter used the phrase on his business card when he started a design and glass-fibre moulding business, the Vetter Fairing Company, at Rantoul, near Urbana, Illinois.

By the end of May, Brown invited the young designer to New Jersey, and explained what he was looking for. His task was made easier because Vetter was an ardent admirer of the sleek US-specification Triumph Bonnevilles of the mid-sixties. Brown recalled:

> I told Craig I wanted a design that looked like it was moving even when standing still. It ought to have a light, lean look and symmetry of lines was important. They were the fundamentals I had heard Edward Turner lay out many times when I was sales manager at Johnson Motors between 1956 and 1965.

Vetter came away from the meeting with a loaned Rocket 3, an early production model recently lent by BSA to convey English celebrity Lord Montagu from his plane to New York's Empire State Building in a *Daily Mail* transatlantic air race.

It was agreed that Vetter would have access to BSA parts from the stores at Nutley, and his out-of-pocket expenses would be refunded. The finished machine would become the property of BSA Inc.

He was expected to make weekly progress reports to Brown and to log his work time so that if the design were to be accepted for production, he could be paid accordingly. Vetter's proposed figure of $17.50 (then about £7.30) per hour was agreed.

Vetter had expressed anxiety that the big BSA corporation would grab his ideas and not give him any credit. However, Brown allayed these fears in a letter, although he had not at that stage divulged his plans to his fellow BSA managers.

The long ride back to Illinois pointed up the Rocket 3's faults to Vetter, who found it overweight, the seat too wide and the footrests badly placed.

## Creating the New Look

Back at his modest 50 × 50ft premises, he started work. Removing the fuel tank, seat and side panels, he found that the BSA already looked more exciting.

After making preliminary sketches, he designed a single moulded unit to form the fuel container, seat and side panels.

The instrument binnacle was scrapped in favour of separate instruments, which Vetter envisaged as having an adjustable angle of tilt to suit the rider. Taking off the flat-backed headlamp, he put on a traditionally shaped chromed unit, prominent in the way Brown had envisaged, and held on a tubular Y-support from the fork bottom yoke. Vetter knew that BSA was planning a switch to a new front fork with alloy sliders, modelled on the Italian Ceriani type widely used on motocrossers and dirt track racers, so he obtained a Ceriani fork from BSA.

'Cylinder heads are much too timid looking,' was one of many notes Vetter made as he studied his raw material, and he addressed the fault by extending the fins, mocking up their new profile by glueing on pieces of shaped plastic. The head was given further prominence by painting the cylinder barrel black.

Several ideas were sketched out for replacing the ungainly ray gun silencers.

'I wasn't sure about the exhaust. But Brown suggested he could send me pipes used by Jim Rice for flat-tracking,' Vetter told the author in 1996. The actual system used by the Team BSA rider, with all three separate pipes and racing megaphones swept to the right side, formed the basis of Vetter's rakish system. 'I figured BSA's engineers could make it quiet,' Vetter said.

By mid-June Brown, had already offered *Cycle World* magazine an exclusive story on the design exercise, should it prove satisfactory. Early on in the venture, Brown realized that Vetter had strong ideas and knew what he was doing, and that minimal interference was called for.

However, in a letter dated 23 July 1969, Brown listed some of his personal criticisms of the design so far. They included the comment that 'the machine appears to me to be front end heavy, in that it seems to be slanting foward.'

The effect was due to the relatively short Ceriani front fork, so Vetter extended the stanchions by inserting 2in lengths of tubing. The length of the fork was effectively increased further by the shape of his alloy fork clamps.

Perfecting the curvaceous, organic shapes of his main bodywork moulding, Vetter had a complete rolling 422lb prototype by the end of the summer. Brown had favoured yel-

low as the main colour scheme, but Vetter preferred a reddish orange – actually Camaro Hugger Red – for the main moulding. Having removed the side reflectors from the oil cooler, and replaced them with BSA piled arms logos, he satisfied the road regulations by applying shaped strips of gold Scotchlite reflective material on the orange. They ran along the top of the fuel tank to form a background for the main BSA decals, and swept down onto the side panels to taper off where '750cc' decals were applied.

## Back to BSA

Word of what was going on got out at Nutley and Brown was summoned to see BSA Corporation Inc.'s US president Peter Thornton who had been installed in July 1969. He was asked to explain himself. 'I simply handed Thornton my file,' Brown says. Thornton's response was to ask Vetter to bring the results of his work to New Jersey.

This he did, although the BSA was not ridable, having a mocked-up wooden oil tank and plastic head fins. It was hauled east in a Volkswagen camper van by the long-haired, casually dressed Vetter, who was still wary of dealing with a large organization.

Joe Parkhurst's book *A Hurricane named Vetter*, which details the whole BSA project, relates how the machine was greeted in silence by Nutley staff, until Thornton arrived to inspect it. He pronounced it as the most exciting thing he'd ever seen, and that it should be sent to Small Heath to study straight away.

In January, Brown left BSA, not convinced of ex-advertising agency man Thornton's policies. Before his departure, he had given UK-based BSA Group chairman Eric Turner an undertaking not to discuss company matters with the press, partly (Brown thinks) because efforts were being made to conceal the true state of the company from people in America.

In return, Brown asked Turner to make sure that if the Vetter project went ahead it would stay faithful to the original design and that Vetter would receive credit for his work – and payment.

Vetter eventually heard from BSA, and a meeting was arranged with Brown's successor Tony Salisbury, in Michigan. He was told that a run of 500 special-trim, premium price Rocket 3s based on his prototype would be made at Small Heath, and launched as a market-testing experiment in 1971. There would be no need for Vetter to visit England. A few weeks later in the spring of 1970, after intervention at BSA by Brown, Vetter was sent a cheque for $12,000 (then about £5,000) to pay for his work.

## Slow Progress to Production

Work proceeded at Armoury Road on measuring up Vetter's prototype and preparing drawings so that special parts could be manufactured. Mitchenall Bros, the Wiltshire-based glass-fibre moulding company known in the UK for its Avon fairings, took on the job of making the prototype tank and seat unit. Doubts about the suitability, or legality, of using a moulded fuel tank meant that a steel container had to be devised to be supplied by Homer and moulded into the plastic. Non-metal fuel tanks would be banned on new motorcycles in the UK in 1973.

Two pre-production examples with five-speed gearboxes were completed at Small Heath by early 1971. Coded V75V, the model was referred to in factory documents as the Rocket 3 Chopper, reflecting BSA staff's bemusement at such a radical machine and the effect of the elongated front fork. As on Vetter's sample, the forks were lengthened by 2in, but this time over the standard BSA stanchion, already longer than the prototype's Ceriani type.

Meanwhile, Vetter's prototype had returned to the States to be photographed for the *Cycle World* article promised by Brown a year before. The orange BSA was featured on the cover of the monthly's September 1970 issue.

In the article, Vetter revealed the philosophy behind his work. He contrasted the age-old traditions of the British motorcycle industry with the underground youth culture then influencing young America'a tastes. And he emphasized the importance of his curvy tank and seat unit as a 'buffer zone' between the hard lines of a machine and the soft lines of a human rider.

Salisbury confirmed the market research aspect of the project, telling *Cycle World*:

> People have seen bikes like this before – customs – but never from the manufacturer. We want to know if the consumers agree with the design. We want to get letters from people. If we get a positive reaction it may go into production.

Letters arrived at the magazine by the sackload, but BSA's intended 1971 Vetter Rocket launch went by the board, a victim of the BSA Group planning bungles that saw even the established 650cc BSA and Triumph twins miss the US selling season.

*The world's first factory custom, and a major influence on subsequent mainstream design: the Triumph X75 Hurricane.*

The finished product stayed close to the Vetter concept, although the current conical hub brakes replaced the earlier type on the Vetter machine. When testing one of two pre-production machines at MIRA in December 1971, BSA staff recorded a best one-way speed of 122.90mph (197.75km/h), but following the close-down of complete motorcycle production at Small Heath, there would clearly be no new BSA triple, and the Vetter was transferred to Meriden for further development. However, a BSA pre-production counterpart was shipped to the US and was exhibited to sound out public opinion further at an American dealers' convention in February 1972.

## Hurricane Blows

Dr Felix Kalinski, who had replaced Thornton as permanent overall boss of American operations in May 1972, saw great promise in the Vetter Rocket. Attending a meeting at Small Heath in mid-1972, he suggested that it should be promoted at the expense of the Trident, with 3,000 examples to be shipped to the USA for 1973 if possible. He added that a triple with electric start and disc brakes was also needed.

At the same meeting, Bert Hopwood commented that the Vetter triple's handling was not as good as the conventional model's. Early trouble, caused by a weak joint between the lower alloy fork yoke and the steel steering stem, had been cured, but factory testers still concluded that the long fork fork and ribbed front tyre upset the machine's steering and general roadholding. But, as former Meriden man Harry Woolridge told the author: 'They rode it like an Isle of Man TT bike, which it wasn't meant to be.' Also, noise from the three-pipe exhaust caused major concern, as new emission restrictions were due to take effect in the US from January 1973.

When volume production started at Meriden in September 1972, the official model name was the Triumph X75 Hurricane, following a meteorological theme set by BSA's earlier Cyclone, Lightning and Thunderbolt twins. However, the V75V code was retained for the first few hundred models' serial numbers before being altered to TRX75.

Hurricane production finished in mid-January, and former Meriden design boss Brian Jones told the author that machines built in the new year for the US market had to be back-dated to avoid falling foul of the 1973 noise controls.

Vetter visited the Meriden plant in late November and early December of 1972, to witness something he'd never really expected: volume production of his 1969 project. He was dismayed that Triumph found it necessary to make the main moulding in two halves, with ugly adhesive tape covering the central join. Nor were the Umberslade-style flimsy steel wire front mudguard stays to his liking, but otherwise he was delighted to see a vision realized. 'I thought it was executed reasonably well, especially considering I had not talked directly with England,' Vetter told the author.

*Craig Vetter tries out a production X75 Hurricane at Meriden during his visit in late 1972. Triple silencers were interlinked to help reduce noise.*

# Triumph X75 Hurricane (1973)

## Engine

As A75 unit, but with enlarged fin area on cylinder head, black cylinder barrel.

| | |
|---|---|
| Engine type | ohv transverse triple |
| Bore and stroke | $67 \times 70$mm |
| Cubic capacity | 741cc |
| Compression ratio | 9.5 :1 |
| Claimed output | 58bhp @ 7,250rpm |
| Carburation | $3 \times 27$mm Amal Concentrics |
| Standard jetting needle | 150 main, .106in needle jet, position 2, throttle slide cutaway no. 3½. |

*Exhaust System*
Three separate downpipes each terminating in a 'reverse cone megaphone' style silencer. All on machine's right side, with silencers interlinked.

## Transmission

Machines with four-speed gearbox as A75.

Five-speed gearbox (as A75V) overall ratios:

| | |
|---|---|
| first | 12.87:1 |
| second | 9.15: 1 |
| third | 6.98: 1 |
| fourth | 5.93: 1 |
| fifth | 4.98: 1 |

| | |
|---|---|
| Gearbox sprocket | 18 teeth |
| Rear wheel sprocket | 53 teeth |

## Cycle parts

Frame: as 1968–72 A75, with minor alterations. Special steel fuel tank enclosed by combined tank/seat unit moulding. Fuel tank capacity: 2 gallons (2.5 US gallons).

## Suspension

Front telescopic fork as 1971 A75/T150, lengthened by 2in (50mm) with polished alloy yokes.

## Tyres

| | |
|---|---|
| Front | $3.25 \times 19$in Dunlop ribbed |
| Rear | $4.25 \times 18$in Dunlop TT100 |

## Brakes

As 1971 A75/T150.

## Dimensions (in/mm)

| | |
|---|---|
| Wheelbase | 60/1,524 |
| Seat height | 31/787 |
| Ground clearance | 5.5/140 |
| Dry weight | 444lb (202kg) |

## Colour scheme

Tank/seat unit self-coloured Aztec Red, with yellow reflective stripes.

---

The main purpose of Vetter's visit was to discuss ideas he had been feeding to Triumph for restyling the Meriden 650cc twin, and to this end he spent much of his time with Jack Wickes, for whom he had great admiration.

Early in 1972, Jack Redmond, Triumph's newly appointed Product Planning Director, had contacted Vetter and asked him to restyle the unloved Umberslade Hall-designed Bonneville. Awed at the idea of dealing with a legendary model, Vetter pro-

*The Bonneville TT twin Vetter designed for Triumph (left) stands alongside a standard T120 twin. Vetter's ideas for the TT, especially the tank and raised instruments, were adopted on the T160.*

posed a machine based on the old US market-only Bonneville TT Special racer. 'When I was a kid, that was the hottest motorcycle you could get in America,' he told the author. For further inspiration, he obtained photos of Gene Romero's 750cc Triumph TT dirt track twin from Pete Colman.

A prototype of the Bonneville TT 750 twin was made and flown to Britain and Vetter followed it. The twin was later toured round American shows to gauge market reaction, but despite a favourable response, the crisis following the NVT merger stopped it in its tracks.

The spirit of the TT survived, however, in the Trident T160, for by the time of Vetter's visit, Wickes was styling the new triple, using a fuel tank shape based on the Vetter Bonneville's, and also copying its up-tilted instrument cluster.

Meriden was, and is now, a rather prim Warwickshire village, and Brian Jones recalled an amusing episode when Vetter was taken for dinner at the local Manor Hotel. The young American's hair and fashionable clothing frightened the staff. Jones recalled:

We had booked a table, but they wouldn't let Craig in the dining room with his big leather hat and loose-fitting suit. We ended up going somewhere else, where they hid him behind a pillar. It was so silly, because we all found him to be such a nice chap.

No more than 1,154 Hurricanes are thought to have been made and confusingly, their serial number sequence was spread amongst the general 1973 T150V output.

Doubts over the Hurricane's handling spread to the USA, where fork modification kits were distributed to dealers to address the problem. High pricing – $2,195, against the conventional Trident's $1,900 and the even cheaper Honda CB750 – meant that the limited edition of X75s was not snapped up as quickly as might have been hoped.

Hurricanes were also sold in small numbers on the Canadian and Australian markets, and some went to Europe, where one pre-production machine had been displayed at shows. Fewer than forty Hurricanes were supplied on the UK market.

## BSA and Triumph 750cc triple production figures

First built 23 August 1968, last 28 April 1976.

| | BSA A75 | Triumph T150 | Triumph T160 | Triumph X75 |
|---|---|---|---|---|
| Aug 1968–Aug 1969 | 3,543 | 3,943 | | |
| Aug 1969–Aug 1970 | 137 | 287 | | |
| Aug 1970–Aug 1971 | 1,047 | 1,297 | | |
| Aug 1971–Aug 1972 | 1,170 | 4,321 | | |
| Aug 1972–Aug 1973 | | 5,166 | | |
| Aug 1973–Mar 1974 | | 4,165 | | |
| Nov 1974–Apr 1976 | | | 7,211 | |
| Sep 1972–Jan 1973 | | | | 1,154 |

Totals   27,544 Triumphs, 5,897 BSAs

Full total: 33,441. These figures are from company records, but allowance must be made for engines taken for racing, and possible inaccuracies in record keeping.

Prefixes on A75 and T150 serial numbers indicate the date of build. The actual month of build is shown by the first letter, whilst the second prefix gives the model year. As production for sales in the following year began in August, the prefix AC indicates a 1969 model built in August 1968. All machines' frame and engine numbers matched when they left the factories.

| First letter | Second letter |
|---|---|
| **A** January | **C** 1969 |
| **B** February | **D** 1970 |
| **C** March | **E** 1971 |
| **D** April | **G** 1972 |
| **E** May | **H** 1973 |
| **G** June | **J** 1974 |
| **H** July | **K** 1975 |
| **J** August | **N** 1976 |
| **K** September | |
| **N** October | |
| **P** November | |

It is not just the X75's rarity that has made it a sought-after motorcycle with almost cult status. Today, it is one of the most desirable triples because of its bold individuality and its fascinating history. Vetter and his company went from strength to strength, particularly with his popular Windjammer motorcycle fairing, and more recently with a wing-shaped 'flairing' for Harley-Davidsons. By 1980, the practice of flowing the lines of a motorcycle fuel tank into the seat and side panels had become the norm for many manufacturers.

Looking back on the Vetter project, Don Brown said he saw it as a return to the lean and light Turner and Wickes style after the lunacy of the Ogle experiment:

I never had the intention of insisting that BSA make it, after all, my job was selling. But I thought something should be done. The company seemed to spend zero time thinking about what the public actually wanted.

# 5  Race Against Time

A major road-racing campaign was the last thing anyone had expected from the British industry in 1969.

There had been a golden age for factory participation in international grand prix competition in the mid-sixties, when Honda, Suzuki and Yamaha mounted intensive campaigns that made even the no expense spared efforts of the Italian MV Agusta factory look modest. But in time, even these thriving makes had decided it was wise to scale down the expensive GP activity.

So the idea that a major British factory would attempt to field a world class race team with a fleet of highly competitive machines seemed unthinkable. And yet that is exactly what was about to happen in the early seventies, when the BSA and Triumph triples achieved legendary status on the world's circuits.

Historically both companies had been cautious of involvement in road racing, a notoriously costly activity. Then a change in the BSA Group's philosophy had come when Harry Sturgeon was installed as Chief Executive in 1964. A firm believer in the philosophy of sports involvement as a selling aid, he encouraged official road racing activity.

But, whilst acknowledging how companies like Honda had built worldwide sales by racing exotic and expensive grand prix machinery, Sturgeon's preferred plan was to enter familiar showroom models in suitable events. If they won on the track, he reasoned, potential buyers would be convinced of their superiority on the road.

This policy was music to Doug Hele's ears, for he had been interested in the racing potential of multi-cylinder roadsters since

his Norton days, and was already applying what he had learned to the Bonneville at Meriden.

By the time that the Rocket 3 and Trident were launched, Triumph 650 twins were a dominant force in Production racing, a class that was attracting growing interest.

Egged on no doubt by the motorcycle industry, British racing's governing body, the Auto Cycle Union, had added a national Production race to the programme of the Isle of Man Tourist Trophy in 1967. The TT, run over the Island's unique machine-hammering 37.73-mile (60.71km) public roads Mountain Course, was still the world's most important road race meeting at that time, and Triumph headed the 750cc Production category with subtly modified Bonnevilles from the outset.

The UK's Production class had grown out of specialized racing held annually at Thruxton, Silverstone and other circuits since the fifties. Endurance events, traditionally of 500 miles (805km) at Thruxton and 1,000km (600 miles) at Silverstone were run for dealer-entered standard road machines, ridden by two-rider teams. Triumph had won the important Thruxton race, promoted by the Southampton Club, several times.

And, with the justification of boosting American sales, Hele had developed a useful open-class 500cc racer out of Triumph's Tiger 100 twin. Wins over native Harley-Davidson machines were achieved in the prestigious Daytona 200-mile (320km) event, where Harley had influenced the rules to the extent that ohv machines competing against its side-valve 750cc twins were restricted to 500cc.

From that machine, Hele derived a twin for open class British and European events, where the half-litre class was the premier category in world championship Grands Prix held mostly in Europe. Ridden by Percy Tait, a 500cc ohv Triumph scored an astonishing success at the 1969 Belgian Grand Prix, finishing second to Italian Giacomo Agostini's works dohc three-cylinder MV Agusta.

At BSA, there had always been an official Competition Department, although it had concentrated on trials and motocross, with world-class successes in the latter. But under Sturgeon's regime there was also a highly active Production racing programme run by a group of keen employees. Small Heath's 654cc A65 was acknowledged to be fast, and BSA had reaped useful publicity when Mike Hailwood won the Production race in the 1965 Hutchinson 100 international meeting at Silverstone on an A65 Spitfire twin. Forays to Daytona with specially prepared A50 twins were less glorious, but larger-capacity BSA engines were prominent in sidecar road racing on British circuits, including the Isle of Man.

It might have seemed the obvious course for both factories to pitch the Trident and Rocket 3 into Production racing as soon as they went on sale to the public, especially as they were full 750s, like their Norton Commando rivals. That didn't happen, despite the triples' power and speed improvement over the A65 and T120.

Many hours and miles of development, and clever interpretation of the ACU rules, had produced 650cc Triumph racers with nimble enough roadholding to lap the TT Course at over 100mph (160km/h) in 1969, and sufficient reliability to win Spain's gruelling Barcelona 24-hour race. Similarly, BSA twins continued to head the factory's Production racing campaign.

But realization that the 650 twins were reaching the limit of their performance was reinforced by the Meriden team's experiences in the 1969 Production TT. Malcolm Uphill won on a T120, making history with an opening lap from a standing start at 100.09mph (161.04km/h), the first ever accomplished by a 'Proddie' machine and a superb advertisement for the Bonneville and for Dunlop's K81 tyres, developed for the

*The highly modified T100 engine in Tait's 500, with oil cooler and front-mounted oil tanks. A special timing cover carries ignition points on an extra bearing for accurate timing.*

*Tait racing the Rob North-framed experimental 750cc Triumph twin at Mallory Park in 1968. This chassis was the starting point for the triples' racing frame.*

triples, which were subsequently marketed under the TT100 name. But after four TT laps (150 racing miles (240km)), a short race by TT standards, the pistons in Uphill's Bonneville were cracking up badly enough to have made completing another circuit an impossibility. And something few spectators were to know was that the fast 650 engines were being stripped and rebuilt, often with new main engine castings, for every important race. Rod Gould's Bonneville had been tipped to win, but after flying through a slightly downhill speed trap at over 140mph (225km/h), it dropped out of the race with a snapped crankshaft.

Hele recalled tentative early race circuit testing with a near-standard Trident early in 1969. The venue was Thruxton, where Triumph were also shaking down 650 twins in a practice session. The rider was 1968 750 Production TT winner Ray Pickrell, and he lapped the T150 triple at almost the same speed as the lighter and more compact Production Bonnevilles, despite the handicap of a four-speed gearbox with road ratios. Eventually Pickrell cranked over so far on a fast curve that the front end of an exhaust pipe grounded, and he crashed heavily, destroying the machine.

In August 1969 a modified Trident was ridden by Percy Tait in a twenty-lap Production race at the Brands Hatch Hutchinson 100 meeting. Although the triple was equipped with a half-fairing, a large aluminium alloy fuel tank and cigar-shaped Production Bonneville silencers in place of ray guns, it was still on standard gearbox ratios.

Competing for the first time in a new Bell helmet, which had replaced his traditional 'pudding-basin' lid, Tait finished sixth on the Trident behind BSA, Norton and Triumph twins. Whilst Hele didn't view the outing as a serious racing venture, he was nevertheless happy that the machine was proving reasonably competitive.

## DAYTONA DEADLINE

Suddenly the triples were thrust to the fore in the BSA Group's increasingly ambitious racing plans. The impetus had come from America where former advertising executive Peter Thornton had become president of BSA Co. Inc. in the States in July 1969. He was all for the glamour of racing as a promotional activity, and rule changes made by the American Motorcyclist Association had opened up the Daytona 200 and other State-side road races to the triples.

The old format of running overhead valve 500s against side-valve 750s had been scrapped in favour of a new 750cc roadster-based formula, destined to exert a huge influence through the seventies, even rivalling the traditional 500cc Grand Prix class in Europe.

Free of valve layout restrictions, the new formula admitted two-stroke and four-stroke machines with any number of cylinders, provided engines were of a type being made available on the market in significant numbers. Racing chassis, exhausts, and other high performance aids were allowed.

With Harley-Davidson preparing a new ohv XR750 to replace the factory's rapid side-valve 750, and Honda planning to compete with the ohc CB750 four, BSA/Triumph's three-cylinder 750cc engine looked like the only realistic proposition for a British road-racing invasion.

Thornton's ambitions went well beyond the Daytona 200. Encouraged by Pete Colman, head of national racing activity for BSA Inc., he stated that it would be the intention of Team BSA and Team Triumph in the USA to completely dominate the AMA Grand National championship in 1970.

The country's foremost series incorporated a mix of road race and dirt track events, with as many as twenty-five rounds in a season. Triumph and BSA were already highly competitive on the dirt, where British twins of up to 750cc had been able to contend with Harley's V-twins.

But the stakes were high in tarmac racing. Although Triumph had trounced Harley's side-valvers with 500s at Daytona in 1966 and 1967, the Brits had been knocked off the top rung in the subsequent two years. Tuned by Harley's brilliant Dick O'Brien, the Milwaukee KR flat-heads were outpacing the little Triumphs by as much as 15mph (24km/h) on top speed. And the new XR overhead engines were expressly designed for racing, while the triples still required development time. Honda's prospects for the new formula looked good, too, with incredible horsepower claims being made for the CB750 engine, with its four cylinders and overhead camshaft.

Regardless of the BSA Group's mounting problems at home, the go-ahead was given for a serious onslaught in the new 750cc US formula class, taking the triples as a basis.

## Developing a Racer

A proper racing department had come into being at Meriden, thanks to the official Production campaign, so many of the necessary facilities were already in place for the hectic four-month programme launched by Hele in the autumn of 1969. The target: to create a three-cylinder 750 racer in less than five months and beat the opposition in America.

For the BSA Group's marketing purposes the team machines were to be built in both BSA and Triumph forms and at the outset it was planned to build three of each marque. Activity was concentrated wholly at Meriden, where staff and facilities that would normally have engaged in creating and prototyping future road machines were employed exclusively on racing work.

Most of the Experimental Department was given over to the Daytona project, as Les Williams, then a chargehand in the department recalled in 1995: 'By November we were working until 10pm at night, and living on Chinese takeaways. Sometimes, on a Saturday afternoon, my wife Joan would cook dinner for half a dozen of us.'

A higher-performance roadster version of the original T150 – coded P2S – had been mooted, but now Hele's sights had been raised to an out-and-out racer. As was required by the rules of the new formula, the starting point would be standard T150 and A75 engines taken off the Small Heath assembly bench.

Lessons learned with the 500cc racer were immediately applied to the 750. One of the most important factors in gaining power was camshaft design, governing the timing of valve opening, closing and overlap. On Triumph's racing twins, Hele had used a BSA cam form, but with a tappet having a larger radius than normal, and the profile further smoothed to boost revs. The resulting cam form, coded TH6, and first used in Rod Gould's 500cc twin racer, was adopted for both the inlet and exhaust on the racing 750. Racing cams were treated with the Eutectic metal-spraying process for longevity. This job was done at Meriden, mostly by Experimental mechanic Arthur

*A Trident racer at Meriden in 1970, showing the 250mm Fontana double-sided front brake, moulded Screen & Plastic fuel tank and mechanical rev-counter.*

Jakeman, using a gas torch and a rig to turn the cams, which was powered by a car windscreen wiper motor.

A battery-less ignition system was devised for the triples, powered by the alternator. The standard sets of three Lucas contact breakers were retained, with a trio of 12-volt ignition coils. Lightening procedures normal in four-stroke engine tuning were carried out on the valve train, with holes drilled in the timing pinions, and the cam followers and some metal removed from the rocker arms, which were also polished. The oil pump drive gears were also lightened, and as much excess metal as possible removed from the primary drive assembly. Cooling holes were made on the cover plate of the standard clutch.

*BSA built for Daytona 1970, showing the positions of the oil cooler and two of the three ignition coils.*

For maximum gas flow at large throttle openings on Daytona's ultra-fast banked track, Amal Grand Prix track carburettors as fitted to the 500s were specified. They were flexibly mounted to the engine on hoses, and supplied by a single Amal matchbox remote float chamber. The instruments' choke size was 1³⁄₁₆in, the equivalent size to the 27mm bores of the Concentrics fitted on triples as standard.

Cylinder heads were stock castings taken to the race shop for final machining and fettling, with centre spark plug holes set at the same angle as the outers, to obtain equal compression ratios on each cylinder. The inlet valves' heads were dropped slightly into the combustion chamber to ensure maximum unmasked gas passage at small openings. Standard cast-in valve seat inserts were to prove unsuitable for racing, and they were supplanted by shrunk-in rings of a harder material.

High compression pistons raised the ratio to 11:1 or higher, with slight variations between individual units. Because AMA rules allowed engines to run on their maximum rebore oversizes, Hele used plus-0.040in pistons in American racing, taking the triples' capacity to approximately 760cc.

Two of the three Experimental Department dynamometer test beds were commandeered for the race programme and, as usual in a Hele-supervised operation, everyone involved chipped in with ideas and concentrated on their strongest skills.

Weeks of work went into devising a racing exhaust system. Hele started out with a three-pipe system, but he learned of promising results gained in America with pipework that blended three header pipes into one single outlet. Later to become standard practice on high-performance motorcycles, branched exhaust systems were then rarely seen outside car racing. In the US, however, some dirt track twins had been tried with two-into-one systems, and experiments with the

# Don Woodward – sheet metal wizard

Most petrol and oil tanks for the works racers were fabricated by Don Woodward. A Lincolnshire-based self-employed sheet metal specialist, he had made body panels for BRM Formula One racing cars since 1954, including those for Graham Hill's world championship-winning machines of 1962.

Before the triples campaign, Woodward had fabricated alloy tanks for Triumph's twin-cylinder racers, including large 5.7-gallon containers for the factory's T120 Bonnevilles to use in production TT. Elder brother of Meriden Experimental Department fitter John Woodward, Don took over alloy fabrication when Triumph's former supplier Bill Jakeman retired. The earliest 1970 Daytona triples had glass-fibre fuel tanks supplied by fairing and seat makers Screen & Plastic, but during that season Woodward's alloy items were adopted. A North frame was taken to Woodward's workshops for use as a pattern, and later a simple fitting jig was used for fuel tanks, replicating the top section of a frame. A dummy fuel tank, carved from lightweight material, was provided as a guide for its shape, and Don has preserved it at his workshop.

Using 16-gauge S1C alloy sheet, Woodward made fuel tanks in segments, using a wheeling machine to form curved areas. Sections were then joined by gas welding, and the joins smoothed and polished. Transverse baffles were placed inside to prevent fuel surge under heavy braking.

For short-circuit racing in the UK, Woodward designed a smaller reservoir to fit the North chassis, holding approximately 3½ gallons. His oil tanks were tailored to individual chassis, to allow for the variations between North's handmade frames. They contained return pipes placed so they could be readily checked by looking into the filler orifice.

Monza quick-release filler caps made by Enots were fitted to petrol and oil tanks. For Daytona in 1971 tanks were made with a 2½in cap on one side and a 2in cap on the other. The smaller cap allowed air to escape during quick fill-ups as well as letting pit crews see the fuel level.

Woodward made special five-gallon dump-cans with 2in butterfly valves for use in pit stops at long races, and some one-off components such as fabricated fork yokes, exhaust megaphones and an all-alloy fairing complete with air ducts. He also supplied Bonneville-based tanks for both Rocket 3 and Trident factory production class racers. A quantity of these were also produced for dealers, as they had to be available for non-works use to satisfy ACU production rules. 'That was a good thing as fas as I was concerned!' Woodward told the author. He recalled an excellent relationship with the Meriden race shop, mainly through Doug Hele himself.

At an Anglo-American match race meeting, Woodward was approached by Danny Macias, boss of the US racing division. 'He asked me if I was the guy who made aluminium gas tanks. I told him I was. He said he had some work for me and gave me a cheque for $1,000 there and then,' Woodward recalled.

Since joined in business by his son Alan, Woodward made tanks for Norton Rotary team racers of the late eighties and early nineties. As well as fabrications for modern and classic racing machines, fuel tanks for the LP Williams Legend and Renegade triples are made at the Woodwards' premises in Morton, Lincolnshire.

triples followed. A system devised for the Trident by Texan Jack Wilson was despatched to Meriden from Triumph's HQ in Baltimore and studied carefully by Hele.

He decided that its efficiency centred on the design of the collector box, and drew out a version that would be easier to make, with more equal gas distribution. 'It worked even better than the American one in brake tests,' Hele recounted to the author. He found that the three-into-one exhaust terminating in a megaphone gave a boost of 4–5bhp over a

*Don Woodward wheeling an alloy mudguard for a car in 1996.*

three pipe system originally proposed, as well as saving weight.

Five-speed close ratio gearboxes were an absolute necessity, and components were already available in the form of internals supplied for the racing 500s and Production 650s by Kent transmission specialist Rod Quaife.

In road racing, power can only be used to best effect if the cycle parts permit. Precise steering, efficient braking, ground clearance, and even rider comfort all make their contribution to fast lap times. Although the Daytona formula insisted that machines were closely based on models sold to the

public, the use of a special racing chassis was allowed.

Hele felt that a pukka purpose-built frame was needed. A compact track chassis had been made for Tait's 500cc GP racer by Ken Sprayson of Reynolds Tube, the Birmingham manufacturer of Reynolds 531 tubing. However, Sprayson recalled in 1996, Reynolds were unable to cope with Triumph's Daytona time-scale, which required six chassis to be designed and built in as many weeks. The solution for Hele offered itself in the form of a one-off brazed duplex frame, which Tait had been racing since mid-1968.

He had commissioned it himself from a fellow member of the racing fraternity, independent constructor Rob North, to house an experimental Bonneville-based 750cc twin-cylinder engine. Percy Tait suggested to Hele that a frame on similar lines could house the triple, and late in 1969, a 750cc engine was sent to North's base, a few miles from Meriden, to be measured up.

Hele stipulated what type of chassis he envisaged. He required full boxed-in fabrication of the swinging arm supports on each side, and steady brackets to secure the top of the engine to the tubework. The resulting frame was a strong and tidy construction, with rigid bracing between the three points that most affect roadholding, the steering

*Forerunner of the North frame? Doug Hele had a hand in designing this chassis for a 250cc BSA racer in 1954. In the region of the swinging arm supports, it resembles the triples frame of 1970.*

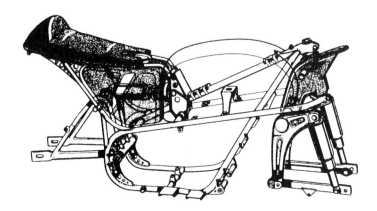

# Rob North – framing a legend

When Rob North was asked to make a small batch of frames for Triumph he could never have dreamed how famous his name would became throughout the motorcycling world. At the time he was twenty-nine and working from a tiny workshop. Formerly the clocking-on shed for a coal mine, it was on Colliery Lane, Bedworth, five miles north of Coventry. During 1970, North moved to a dis-used cimena in Short Street, Nuneaton, which visitors always remembered because of its sloping floor, and a ferocious German Shepherd dog.

A gifted welder, whose product was always robust, North's main work had been in making speed-way frames patterned on the contemporary Eso chassis. They were favoured by several UK First Division speedway riders, and he also built sidecar road racing chassis for leading competitors, including Chris Vincent, who housed a four-cylinder 750cc dohc Fath URS engine in North tube-work.

North had served a five-year apprenticeship at the Alfred Herbert machine tools company, before becoming a successful national-level sidecar pilot. He built a Triumph-powered outfit using a cut-down version of the famous Manx Norton featherbed racing frame.

Breakages in tubes near the steering head persuaded him to change their layout. On the feath-erbed, the top tubes and downtubes cross, with the top tubes meeting the lower portion of the head-stock, and the downtubes reaching to the upper part of it. North reversed the layout, taking the top tubes to the upper part of the head, and the bottom tubes to its lower end. This put a stop to the frame tube fractures.

The same layout was used when North was commissioned to make a solo racing frame for Percy Tait's 750cc Triumph short circuit racing twin, first aired at Mallory Park in September 1968. He told the author:

> That was the first frame I made in the wrap-around style, with the top tubes passing on either side of the engine. Also, that frame had three tubes running to the top of each rear suspension mount. We thought a stiffer subframe would make a bike handle better, but dropped that idea later.

When North agreed to frame the three-cylinder racers late in 1969, Triumph provided him with an engine and a spare front frame section. The latter was used, in collaboration with Tait, to determine the position of the engine relative to the steering head. 'Percy wanted it slightly higher and further forward than standard, to get weight forward and for better ground clearance,' North recalled.

Unwittingly, he replicated the steering head angle on the pattern roadster frame, which was a scrapped item of the abandoned 65-degree type. With the exception of this oversight, the frames were designed in close collaboration with Doug Hele.

As North had no pipe-bending machines, he filled lengths of tubing with sand, heated them and made bends on plywood formers. He was renowned for his skill with a gas torch, and joints were brazed on all works racing frames. Each frame was individually made, and the minor variations between them meant that parts such as oil tanks were not interchangeable between machines.

After making the initial batch of six frames for the 1970 Daytona meeting, he made one extra at the last minute:

> Percy told me that his machine had been commandeered by the American team, and he had lost his ride. That was on a Friday. I made a frame over the weekend and delivered it to the gate at Meriden at one o'clock on the Monday morning. It was built up into a machine and shipped on the Wednesday.

North also made cast alloy wheel hubs for racing triples and, when Lowboy frames were made for 1971, North devised new wider fork yokes to make room for the disc rotors on each side of the front wheel.

North estimates a total build of fifteen works frames for the 1970 and 1971 seasons. He charged £145 per frame, and his contract prevented him from making his triples solo road racing chassis for anyone other than the BSA Group. A Honda chassis on similar lines made by North in 1972 is believed to have survived.

Drawings were made from a completed frame at Meriden, and copies subsequently sent to the American BSA and Triumph racing headquarters at Duarte, so that editions could be produced as required in the States. US privateer racers put pressure on for frames, which they were meant to be able to buy from the manufacturer under AMA rules.

North told the author that Bert Hopwood once asked him if he would prefer an outright payment or royalties if his frames were to be produced in much larger quantities, but no deal transpired. One chassis was supplied with a removable frame tube to make engine fitting easier, and North speculated that it was a prototype for a road machine.

When the offical BSA/Triumph race team was disbanded, North was free to make the triple racing frame for other customers. However, he emigrated to America during 1973, and in October of that year his former business partner, Stuart Ashford, passed on the road racing components business to Stan Shenton of Kent's sporting dealer Boyer of Bromley.

Working from a base in Chula Vista, Southern California, North estimated that by early 1996 he had completed a total of ninety-one chassis for the triples. To see his influence on motorcycle development he only has to look at any modern sports machine, which is sure to echo the line of his famous 'wrap around' chassis.

*Still busy: Rob North in 1995.*

head and each of the two swinging arm supports. The curved tube in the area of the latter bore a strong resemblance to the frame of the experimental 250cc BSA MC1 racer, which Hele had designed in the early fifties. At the outset, a total of six frames would be required from North, all to the same pattern regardless of whether they were for BSA or Triumph badged racers.

The most effective proprietary racing brakes available at the time were large 250mm diameter drum units made by Daniele Fontana in Milan, and several sets were ordered in October 1969. Wheels with alloy rims were built in the 18in size, WM2 width at the front and WM3 rear, to accept the Goodyear tyres that US riders were contracted to use. Front forks were selectively assembled using stock T150 components.

For rear wheel braking, hydraulic disc brakes, then a relative novelty in motorcycle racing, were adopted. About four years earlier Hele had organized trials of disc brakes made by racing constructor Colin Lyster on a Triumph twin and had been deeply impressed. But riders criticized early disc front anchors for their lack of feel at the hand lever. The Daytona machines carried a two-piston caliper and cast iron rotor provided by Automotive Products.

Efficient streamlining was essential for the high-speed banked sections at Daytona. Development of an aerodynamic glass fibre fairing to suit the North chassis was put in to the hands of the technicians at Umberslade Hall, the BSA Group's research facility.

Mike Nedham, the Group's Engineering Director, had worked at the Scott motorcycle factory in his youth, but his career background was in aviation, working at aircraft maker Bristol and on Bloodhound missile ram-jet engines before joining BSA in 1968. He arranged for a small group of technicians, headed by Graham Nicholson and Trevor Winship, to work on the fairing project. At times they used the sub-sonic wind tunnel at the Royal Aircraft Establishment research centre in Farnborough, Surrey. This installation was able to run at higher speeds than MIRA's tunnel, which could only replicate road speeds in the region of 100mph (160km/h).

Aware of the need to maintain a stream of cool air around the engine, the fairing designers tried to shape the fairing accordingly. They also produced special seat tail mouldings. Much bigger than the tailpieces conventionally used for circuit racing, they were designed to streamline the area of the machine immediately behind the rider, reducing turbulence and boosting speed on Daytona's flat-out sections.

Manufacture of fairings and moulded fuel tanks was carried out by Screen & Plastic, the glass-fibre moulding company that had made enclosures for the Production twins.

A completed, but unfaired, North triple prototype circulated MIRA's banked test track at 140mph (225km/h) on high gearing,

but a more spacious venue was needed to test the fairing at the higher speeds likely to be achieved at Daytona.

One freezing Saturday morning in January 1970, Hele's team took the faired prototype to RAF Elvington, near York, where the 2-mile (3km) bomber runway was occasionally made available for record attempts and testing. The ever-stoical Tait was to make timed runs; Hele tells the story:

> The strip was covered in snow, and I rang up the RAF controller and asked if they couldn't bring out a sweeper, but they wouldn't. By about midday it seemed to have cleared, and Percy made his first run.
>
> We timed him at 164mph [264km/h], which was not the sort of speed we were used to in those days! The lights we had only worked one way, so we had to set them up for a run in the opposite direction, which appeared to be slightly downhill. It was nearly 3 o'clock when Percy set off the other way. As he approached the far end, he fell off, but got up and walked away.
>
> I'd noticed that the lights only showed something like 157mph [253km/h], and I thought a tappet might have closed up and slowed him. But Percy said he had thought the clutch was slipping, until he realized it was wheel-slip because of frost on the runway. And that's what had brought him off!

The 160mph-plus (257km/h+) run had proved the aerodynamic qualities of the fairing, although the low temperature at Elvington had failed to test the effectiveness of the cooling air flow inside it.

With only six weeks left, a full squad of six machines had to be built and prepared for Daytona, but engine development was still progressing. The output of engines had been readily hoisted from the 60bhp of a good standard unit to near 80bhp, but work progressed to wring as much horsepower as could be had. At Meriden, output was usually measured at the drive-side engine mainshaft.

As the Florida deadline approached, the fleet of three BSA and three Triumph works racers took shape under Hele's direction, meticulously assembled by the factory's best fitters. For simplicity, Triumph gearbox end covers were fitted to all six, and the only differences between the marques were the BSA version's inclined cylinders and the paintwork. Following tradition established by the American racing teams, the BSAs' paintwork was red and white and the Triumphs' blue and white.

## Turning up the Heat

The Daytona International Speedway is an extraordinary place. Built on the western outskirts of Daytona Beach, a coastal resort about 200 miles (320km) north of Miami on Florida's eastern seaboard, the circuit was designed primarily for top-level stock car racing. Its dominant feature is a huge 'tri-oval' saucer of tarmac, surrounding an arena reached by tunnels under the structure. In places the oval's track is banked at 31 degrees to allow extremely high speeds to be maintained through the three turns.

For the AMA's Daytona 200 motorcycle race, held annually in early March, a substantial portion of the bankings is used, combined with a flat, twisting infield section, creating a 3.8-mile (6.1km) circuit to test a machine's brakes and handling as well as flat-out ability. Although bikes appear insect-like against Daytona's expanse of banked track, their speed and the reverberation of exhaust noise creates an eerie atmosphere.

## The Team

Riders allocated triples for Daytona in 1970 were drawn mainly from the ranks of BSA and Triumph's top American professionals. To obtain maximum publicity, BSA's marketing department also approached Briton Mike Hailwood, the legendary nine-times

world champion grand prix rider who had retired from full-time motorcycle racing two years previously. Hailwood's presence would guarantee worldwide coverage of the Florida race, and his ability to win was not in doubt.

The Oxfordshire star knew the Speedway well, having set a world one-hour record of 144.222mph (232.053km/h) aboard a works MV Agusta on the tri-oval in 1964. He also won the 500cc US Grand Prix held on the circuit in that year aboard the Italian four.

As Hailwood was due to compete in the Sebring car race in mid-Florida on the following weekend the plan suited him, and he agreed to compete. He told the press that Daytona 1970 was to be his last ever motorcycle race, a prophecy that was to prove rather inaccurate.

BSAs were also provided for David Aldana and Jim Rice. Aldana, a twenty-year-old Californian in his first year as a senior normally campaigned 650cc BSA twins. A fearless and sometimes wild full-throttle dirt rider, he lacked road racing experience. Rice, also from the west coast, had three 1969 Grand National wins to his credit, all on the dirt aboard Team BSA twins.

Team BSA were negotiating to hire Dick Mann, a wily veteran of the Grand Nationals since the fifties, for 1970, but for Daytona he had signed to ride a Team Hansen-entered Honda CB750 four, along with British riders Ralph Bryans, Tommy Robb and Bill Smith.

Triumph's top gun for the triples' US debut was Gene Romero, a Californian maestro of the dirt-tracks who had been Triumph supported since 1968 and was AMA Grand National runner-up in 1969. Romero and Aldana called themselves 'Team Mexican' because of their shared ancestry, but were strictly rivals on the track.

Oklahoma boy Gary Nixon, one of America's very best all-rounders, had the best credentials among the three US Team Triumph riders, having won at Daytona on the Hele 500cc twin in 1967, and having delivered Triumph two AMA championships in 1967 and 1968. But Nixon had suffered a serious leg injury in a crash on the Santa Rosa Mile flat-track in 1969.

The other teamster on a blue and white triple was Don Castro, a promising twenty-year-old, also from California.

A seventh machine in Triumph colours was belatedly shipped to Florida for Percy Tait to ride, although officially he was present at Daytona primarily as an adviser to the six main team riders, who had no previous experience of the factory threes. Not everyone in the American camp approved of British riders competing, as their one-off rides would not contribute to the overall plan for the season of amassing Grand National points.

Hele's team of mechanics in America were Arthur Jakeman, Jack Shemans and Fred Swift, all veterans of twin-cylinder racing. Senior BSA Group engineering staff, including Mike Nedham, were present, and Lionel Jofeh flew to Florida for the race.

Machines ridden by US riders were put in the care of American fitters and tuners, the latter making decisions on jetting, suspension and tyres.

The Team BSA and Team Triumph squads were formed from personnel based at east and west coast arms of BSA Co. Inc. In charge of them was Pete Colman, a former racer and Vice President of Engineering and Director of Racing under Thornton, based at Duarte, California. Although the racing programme had officially been unified between BSA and Triumph, old rivalries still simmered. 'In spite of the organized effort, there continued to be dissension among former Triumph East and Triumph West service personnel and BSA East and West personnel,' Colman told the author.

During the week's training, it became clear that overheating was causing the triples problems. The Florida spring weather, often as hot as the English summer by March, was becoming warmer. On some machines, ductings inside the fairings were removed in an attempt to make the engines run cooler.

## Ready to Run

There was a last-minute hiccup concerning the five-speed gearboxes and their legality in the race, which depended on an homologation rule. At least fifty five-speed boxes needed to have been made publicly available for them to be eligible. Although the quota had apparently been manufactured, none had yet reached America.

The rival Honda equipe threatened to make an issue of this, but never did. Tommy Robb crashed his CB750-based racer in practice and it burst into flames. Fire crews were slow to deal with the incident, and the four's main engine cases were so thoroughly destroyed that those who saw the wreckage, and plenty did, realized that they must have been made of rule-stretching non-standard magnesium alloy.

Team Hansen boss Bob Hansen told the author in 1996 that the factory-prepared Hondas did include magnesium and titanium 'goodies'. The five-speed issue caused Hele some last-minute anxiety:

> The night before the race Jofeh told me we couldn't race with the five-speeders because the fifty issued by the factory hadn't yet reached the States. He said we would have to change all the bikes back to four speeds.
>
> I told him that was impossible. It would have meant keeping the mechanics up all night, and then we would have had to start from scratch in calculating our gearing, with no practice whatever on four speeds.
>
> I risked the sack by not changing the boxes. But the next morning we heard that the shipment had arrived in the States.

Despite these tribulations, the astonishing speed of the British triples made a terrific impression. A high-speed qualifying session for grid positions was held on a 2.5-mile (4km) all-banked circuit without the infield section (1970 was to be the last year this was done). Riders were allowed a warm-up lap before their timed flying lap, which was followed by a slowing-down circuit.

The record qualifying speed had been set in the previous year by Canadian Yvon DuHamel at 150mph (240km/h) on a 350cc air-cooled Yamaha open-class two-stroke. But the roadster-based 750s easily exceeded that speed on the Friday before Sunday's race day, with triples qualifying in the first three places. The best five laps were:

| | |
|---|---|
| Gene Romero (750 Triumph) | 157.34mph (253.16km/h) |
| Mike Hailwood (750 BSA) | 152.90mph (246.02km/h) |
| Gary Nixon (750 Triumph) | 152.82mph (245.89km/h) |
| Dick Mann (750 Honda) | 152.67mph (245.65km/h) |
| Kel Carruthers (350 Yamaha) | 151.72mph (244.12km/h) |

Even more dramatic was Romero's flat-out speed clocked through an unofficial trap at the end of one banked section. It recorded his Triumph streaking by at 165.44mph (266.19km/h) a moment before shutting off to take a turn. Romero's tuner, Pat Owens, a senior west coast Triumph technician, had fitted narrow ribbed Goodyear tyres front and rear, pumped up to over 40psi pressure, for the qualifier. Whilst marginal for safety and clearly unsuitable for the infield section, the temporary modification proved ideal for achieving a maximum speed on the bowl. Fred Swift recalled that Romero's machine had grease removed from its wheel bearings to reduce friction, and even had its fairing polished to reduce drag.

The threes lost out slightly to the 350 Yamahas when it came to flicking through infield twists, but a wide band of usable power from 4,000rpm to 8,800rpm made them superbly tractable through the slower sections. And the sound from their megaphones, a husky bellow that rose to a full-blooded howl at high revs, was truly awesome.

## Mixed Fortunes

Springtime Florida sunshine bathed the Speedway for Sunday's big 53-lap race. But the warmth, whilst pleasant for the record crowd of spectators who had flocked to Daytona took its toll on the triples, set up in England's bleak mid-winter.

*Triumph engineer Pat Owens (on machine) briefs Gene Romero before his 157mph (253km/h) qualifying lap.*

Early in the race, Hailwood and Nixon diced for the lead, lapping at 106mph (171km/h), but Mike's BSA engine only withstood the pace for a dozen laps before making unwelcome noises, so he pulled out. The tip of a valve had broken up. Nixon, who had proved that an American could ride as fast as the man many acknowledged as the greatest road racer ever, nudged his lap times up before his motor failed after 32 laps.

Percy Tait had called it a day after only nine circuits, frustrated by an engine that refused to run cleanly. When shipped over, Tait's machine had been brand new and its motor not even bench tested, but during practice the engine was switched with the unit in Castro's Triumph. As a Triumph employee, Percy would often have to give up machines or engines when circumstances dictated. He himself was also detuned for the race by having injured an arm in a practice spill.

It wasn't just the BSAs and Triumphs that struck troubles in the long, hot race. Honda riders Bryans and Robb both dropped out, their fours succumbing to the camshaft chain tensioner failures that had started in practice. Potential victor Kel Carruthers suffered a seizure on his Yamaha and expatriate Briton Ron Grant terminally damaged the engine internals of his two-stroke Suzuki by running out of fuel while leading.

By the closing stages Dick Mann led on his Honda, but he was being pressed hard by Romero, who had lost crucial seconds running off the track in an early race incident. Mann was losing power as his cam chain, fitted new for the race, had stretched and disrupted the valve timing. On the final lap Romero wore Mann's lead down by several seconds, but he trailed the Honda over the line with Castro and his Triumph securing third place.

Aldana finished twelfth after an eventful time in his first road race. He ran off the

*BSA teamsters Jim Rice (left) and Dave Aldana look apprehensive at Daytona.*

track when dicing with Mann despite being some laps behind the Honda rider. High-siding the BSA while trying to ride off the grass, he picked the machine up and remounted to call at his pit for repairs before continuing.

Harley-Davidson's team meanwhile was hit by valve problems and overheating of the XR750s' rear cylinders.

The troubles that had afflicted the triples were also mainly to do with overheating. Inefficient cooling in the area behind the cylinders was blamed for fuel boiling in the carburettor float bowls. Also, the standard ignition contact breakers had proved unable to maintain consistent spark timing at high revs and in hot conditions.

The original set-up, with the points unit mounted on a taper on the end of the inlet camshaft was prone to waver as the shaft flexed. This disturbed the timing, which has to be completely accurate on a high revving racing engine.

Back at Meriden, Hele devised a more accurate location method, mounting the

*Aldana takes the flag to finish in twelfth place after crashing and remounting.*

*Percy Tait prepares to bump start one of the BSAs at Daytona, where his role was to advise US riders.*

points on a long quill-drive shaft that passed inside the hollow camshaft and located on a peg halfway along it, where flexing was minimal. The team also junked Lucas points in favour of US-made Bendix items, which had short, straight springs and proved far more reliable.

## THE OTHER AMA RACES

The next AMA road race was at Kent, in Washington State, a tricky, narrow circuit, where Gary Nixon took third on his Triumph triple behind Ron Grant's Suzuki and Yvon DuHamel's Yamaha.

At Talladega, Alabama, in May, Aldana scored the first race win for a BSA triple in the 200-mile (320km) road race at an average speed of 104.589mph (168.284km/h), making it America's fastest road race. The victory scooped him a $5,000 incentive bonus from BSA, which riders had been told of on the starting grid, on top of his prize money. Aldana's machine was his Daytona mount, prepared by Bob Tryon, a senior Duarte technician, and Aldana's regular spanner man Dallas Baker. 'My bike was about the fastest thing on the track. It had enough horsepower to make up for my mistakes,' Aldana recalled. A sticking throttle caused Nixon to crash.

Dick Mann, now in the BSA team, competed at the Alabama track on the ex-Hailwood machine, which had been fitted with the points modification in Britain. But there was still a misfire at high revs, and Mann, who was also overgeared, only managed to finish fourth behind Rice. Gene Romero was seventh on a Triumph that had been hastily repaired by Owens after a practice crash. According to Colman, some Triumph personnel expressed annoyance at Hele for bringing a reworked BSA from Britain, and not a triple in Triumph colours.

The remaining AMA championship road race round in 1970, a 100-miler (160km) at Loudon, New Hampshire was won by Nixon. It was to be the only Grand National win scored by a Triumph-badged triple.

## SLOW START IN BRITAIN

BSA and Triumph's racing in Britain got a boost from the bullish 1970 policy. Triples were immediately fully launched into production racing (see Chapter 7), but the North-framed machines did not make an impact on UK circuits until later in the year.

Percy Tait's racer, No. 7 in the build sequence, returned permanently to the factory from Daytona for his use in UK events. He had only limited success in 1970, and told mechanics that he was not convinced of the triple's advantage over a twin for short circuit racing. In the 1,000cc Carreras International Trophy race at the post-TT Mallory Park meeting, Tait finished a lowly thirteenth on his Daytona machine, although he was to get better results later in the season.

Paul Smart, who had already shown well on a production Trident was signed to ride a second UK-based North-framed racer, and made his first acquaintance with one at the Brands Hatch Hutchinson 100 meeting in August 1970. Its steering head angle had been changed immediately before the meeting and hastily tested at MIRA. The Triumph certainly suited the talented twenty-seven-year-old Kentish racer, who took a second at Brands and then won second time out on it in a day of record breaking at Crystal Palace in September, the first UK short circuit victory for a works Daytona triple.

Gary Nixon flew to the UK for the late-summer Mallory Park Race of the Year meeting and was lent Tait's racer, but complained of poor handling. Between practising and race day it was taken to Rob North's workshop, not far from the Leicestershire circuit, where its steering head angle was altered to be like that on Smart's. The job was done with the engine left in place, and according to Fred Swift, it was found later in the season that the cylinder head of Tait's machine could not be removed whilst the engine was in the frame because of the rushed steering head changes.

In what he described at the time as one of the hardest races of his life, Nixon finished fourth, 12 seconds behind winner John Cooper on his Seeley-framed 350cc Yamaha two-stroke. Phil Read, also Yamaha-mounted, was second and Paul Smart third. Used to the clutch start normal in US 750 formula racing, Nixon had to master push starting his Triumph, a strenuous job because of its weight and high compression ratio.

Ray Pickrell, who had occasionally raced for BSA and Triumph, left the Dunstall Norton équipe to be a full factory rider on triples – mainly in BSA livery – in time for the Race of the South season-ender at Brands Hatch. At that meeting he rode a production-type Triumph that had been raced at France's *Bol d'Or* event.

## Tait's Triumph tested

David Dixon, racing machine tester for the UK weekly *Motor Cycle*, tested Tait's 1970 works racer at the Snetterton circuit in August, before its steering geometry was changed.

Dixon, who had waited five months to get aboard the Triumph, said he had never been down the Norfolk circuit's Norwich Straight so quickly. Finding the engine supremely flexible, he reported trickling round the hairpin at under 4,000rpm in second gear and screaming to 9,000rpm with ease. He found the engine smoother and, surprisingly, more tractable than the standard Trident roadster's.

Considering it was in early stages of development, Dixon said prophetically that if the FIM, governing body of international racing, followed the AMA's initiative in promoting the 750cc Daytona formula, the triple could put Britain back on the big-time international racing map.

Slightly daunted by the Triumph's weight, about 380lb (170kg), Dixon said that the machine's front fork chattered on corrugated surfaces. However, he praised the brakes, which on Tait's 1970 UK circuits 'hack' included a 200mm Fontana rear drum, fitted because Tait found his disc liable to lock on too readily.

With some of the best road racers available on the team, and machine development pushing ahead, the BSA and Triumph race team's prospects were excellent for 1971.

## US DIRT TRACK

### Mile Monsters

Contestants in American national series in the 1970s had to be versatile. A typical season of AMA championship rounds included five road races and more than twenty dirt track events. The AMA dirt nationals fell into four categories (which still apply today), each demanding particular riding skills and machine preparation.

TT Steeplechase races were run over tracks incorporating left and right turns, with one or more artificial jumps. Machines were equipped with front and rear brakes.

Flat track rounds were held on short-tracks, ovals of less than half a mile round, a half-mile, and a mile. Front brakes were never fitted, but from 1970 flat track machines had the option of running with rear wheel brakes.

The Mile can be one of the most exciting spectacles in any form of motorcycle sport. By the late sixties, 750cc Harley-Davidson V-twins and 650cc British parallel twins were lapping firmly surfaced tracks at 95mph (153km/h), sliding through the two turns and exceeding 120mph (193km/h) on the straights between. Racing was often breathtakingly close, with riders bunched into 'freight trains' in order to tuck into each other's slipstreams on the straights.

Overhead valve 750s were permitted on the dirt in 1969, a year before the new rule applied to road racing, and it was usual for BSA and Triumph team riders and their tuners to use cycle parts and engine modifications of their choice. When the production triples arrived in the USA, their outstanding speed made them tempting propositions for Mile racing. Managers reasoned that sporting success would help boost sales, emphasizing the new 750s' superiority over twins.

## Tools for the Job

In 1969, official dirt triples appeared both with standard BSA and Triumph road frames, and with the more suitable purpose-built Trackmaster chassis. Made by Ray Hensley in California, the oil-in-frame Trackmaster was a popular choice for installing on British twins, but special versions were tailor-made for triples. Tuner Tom Cates built an A75-engined Trackmaster with a Ceriani front fork for BSA West, salvaging engine parts from road machines returned to Duarte under warranty.

Team BSA rider Jim Rice power-slid the Cates machine to an AMA national win on the Mile at Sedalia, Missouri, in 1969. But despite this early success Rice did not take to the triple as a dirt mount, and later only rode it under pressure from BSA. On California's Sacramento Mile in 1970, poor placing on it may have cost him the AMA Number One plate. By then the A75 engine carried Victor Products distributor ignition with single points and a single coil. This sys-

tem was also temporarily tried on some US tarmac racing triples.

David Aldana recalled riding an A75 Trackmaster at Nazareth, Pennsylvania, in 1969 to win an Amateur class race in the same season. 'I left it in second gear all the time. It just kept pulling and it was as fast as Don Castro's Triumph twin,' he told the author. For the 1970–1 off-season the Cates Trackmaster triple was converted into a

*Above right: Jim Rice sits on his Trackmaster triple (24), while fellow BSA rider, Dave Aldana, stays aboard a twin. Rice's machine has a single points ignition system with a distributor.*

*Right: Tom Rockwood guns his Trackmaster-framed Trident on the Mile in 1969.*

road racer with a Fontana front brake for BSA signee Don Emde to use as a practice machine. A truly versatile motorcycle, it had been used by journalist Bob Braverman to make at run of 144mph (232km/h) at Bonneville Salt Flats late in 1969.

Nutley-based BSA tuner Herb Neas had two A75-engined machines out in 1969. A Trackmaster was ridden occasionally by Yvon DuHamel, while Dallas Baker had some success on a standard-framed Rocket 3. Two Triumph T150-powered Trackmasters were also assembled for Johnson Motors, one by Norm Lee for rider Ralph White, and the other by Joe Dudek for Tom Rockwood.

Gary Nixon raced a Cliff Guild-built Triumph Trackmaster triple in 1969, bringing it out at the 1⅛-mile Nazareth track, but was unable to better the side-valve Harley-Davidsons. And in 1970, the dirt Triumph's wide engine dug in and flung him off when he was lying second in the season's final Mile at Sacramento, California.

## Hard to Handle

During 1970 four of the factory North-framed road racers, two BSAs and two Triumphs, were converted for dirt racing in the Duarte workshops. Fairings were removed and high handlebars fitted along with suitable wheel rims and tyres. Brakeless Barnes front hubs were used, dirt-proof air filters were added, and protective shields placed over the ignition coils. Brake pedals were resited on the right, below the gearchange levers, since flat track riders only turn left.

Aldana recalls opting to ride a converted triple midway through 1970, on the Mile at Santa Rosa, California, mainly because he felt it could be more reliable in 20-lap races. One event ended in a typical Aldana crash spectacle when the throttles stuck open.

'The bike looked like a truck had run over it,' recalled Aldana, who broke two fingers and a thumb in the practice crash and opted for his familiar twin in the main event. 'The triple was too squirly on the dirt, the head angle was wrong and it just didn't handle,'

*Gary Nixon leads the pack on his Trackmaster T150 in a heat at Sacramento in 1970. Behind him are Chuck Palmgren (650 Yamaha), Jim Rice (Trackmaster BSA) and Tom Rockwood (750 Triumph twin).*

*Triumph teamsters on triples in 1970: Don Castro on a converted road racer with Ceriani forks and Gary Nixon with his Trackmaster.*

he said. 'And it was heavy and awkward to ride, the seat was uncomfortable and the road race tank was too big.'

The BSA teamster only had three dirt outings on triples that year, the others being at Sedalia and Sacramento. Saner riders came unstuck dirt-sliding triples, too. Don Emde thought, wrongly as it was to transpire, that he had blown his chances of a works BSA ride when he crashed a triple at 100mph (160km/h) on the Nazareth oval in 1970. Still ranked as an Amateur, he had been offered a triple when some of BSA's Expert riders chose to race twins.

'I thought it was my big chance,' Emde recalled. 'In practice I found out two things … the triples had more than enough power, but they were also very heavy compared to our A65 twins.' His Rocket 3 debut ended when he dabbed his brake to steady for a turn and was rammed from behind by a brake-less Harley-Davidson rider and both machines slammed into a wall. Emde escaped unhurt.

In the same meeting, Rice won his heat on the Cates A75, setting a new lap record, but his primary drive failed in the final. Triumph rider Don Castro managed third, the best result achieved on a North-framed dirt tracker.

Triumph's Gene Romero practised on, but didn't race, a dirt triple. He was quoted in mid-1970 as saying the North-framed dirt threes needed more development. Romero didn't need the hassle of wrestling one, for he had a sensationally fast big-bore 750cc Triumph twin tuned by C. R. Axtell in California. BSA teamster Dick Mann never raced a triple on the dirt. 'David (Aldana) wrecked the BSA I would have had to ride, and I'm thankful to him for that!' Mann told the author.

By the end of 1970 it was clear that the triple just wasn't suitable as a dirt tracker. The engine was too wide and too heavy, whilst its power characteristics were too fierce and less tractable than a grunty parallel twin or V-twin. Talking to Mike Nicks of *MCN* in 1972, Romero summed up most racers' opinion of the dirt triples: 'I told Triumph to take them home,' he said.

*Early Trident converted with styling kit supplied to American dealers. Changed parts include fuel tank and silencer.*

*Engine unit of 1968 'beauty kit' Trident restored by Clive Humphreys of Motorcycles of Kenilworth.*

*First type of 8in twin leading shoe front brake fitted to the Trident. The cable layout was altered early in production.*

*BSA Rocket 3 in final 1972 form with UK market fuel tank and restyled side panels.*

*The alloy cap replacing the plated points cover shows that owner Kim Williams has converted this 1972 Rocket 3 to electronic ignition.*

*Megaphone silencers were fitted to the Rocket 3 in 1971 and 1972.*

*Restored 1973 Trident T150V, with modifications made by owner Tony Sanderson.*

*Modernizing parts on the Sanderson Trident include handlebar switchgear and rear-view mirrors.*

*Twin disc conversion fitted to the 1973 T150V uses Italian Grimeca calipers.*

*Front end of a standard T160, with single disc brake, gaiterless front fork and tilted-up instruments.*

The facia between instruments carries warning lights and ignition switch on the T160.

The annular discharge silencers on the T160 were originally developed for Norton.

The T160-based LP Williams Renegade, with Legend cycle parts, luxury seat and Grimeca front and rear drum brakes.

The oil pressure gauge is added to the Renegade's instrument panel. This machine is owned by Trevor Gleadall, proprietor of LP Williams.

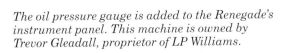

Tony Jefferies rides to victory on his Triumph in the 1972 F750 TT.

Paul Smart at Daytona in 1971. His Triumph retired when leading the 200-mile race.

American BSA teamster Dave Aldana was allotted a drum-braked 1970 machine for 1971

BSA guest rider Mike Hailwood aboard one of the latest triples at Daytona in 1971. After a fast start he hit machine trouble.

UK Triumph team riders Paul Smart (10) and Percy Tait at Mallory Park in 1971. Both triples riders notched up many wins during that year.

Slippery Sam, the legendary production class works racer, in its resting place at the National Motorcycle Museum.

Duelling Triumph triples in UK classic racing. Richard Peckett is just ahead of Phil Davenport at Brands Hatch in 1990.

*The 750cc Triumph Legend of 1984, built by LP Williams around the T160 frame and engine.*

*High-speed Hinckley triple, the 900cc 113bhp Triumph Daytona Super III.*

# 6 Works Racing 1971–2

Through the 1971 season, The Year of the Triples, racetracks in Europe and America resounded to the howl of BSA and Triumph threes as they notched up victories in one of the biggest factory campaigns road racing had ever seen.

But there was an element of a 'double or quits' gamble in the BSA Group's continued subsidy of sport. BSA Co. Inc. boss Peter Thornton told *MCN*'s Mike Nicks in January 1971 that his budget for blitzing American AMA events was $1m, then approximately £420,000. Showing less than full confidence in the 750cc roadsters, he went on to say: 'If we had to sell the triple dollar for dollar against the Honda four, we wouldn't sell one. We would go out and hang ourselves.'

And in Britain, the BSA Group opted to try sport as a sales tool again, despite multifarious industrial problems delaying its redesigned roadster range.

Work started at Meriden on new F750 racers for 1971 in November of 1970. The principal objective was Daytona, where four of the latest machines, two BSAs and two Triumphs, would join forces with the six American-based 1970 machines that had been modified and updated by the teams in the US.

Components were shipped from Meriden, but other purely American alterations were made to American-based 1970 triples. They included adding braces to the front forks and changing the rear disc rotors to a 10in Honda type. Other changes, not necessarily made across the board, were made to the cycle parts. New tanks and fairings were fitted, and front brakes would gradually be converted from drums to discs during the season, usually with calipers set ahead of the fork sliders. Some machines had Victor Products ignition with single coils, single points and distributor units fitted to their timing covers, and engines received internal engine tweaking in line with American tuning ideas.

## MERIDEN'S NEW RACERS

In Britain, Doug Hele made various major improvements in building racers for the new season, based on lessons learned during the previous year, with general weight reduction a prime objective. The use of magnesium alloy main engine and gearbox castings had been discussed at Umberslade Hall in mid-1970, and rejected because there was insufficient time to make 200 sets for homologation.

Rob North again supplied the frames, all with the 62-degree steering head angle. They also carried fabricated front fork yokes made by North, wide enough to accommodate the twin disc front brakes, perfected on factory triples during the latter part of the UK season. The Fontanas would progressively fade during a race, a typical failing of drum brakes, and they were also weighty. The most effective solution was discs all round, and Hele's were the first road racers to be equipped with a total of three disc rotors. For the new front brakes, Automotive Products supplied alloy calipers and rotors made from light alloy metal-sprayed and finished by machining.

Ron Hammond, who worked in AP's competitions department at the time, recalled that the weight-saving discs were expensive, especially as the coating process had to be even, and a 50 per cent success rate in manufacture was not unusual. Suitable hubs were turned from alloy billet in the Meriden tool room, and some machines acquired extra-lightweight magnesium hubs specially made in a limited batch.

Revised geometry and a shorter front fork lowered the front end of the 1971 racer by more than an inch. Road triples were now equipped with a racer-look fork, but the racers were still based on the traditional Triumph type with steel sliders.

The newer frame was to become known as the lowboy, and the earlier type the highboy, although this was not official Meriden terminology. Reducing the machine's frontal profile meant that there was no longer room for the oil cooling radiator in its previous location just ahead of the exhaust rocker box. The cooler was therefore moved into the nose of the fairing, a much better site as it could receive a blast of air through a rectangular opening under the front number plate, soon dubbed the 'letter box', However, it was fitted lying flat with the oil hose unions at the back, and not upright with the unions at the bottom as on road machines. On entering the slot, the air met the lower face of the cooler.

Hoses were arranged above and behind the radiator to conduct warmed air straight out through vents in the sides of the fairing, rather than let it heat up the engine and carburettors. The front opening slightly spoiled the streamlining's wind-tunnel aerodynamics but after the problems of 1970 every effort was being made to try to avoid overheating at Daytona.

For lighter throttle operation and cleaner mid-range performance, sets of Amal Concentric carburettors were prepared for the racers to replace the GP instruments. Both systems were to be taken to Daytona for practice testing.

Some Daytona engines were built with 'line contact' rockers, a refinement Hele had tried successfully on 500cc racers, and then for increased reliability on production racers competing in the 1970 *Bol d'Or* 24-hour event (*see* Chapter 7) The clearance adjuster was sited on the upper end of each pushrod instead of being on one end of the rocker, so better rubbing contact between the top of the valve and the plain end of the new lightweight rocker was achieved.

Crankshafts in factory racers were usually about 4lb (1.8kg) lighter than standard, but ultra-light types were also tried during 1971. Most riders found they preferred the flywheel effect of the normal 'heavy' racing crank. Similarly, a new cam form was to be experimented with in 1971. Coded TH13, it was usually fitted to the inlet side only for maximum top-end performance. Although Percy Tait preferred it to the TH6, many riders stuck with the earlier type for flexibility.

'Squish' combustion chambers were also to be used frequently on works triples in 1971. Squish is the term for a configuration featuring an extremely close piston-to-head clearance around the periphery of the piston crown, called a squish band. The result, when carried out correctly, is to create useful turbulence and promote more efficient combustion. Hele's experience with it dated from his Manx Norton development days, and squish had been used successfully on the 500cc Triumph twin-cylinder racers.

Drawings for three-cylinder squish heads had been completed early in 1970, and early trials carried out by altering existing Triumph pistons. Following that, specially cast pistons were supplied to Meriden by a Coventry company.

'Squish pistons immediately gained us another couple of bhp,' Hele told the author. By 1971 the best Daytona specification factory engines were producing 85bhp, measured at the crankshaft. Two squish engines were given a pre-Daytona tryout in South Africa in February 1971.

International meetings were held there during the southern hemisphere's summer, and despite widespread sporting boycotts of South Africa in those days, some major teams and top riders attended the South African TT at Durban's Pietermaritzburg circuit and the South African GP at Kyalami near Johannesburg, held on successive weekends. The races were an opportunity for pre-season testing in warm weather, and BSA was in favour of attending for publicity purposes. Testing of new 'sticky' compound tyres for Dunlop was also part of the plan.

Experimental gaffer Les Williams took two machines with 1970 chassis on the winter tour, one with a squish engine. He had strict instructions to lift the cylinder barrels and check its pistons for cracks after every race. Williams recalled going to a philatelic shop to buy a powerful magnifying glass for the purpose.

Ridden by Ray Pickrell and Paul Smart, the triples ran up against Italian world champion Giacomo Agostini and his 500cc MV Agusta triple for the first time in South Africa. The MV was an exotic purpose-built grand prix racer with a dohc engine, probably 110lb (50kg) lighter than the British ohv 750s, and a few miles an hour faster on top speed. But Meriden's roadster-based ohv triples, particularly Smart's Triumph, made life difficult for Ago at both meetings, pushing him to record lap speeds.

As Triumph's number one European rider, Smart was entered for Daytona on one of the new racers, with a squish engine. Thornton had also invited Mike Hailwood to contest all seven road races in the 1971 AMA calendar. The ex-champion had declined, but agreed to another one-off Daytona outing, for which he was given the machine built for Ray Pickrell to ride in Europe in 1971, one of the new lowboy Rocket 3s with squish heads. The other new BSA was allotted to

*Push! Starting Paul Smart's squish-engined Triumph in 1971 Daytona training.*

Mann by Team BSA manager Danny Macias.

Aldana and Rice had to be content with 1970 machines worked over at Duarte, as did twenty-year-old BSA recruit Don Emde, son of 1948 Daytona Beach race winner Floyd Emde. The second lowboy Triumph sent to the USA was allocated to Romero on its arrival in Florida. (A third 1971 Triumph was kept for Tait's use in the UK). Three Duarte highboys were ridden by teamsters Castro and Nixon, with newcomer Tom Rockwood, a young Californian ranked ninth in the 1970 AMA table, on a Fontana-braked 1970 bike.

American riders were on highly rewarding contracts for the season, which included continued payment in the event of being sidelined. Hailwood and Smart had their every need catered for, and BSA/Triumph's huge teams let rip at Daytona with numerous costly receptions and parties.

## THE BRITISH TRIPLE WHAMMY

With the one-lap speed bowl qualifier dropped for 1971, Smart put himself on pole position by completing a confident lap of the full 3.8-mile (6.1km) circuit at 105.80mph (170.23km/h). But hot engines and boiling fuel were again a problem, so air deflectors were added inside fairings during practice. These were to force cooling air into the finning, and keep hot air from collecting in a 'hot spot' near the carburettors. Brakes caught Hailwood out in practice when he crashed when slowing from 120mph (193km/h).

The alloy brake discs had a hazardous tendency to grow in diameter when hot and snag in the calipers, so a senior US Triumph technician, Rod Coates, phoned an urgent request for cast iron discs to Meriden. With help from senior production staff, Les Williams managed to obtain a batch from

*BSA team riders at Daytona in 1971. From left: Don Emde, Mike Hailwood, Dick Mann, Dave Aldana and Jim Rice. Machines bearing numbers 3 and 2 are 1970 racers, Rice's having an added fork brace.*

the Standard Triumph car factory, and had them skimmed to the correct thickness, re-drilled and despatched by air to Florida.

In the race Smart and Hailwood howled into the lead to set a searing pace, their squish-engined triples bellowing round the bankings in close company. But Hailwood's BSA went sick after covering barely a quarter of the 200 miles (320km). His engine's line-contact rockers had begun to show signs of trouble in practice, with increasing clearances. A post-race check revealed that the opening-up problem had continued during the race.

Smart looked like a sure winner as he maintained a clear lead, until his engine blew a piston 11 laps short of the flag. The compression ratio of Smart's engine was particularly high at over 12.5:1: the Champion plug company's expert at Daytona, Bobby Strahlman, had warned Hele of the risk. Weak mixture may have contributed to the blow-up, as the Amal Concentric carburettors fitted on his engine were found to run leaner than GPs.

Mann overshot a bend during the race, but got back into contention and saved the day for BSA by winning at 104.737mph (168.522km/h) with a non-squish engine equipped with GPs and a 'heavy' crank, which, though slightly down on speed compared with the Hailwood and Smart bikes, was clearly more reliable that day. Mann had geared his BSA high to improve his chances of finishing.

Two more triples filled the Daytona Winners' Circle, giving BSA and Triumph an incredible Daytona 1-2-3. Romero repeated his second placing of the previous year, proving his tarmac credentials. His Triumph's engine was also equipped with line-contact rockers, but they had proved reliable, as they were to be in subsequent use. Emde, who had dearly wanted to win, came home third on his drum-braked BSA, ahead of Harley's best man, Roger Reiman. Nixon,

*Dream result for BSA/Triumph as the top three finishers celebrate in Victory lane at Daytona 1971. Winner Dick Mann (4) shakes hands with second placeman Gene Romero (1) and Don Emde, third on his heavier drum-braked BSA.*

whose machine had been the slowest triple in qualifying, battled magnificently up to fifth spot before his clutch cable snapped on lap 26, and the transmission subsequently cried enough.

American riders had traditionally raced on Goodyear tyres, and received bonuses from the company. But Dunlop attended

*Gary Nixon rides his disc-brake-equipped 1970 machine inside Jim Rice's BSA at Daytona in 1971.*

# Team orders at Daytona

Don Emde, recruited by Team BSA for 1971 as one of America's top road racing prospects, was disappointed to find himself aboard an obsolete 1970 machine at Daytona. He recalled in 1996 how machines were switched on team orders in Florida:

> I spotted my new bike, with my name and number on the fairing, and there was a second lowboy BSA for Mike Hailwood. On the Triumph side of the garage were two lowboys, one for Paul Smart and the other for Gary Nixon.
>
> I spent a few minutes in the saddle of my bike getting the feel of it. Then I noticed a meeting going on in a corner, between BSA/Triumph race chief Pete Colman, team manager Danny Macias and racers Dick Mann and Gene Romero.
>
> A few minutes later, Danny told me they felt it was important to have Mann ride the new BSA and Romero a lowboy Triumph, because they had the best chances for the overall season championship. What could I say? I was only the rookie.

Emde did not complain, although he felt that he and the others given year-old equipment were at a real disadvantage. But he charitably admits that BSA's strategy was ultimately justified, in that Dick Mann went on to win Daytona and the 1971 AMA Grand National title, the last ever to be won by a British marque.

Nixon was apparently relegated to a 1970 Triumph because he was not as physically fit as Number One plate holder Romero, having broken a thigh in a non-racing off-road accident three weeks earlier. His mount was the ex-Romero bike, modified at Duarte with altered steering geometry, disc brakes all round and a reshaped fuel tank with an aircraft-type quick-fill valve.

In an eloquent profile of Nixon in *Cycle*, June 1971, Cook Neilson quoted the American rider as remarking that his Triumph was 'only about 17mph [27km/h] slower than it was last year.'

*The American team at work during 1971. In the foreground is Team Manager Danny Macias (wearing sunglasses), and Don Emde stands on the right with eyeshade. Steadying Gene Romero's bike on the truck tail-lift is leading Triumph tuner Nick Deligianis.*

Daytona for the first time in 1971 and made several converts, including Mann, who used the company's new KR83 rear tyre, developed to keep pace with new generation 750s. Later, other US teamsters switched to the British-designed triangular-section tyres for tarmac events.

Mann and his BSA went on to win the 1971 AMA Grand National series, using his triple to score two more wins and two second placings in road race events.

## TRANSATLANTIC CHALLENGE

The BSA Group found an ideal showcase for its racers in the Anglo-American match races, first held over the 1971 Easter holiday weekend.

A Transatlantic Challenge series, with the possibility of rounds in both Britain and America had been mooted for 1970, but plans had been dropped because of date clashes with Stateside AMA events.

Match races became a reality for 1971, when BSA and Triumph were ostensibly sponsors of the three-day extravaganza,

although the bulk of funding actually came from the promoters, Motor Circuit Developments.

Run over legs at Brands Hatch in Kent on Good Friday, Mallory Park on Easter Day and Oulton Park in Cheshire on the holiday Monday, the series consisted of two races at each venue, with supporting events.

The British team was captained by Percy Tait, after Hailwood declined the job. His men were Smart (Triumph), Pickrell (BSA) and two new triples riders. These were Derby's established short circuit star John Cooper, who had previously ridden production twins for BSA and was given a one-off ride, and former Meriden trainee Tony Jefferies, son of famous Triumph trials rider Allan Jefferies, who was invited to join the team for 1971.

The twenty-two-year-old Yorkshireman had made an impression at the 1970 Race of the Year, when he had harried Triumph star Gary Nixon aboard his private twin-cylinder Norton Metisse in the 1,000cc race. But Jefferies made an inauspicious triples debut at an Oulton Park practice day, flinging his Triumph away at Deer's Leap, fortunately

*Dick Mann makes a point to US team captain Gary Nixon (with arm in plaster) at Mallory. Behind him are UK rider Ray Pickrell and Triumph's Les Williams.*

*Above: Doug Hele looks serious as he listens to new Triumph teamster Tony Jefferies.*

*Above right: Paul Smart steps off his Triumph at Mallory's hairpin in the 1971 Race of the Year meeting. Pickrell escapes on the BSA and Percy Tait takes avoiding action.*

*Right: Match race riders on the grid at Mallory Park. From left: Jim Rice (US), Don Castro (US), Tony Jefferies (UK), Don Emde (US) and Dave Aldana (US).*

without personal injury, although the machine needed a new fuel tank.

Nixon, who had raced in the UK before, headed the American squad of Aldana, Castro, Emde, Mann and Nixon. Romero, who declined to ride for fear of injury jeopardizing his attempt at a second AMA championship, came to spectate and Castro rode his 1971 machine.

All match race competitors would ride BSA and Triumph 750s, providing unforgettable sights and sounds for British road racing fans.

Nixon was easily the fastest US teamster at a pre-meeting Oulton Park session. But he crashed in a wintry practice at Brands, and skippered from the sidelines. The cold conditions caused embarrassment for the

works triples, when their thick R40-grade Duckhams racing oil failed to circulate properly in practice, resulting in big-end failures. Arthur Jakeman told the author that he and fellow mechanic Jack Shemans had to rebuild afflicted engines at Paul Smart's Kent home, not far from the circuit. Larger diameter engine oil feed passages were always used after that.

In the first round of match races on the Brands 1.24-mile (2km) short circuit none of the Americans could keep pace with Pickrell, who won both legs on the 1971 BSA that Hailwood had ridden at Daytona.

New man Cooper had been detuned by a Yamaha crash at Brands, but he soon got the feel of his BSA triple at Mallory, equalling the absolute lap record of 52 seconds set by

*John 'Mooneyes' Cooper leads Castro and Mann in a match race at Mallory Park.*

Hailwood on a 297cc Honda six in 1967. He set it closing on Smart and Pickrell to finish third behind them in the second match race. Mann, who was fourth, looked the best US contestant on his 1971 BSA, although Castro, a newcomer to tarmac, showed well on Romero's Triumph, even though it had a Daytona fuel tank and seat, unwieldy on short circuits. 'I never leaned a motorcycle so far over, and I never braked hard into turns before,' he told *MCN*. He was learning fast!

Smart won both races at Oulton Park, although his wrist was swollen from a get-off in the first Mallory match. Pickrell crashed heavily on his ex-Hailwood BSA, which had to be rebuilt with a new frame. UK teamsters had been asked by BSA managers to ease up at Oulton to allow the

Americans to do better and thus encourage them to return; this request, which Pickrell ignored, may have caused others in front of him to ride more slowly than he expected, causing his fall. To no one's great surprise, the home team were clear winners, scoring 183 points to the US team's 137.

## FORMULA 750 AT THE TT

Urged on by BSA-Triumph, Norton, the press and public opinion, the ACU had instituted a Formula 750 class for UK racing, based on the American rules. As a result, a national-status Formula 750 race was part of the Isle of Man TT meeting for the first time in 1971.

# Yanks abroad

The first that most US team riders knew about the Anglo-American series was when they were handed out itineraries for a planned visit to England at Daytona in 1970. They made the most of the all-expenses-paid jaunt, as 1971 teamsters recalled.

David Aldana:

> That first time we came to England we were just kids, given a lot of money to play with. They put us in a smart hotel near Hyde Park, a real fancy place with silk on the walls – we were used to sleeping in vans. There were Hollywood stars staying there, I think Kirk Douglas was one.
>
> Some of us went round to Shepherds Market [an area of London's Mayfair notorious for prostitution]. We just went wild!
>
> We rolled a rented car at Oulton Park. The English took it real serious – they threatened to ban us for ever. We couldn't understand their attitude. [MCN reported that Jim Rice had flipped a 3.0-litre Ford Zephyr at 50mph, rounding Lodge Corner].
>
> Riding in England taught us a lot, I think it made us better racers. I'd never raced in rain before, but I realized that the technique was simple. If you didn't throttle back, you were an idiot and you deserved to fall down.
>
> People thought I had crashed because I rode with duct tape on my fairing, but that was because my mechanic Lloyd Bulmer dropped the bike bump starting it at Brands Hatch.

Don Emde:

> It was not until we read the motorcycling press on our arrival in Britain that we realized this was going to be serious racing. I had thought there would just be some kind of an exhibition race, and a factory visit. What English fans never knew was that even if we had competitive machinery, which we didn't, we had no motivation to put ourselves at risk. Our contracts were to win AMA championships in the US. We mainly wanted to go shopping and see London.
>
> We got smoked pretty badly in the races. We never had a chance. With Nixon out, that left only Mann on a lowboy against British bikes with small short-circuit gas tanks and Concentric carburettors for better acceleration. I'm told they also had much higher compression motors, and the riders were all so experienced at these tracks.
>
> But the first match races remain one of my best memories of racing. The fans in England were great, and so enthusiastic, unlike those in the United States, where riders were not treated with as much respect.

Dick Mann:

> When I was at the match races in 1971, Fred Swift rebuilt my BSA's engine at the factory and put in a lighter crankshaft.
>
> We were at a disadvantage because I was the only experienced road racer in the team, and I was getting too old to be aggressive. You must remember that some members of the team had hardly done any road racing.
>
> But we did better than we expected. I took it for granted we'd get beaten, but in fact I was surprised at how close we were to the lap records. I said to myself: 'Gee – maybe we're not so bad as we thought!'
>
> And of course in the next year, Cal Rayborn proved that an American could beat the Brits on their own tracks. I think the Match Races were an important moment for American road rac-

The new event was to provide yet another showcase for Hele's team of triples when Jefferies, always superb on the Mountain Course, swept to a win on his 1971-specification Triumph ahead of Pickrell's BSA.

After setting the fastest lap in the three-lap event at 103.21mph (166.06km/h), Jefferies said he found the machine 'perfect'. He also noted that it felt much heavier on fast bends than the typical 350 or 500cc TT racer. Factory-fitted suspension damping modifications had been carried out especially for the bumpy Isle of Man course.

Smart was out of action, having broken a wrist when he crashed a 250 in May's Irish North West 200 meeting. Peter Williams of the rival Norton Villiers team was third, and David Nixon brought the non-factory Boyer Triumph Trident home sixth. The best placed Honda CB750 four was ridden to ninth place by veteran endurance racer Peter Darvill.

BSA and Triumph triples stormed the British short circuits, heartening a generation of road racing fans who had almost become resigned to seeing British makes outclassed in traditional racing classes. *Motor Cycle News* encouraged big-bike racing by running the 1,000cc *MCN* Superbike Championship, in which factory and other triples figured heavily, with Tait clinching the title ahead of Pickrell at the end of the season. Twenty-two-year-old BSA employee Bob Heath, who had campaigned works production triples, was given a North-framed machine to ride in several F750 rounds.

BSA's marketing department could hardly complain! In May, Pickrell had won Britain's first Formula 750 race, a 200-mile (320km) marathon run at the same (Thruxton, Hants.) meeting as the 500-mile (804km) production event. And a Formula 750 race was the highlight of the midsummer Silverstone international meeting, a precursor of the British Grand Prix. A crowd of 27,000, the best ever seen for a motorcycle event at the Northamptonshire circuit, was treated to a works triples walkover, led by a fully mended Smart, who raised the outright two-wheeler lap record to 104.95mph (168.86km/h). Tait was second, Pickrell third and Mike Hailwood, making a well-publicized UK comeback on a 350cc Yamaha, was fourth.

Smart smashed another record in the *MCN* Superbike round at Oulton Park, but after lapping at 93.24mph (150.02km/h), his gearbox went haywire, letting the triples of Pickrell and Tait through. Third finisher was David Nixon on the non-works Boyer Team Trident.

But the first hint that the bubble might burst had come in June, when the free-spending racing enthusiast Thornton was forced to quit his post as chief of American operations.

In the meantime, North-framed machines were eligible for the *Bol d'Or* 24 Hour race in France in 1971. Moved from Montlhéry near

Paris to the 2.7-mile (4.3km) Bugatti circuit at Le Mans, the *GP d'Endurance* round displayed the British triples' long-distance stamina. Budget limitations were beginning to bite, however, as Les Williams remembered:

> There was no new money for the *Bol d'Or* that year, so we built up machines from spares, using old 1970 North frames. I supervised the building of two machines with battery ignition and lighting, and we took them to MIRA for Percy to test. He asked me which one he would be riding and I told him he could choose. That was a new experience for Percy, because as the factory tester he almost always had to hand over the fastest machines to other riders.

The second Triumph was allocated to the French Triumph team competing at Le Mans.

Tait and Ray Pickrell won, ahead of a works Laverda twin, completing 616 laps (1,663 miles/2,676km) at an average of 113.495km/h (70.52mph), despite the heavy rain that fell for half of the 24-hour period. In a traditional Le Mans start, one rider from each two-man team had to hold the

*Les Williams with one of the North-framed Triumphs prepared for the 1971 Bol d'Or 24-hour race at Le Mans. This machine, ridden by the French team of Olivier Chevalier and Gérard Debrock, crashed in the early hours. A battery for lighting was carried in the seat hump.*

machine, and at the drop of the flag the other would run across the track and kick-start it. Tait was left kicking his cold engine as the field disappeared, and only got away as most riders were on their second lap. The Triumph ran on two cylinders for several laps and then cleared, when Tait spent the rest of his stint catching up.

*Paul Smart's engine at the factory, showing the lightweight transmission with the alloy clutch chainwheel and shock absorber in the engine sprocket.*

*Ray Pickrell during one of his stints on the winning Triumph he shared with Percy Tait at Le Mans in 1971.*

Specially prepared to *Bol d'Or* rules, the winning triple was built with the engine used by Smart and Tom Dickie in the 1970 *Bol*, installed in the 1970 North triple-disc chassis used by Gary Nixon at the 1970 Race of the Year and later by Ray Pickrell in South Africa. Lighting was added, including a small lamp to illuminate the right-side number plate to help lap scorers in the night. Another machine had been prepared for the French pairing of Olivier Chevallier and Gérard Debrock, but they dropped out after two crashes.

*Magnesium alloy transmission covers with breather tube on John Cooper's BSA in 1971.*

## COOPER THE HERO

One week after the French victory came a day that will always stand out in British road racing history. The 1971 Race of the Year at Mallory Park, Leicestershire, was one of the triples' greatest moments. Hard riding John Cooper, recruited to the BSA-Triumph team for the Anglo-US series, had requested the use of the BSA again at the September meeting. Nicknamed Mooneyes, because of his helmet design, Cooper was a master of Mallory who had made his name on Manx Norton singles in the sixties, and more recently on a Seeley-framed Yamaha two-stroke. Cooper was enrolled at the insistence of BSA marketing director Peter Deverall. At first, Hele was reluctant to add Cooper to the équipe:

> I felt we had the team we needed the Race of the Year, but Deverall said we must have John Cooper. I was a bit upset at him interfering, but we knew Cooper was a potential winner and provided him with a bike.

Cooper's BSA triple was a second-ranking factory mount with a non-squish engine, previously used in TT practice and raced by Bob Heath and Percy Tait. For the Race of the Year it had the new primary transmission introduced on some works machines in 1971, a compact racing clutch with two Ferodo 5in sintered friction plates supplied for the team by AP. It was carried on an elongated gearbox mainshaft and supported by a ballrace in a special inner primary drive cover. New casings were made in ultra-lightweight magnesium alloy, with a large breather outlet incorporated in the outer inspection cover. The expensive modification saved about 14lb (6.5kg) in overall weight, and it made clutch operation lighter, although on Tait and Pickrell's machines porous castings caused oil leaks.

Hele had to admit his folly in doubting the wisdom of bringing Cooper on board, for the Mallory Race of the Year proved sensational. In front of 50,000 fans, the Derby rider battled head-to-head with world champion Giacomo Agostini and his mighty 500cc three-cylinder MV Agusta. The Italian had come to be seen as invincible in the world championships, let alone UK events.

After 10 of the 30 laps in the day's big race, Coop outbraked Ago into the Esses to head the MV, to the delight of the roaring, programme-waving crowd. But then the Italian repassed Cooper, who nearly blew it when his BSA went into a hair-raising slide

*Triples bump start at Mallory Park in 1971. Guest US rider Gary Nixon (Triumph, 4) is on the right.*

*Cooper in front of Agostini going into Devil's Elbow, during their titanic Race of the Year battle.*

at the treacherous Esses. Cooper fought back and regained the lead in the closing stages, using every bit of his familiarity with the 1.43-mile (2.3km) circuit, holding Agostini at bay to the flag.

The partisan spectators went wild as the BSA beat the MV by three-fifths of a second. A British machine had trounced the world's best, something many race fans thought they would never see again.

Presented with the victor's laurel wreath after the unforgettable race, Cooper gave it to Hele, reportedly saying: 'You deserve it, that bike's a beauty.'

Cooper staged another giant-killing act, defeating Ago again in the 1,000cc Race of the South at Brands Hatch in October, this

time with a squish engine, bored to 40-thou oversize. Coop sliced a fifth of a second off the absolute motorcycle record for the full 2.65-mile (4.26km) Brands circuit, raising it to 91.03mph (146.47km/h).

## ONTARIO EPIC

BSA's new hero had earned himself a ride in the last major F750 race of the year, the Champion Spark Plug Classic in California.

Then the world's richest road race, with a £40,000 purse, the event was at a 3.194-mile (5.139km) circuit with room for 140,000 spectators, laid out at a cost of £10 million the year before at Ontario, east of Los Angeles. The 250-mile (400km) AMA-run race was to be over two 125-mile (200km) legs, with a 45-minute break between them, riders' results being aggregated into an overall order.

Hele took two machines, Cooper's BSA, and a Triumph to the latest specification for Gary Nixon, along with Meriden mechanics Steve Brown and Fred Swift. According to press reports, factory financial problems had prevented a machine being taken for Smart.

Well aware of the ever-increasing threat from two-strokes, especially from favourite DuHamel and his 73bhp, 330lb (148.5kg) 500cc three-cylinder Kawasaki two-stroke, Hele made careful fuel consumption tests in practice, and decided that his machines could take advantage of the fact that they could complete a leg without refuelling – just.

'It was a hell of a risk, but had to be worth it,' Hele said in 1995. US team manager Danny Macias had said that his five official Duarte triples would not risk running right through without refilling, as he gauged their safe range at a maximum of 120 miles (200km).

Hele's gamble paid off in the first leg, won by non-stop Nixon after a battle with Yvon DuHamel who'd had to stop and refuel his thirsty two-stroke.

In the early stages of the second leg, there was a spectacular pile-up on an oil slick, involving nine riders including Dave Aldana, Dick Mann, Nixon and DuHamel but Cooper was not one of those sent sprawling across the track.

Nixon remounted and returned to his pit, where Hele was so preoccupied with trying to clear dirt from his Triumph's throttle linkages that he lost track of the laps and missed giving Cooper his 'last lap' signal.

But Cooper was locked into a titanic struggle with Kel Carruthers on his Don Vesco-tuned 350cc Yamaha and the two exchanged the lead several times in the last 20 laps. On the final circuit, Cooper's howling BSA hauled magnificently out of the last slow corner to out-accelerate the two-stroke and beat Carruthers to the line by a tyre's width. The official winning interval was three-fifths of a second.

Cooper, the first Briton to win a major AMA event, was in line for a $6,050 slice of the prize fund. But rejoicing in the British camp then turned to consternation, thanks to an unexpected turn of events following the race.

Californian road racer Bob Bailey claimed his right, under an AMA 'selling plate' rule, to buy Cooper's winning machine. The rule followed a tradition in US racing dating back to the thirties, under which pure racing machines were discouraged. It is still in force today, and is generally acknowledged to be a useful control in sport.

Under the 750cc Class C formula operating at Ontario, machines were meant to comprise parts available to any rider. To deter the use of highly specialized and exotic components, race regulations included a clause allowing anyone competing in a main event to bid $2,500 (then equivalent to about £1,000) for another competitor's machine.

Manufacturers were meant to comply with the rules by making racing parts available to private riders, and Bailey was apparently frustrated that his repeated requests for special parts from the BSA-Triumph organization, including a North frame, had been refused. He saw the claim as his only opportunity to acquire a competitive 750 racer.

One stated penalty for refusing to sell was to forfeit victory. Hele, who estimated the value of Cooper's BSA at nearer £10,000, recalled his shock:

> I panicked, because there was no way that we could part with the expensive special transmission. In any case it would have

*A freshly made 1971 North frame built around an empty engine, on the floor at Meriden. Machine number 70 behind is the 1971 Bol d'Or winner.*

been too much trouble for a privateer to maintain. I got involved in the argument, because it seemed as though Pete Colman was agreeing to sell.

I had to think quickly, and I realized it was no good taking on the AMA, so I spoke directly to Bailey. I explained to him that Cooper's bike had completed a hard season and that it was clapped out. If he bought it, he'd only have to send it to England to be rebuilt. I told him that we had a better racer back at the factory, and guaranteed that we would ship it over for him.

Cooper's mechanic Steve Brown played his part by staunchly refusing to let go of the machine, and Tony Jefferies' 1971 Triumph was subsequently shipped to America in return for Bailey's $2,500.

## THE END OF THE SEASON

Gene Romero had gone to Ontario with the slimmest chance of notching a second successive AMA Grand National title for Triumph. But a crash in the first leg and a throttle cable failure in the second allowed the title to go to thirty-eight-year-old Dick Mann, his first Number One plate since 1963. Mann had done a great job for BSA, winning 100-mile (160km) road races on his triple at Pocono and Kent as well as the Daytona 200.

American BSA and Triumph team riders had surely given their employers what they had asked for: domination of the Grand National series, with Romero, Rice and Aldana completing the top four national standings.

But during November's American Thanksgiving holiday, letters went out to Aldana, Castro, Emde, Rice and Rockwood telling them that their lucrative contracts were terminated. Only one rider in each team would be retained full-time for 1972, Mann for BSA and Romero for Triumph.

In 1996, Emde recalled his surprise at the sackings: 'I thought I would be riding for BSA a long time, and hoped for new BSA triples in 1972. We were left with less than 100 days to find new rides at Daytona.' Emde went on to win the 1972 200-miler

# Pocono pounce

According to veteran American motorcycle dealer Jim Cotherman, Bob Bailey's Ontario claim was not the first made on a works triple. He told the author of a less well known episode at the Mount Pocono, Pennsylvania, circuit earlier in the 1971 season. Cotherman had a Triumph shop in Freeport, Illinois. He said:

> I wanted a works machine, both to race myself and to use as a pattern for making special parts to sell to privateers. I was riding in the Junior category that year, so I asked a rider in the main race to place a $2,000 claim on Gene Romero's lowboy Triumph on my behalf.

The AMA refused to sanction his claim on the basis that a cashier's cheque was presented, and not a certified cheque as stated by the rule book.

> I kept chasing for a machine, and I got help from Cliff Guild (Gary Nixon's tuner). Eventually, I was offered a 1970 machine, with a choice between BSA and Triumph, and Fontana front brake or double disc. For my $2,000 I ended up with a Triumph with a Honda rear disc, numbered 5 on the oil tank. I think it was Nixon's 1971 Daytona bike.

Disappointed that it was not a 1971 model, Cotherman nevertheless overhauled it and raced it until 1974, when he crashed at Road Atlanta. Since rebuilt and painted white in the colours of Cotherman's C & D équipe, the machine has remained with its owner.

*Three Triumph team highboys and Gene Romero's lowboy (1) stand ready at the Loudon, New Hampshire, circuit in 1971. Privateers were frustrated at the non-availability of parts to convert their triples into full racers.*

(320km) on Mel Dineson's 350cc TR2 Yamaha.

The BSA Group's financial troubles were now deadly serious, and it was clear to Hele and his team that racing must be in jeopardy. In any case, he had realistically concluded from what he had seen at Ontario that the Japanese two-strokes were gaining ground with every race, while his ohv triple was nearing the limits of its capability, certainly in 750cc form.

A simple way to enlarge the engine was to bore it out to 71mm to accept T120 pistons, but when Paul Smart raced an 830cc triple in 1,000cc races on British short circuits towards the end of the 1971 season, it was found that enlarging the Triumph's bores jeopardized its reliability by causing cylinder head sealing problems.

Fortunately for race fans who had been thrilled to see British racers stand up to and beat the might of America, Italy and Japan, there was more triples action to come in 1972.

# Major BSA and Triumph triple road racing wins in 1971

| | | |
|---|---|---|
| Isle of Man | Formula 750 TT | Tony Jefferies (Triumph) |
| Isle of Man | Production TT | Ray Pickrell (BSA) |
| | | |
| Thruxton | 500-mile GP d'Endurance | Percy Tait/Dave Croxford(Tri) |
| | | |
| Thruxton | 200-mile F750 | Pickrell (BSA) |
| Brands Hatch | Hutchinson 100 | Paul Smart (Triumph |
| Silverstone | Formula 750 | Smart (Triumph) |
| Mallory Park | Race of the Year | John Cooper (BSA) |
| Brands Hatch | Race of the South | Cooper (BSA) |
| | | |
| Le Mans (France) | Bol d'Or | Tait/Pickrell(Triumph) |
| | | |
| Daytona (USA) | AMA 200-mile | Dick Mann (BSA) |
| Kent (USA) | AMA road race | Mann (BSA) |
| Pocono (USA) | AMA road race | Mann (BSA) |
| Ontario (USA) | AMA Champion Classic | Cooper (BSA) |

750cc British Championship rounds

| | | |
|---|---|---|
| Oulton Park | March | Tait (Triumph) |
| Thruxton | March | Tait (Triumph) |
| Mallory Park | May | Tait (Triumph) |
| Castle Combe | September | Tait (BSA) |
| Snetterton | October | Tait (Triumph) |
| Champion: Percy Tait | | |

Percy Tait was also *Motor Cycle News* Superbike Champion and Shell Sport Champion.

## MECHANICS' MEMORIES

### Steve Brown – A Taste of Glory

It took courage to work at the Triumph factory clad in BSA overalls, but that is what Steve Brown did on his arrival at Meriden from Small Heath. His transfer from Birmingham to Triumph's race shop was sanctioned by Doug Hele, and had to be cleared with Meriden trade unions.

Birmingham-born Brown had ridden BSAs since his teens and joined the Small Heath workforce in 1965. Employed on rectification, correcting faults on machines as the left the production line for the Packing Department, he also tested them on the small circuit laid out within the Armoury Road complex.

By the time Rocket 3s were rolling off the line, he had started racing his own 650cc Spitfire twin.

'I spent my break times in the race shop picking up tips, and pestering Brian Martin for a job,' he told the author. Eventually Martin, BSA's race shop boss, relented and

Brown became one of four fitters working on road racing machines, alongside a larger team preparing motocross hardware, supervised by Jeff Smith.

Road racing activity had been focused on production twins, campaigned mostly by Pat Mahoney and BSA employee Tony Smith, but for the 1970 season, Brown was involved with a pair of Rocket 3s prepared mainly for the Thruxton 500-miler and the production TT.

'We wanted North-framed bikes as well, but that didn't happen,' he recalled. When road racing activity was scaled down, Brown was offered work on motocrossers. 'I was quite cheeky in those days, and I said I'd rather go and work at Meriden.' His cheek paid off in more ways than one, because the transfer was arranged and he found himself on Coventry's better rates of pay.

His first job at Triumph was working on a BSA, a production Rocket 3 being built to complete a squad of six, comprising three of each make. It had a high-clearance frame assembled from scratch at Meriden, without the weighty internal strengthening tubes fitted to the stock A75 frame.

For the 1971 Anglo-US series Brown was put in charge of John Cooper's North-framed BSA:

> In John's try-out at Mallory the bike misfired all the way round Gerards Bend. Doug Hele was baffled until we realized that Coop, who always moved around a lot on the bike, was accidently touching the handlebar cut-out.

He was proud that Cooper's machine ran well at the freezing 1971 Brands Hatch Anglo-US opener, when other team bikes suffered big-end failures in practice. 'I stayed and warmed my bike up when the others had knocked off and gone to the cafe.'

At the 1971 *Bol d'Or*, Brown was part of the crew looking after the winning Pickrell/Tait machine. He remembers how he burned his hands feeding a new chain over a hot gearbox sprocket during the race.

As Cooper's right-hand man, Brown shared in the glories of the 1971 Mallory Park Race of the Year, the Race of the South and Ontario. At the American event, Brown was about to strip the BSA's engine for official measuring when the Bailey controversy blew up. He recalled:

> I have never taken so long to remove a cylinder head as I did that day. Doug Hele and the American bigwigs were arguing it out, and I knew that bike couldn't go anywhere until it had been measured. I think I held out for about an hour!

The relationship with Cooper resumed for 1972, when the machine was kept at the rider's garage business in Derby. Brown spent Mondays fettling it, and the rest of the week at Meriden: 'I was working on the big-bore T180 project, and a production version of the racing transmission with the two-plate clutch and a duplex chain.'

He returned to Ontario in 1972 with Cooper, and then moved to Kitts Green when Meriden was shut, before finally being made redundant. He continued to work with triples, firstly at dealers' workshops, and then on his own. He bought an ex-Pickrell Production A75, and helped Bee Bee Racing, new owners of the ex-Cooper triple, and other privateers. He also owned Son of Sam, the T160 production racer project originating at Kitts Green.

Brown never lost any of his passion for the racing triples. 'I'll never forget the sound of ten of them racing together in the match races,' he told the author.

## Bill Fannon – Dream Come True

As a Triumph-owning motor mechanic employed at a garage near the factory, working at Meriden was Bill Fannon's dream. It came true when he was interviewed by Experimental Foreman Henry Vale, before starting work in the department in April 1966.

He was Malcolm Uphill's mechanic during the successful 1969 Bonneville racing season, and then he joined the mass effort to prepare triples for the 1970 season. He recalled:

> I was seconded to work with Rob North, helping him get frames done on time, which wasn't easy because he had so much work doing Speedway frames. I was already able to weld, but I learned a lot from Rob in his little hut with holes in the roof. I also worked with Arthur Jakeman, making the three-into-one exhausts – we used to call that job 'snake-charming'!

He became Percy Tait's regular mechanic, but at the 1970 *Bol d'Or* he looked after the Triumph-mounted French team: 'At seven o'clock in the morning, when we were getting sleepy, the rider came in with no first gear. I told him to try and get by without it, and he came back in with a burnt clutch!' Fannon rebuilt the gearbox and clutch in an incredible 25 minutes.

Fannon, like other former team members, also told the author that there was high-level company pressure for BSA-badged machines to take the major wins.

When Triumph wound down, he returned to cars, becoming a technician at Jaguar.

## Arthur Jakeman – the Magic Touch

Riders marvelled at the stability and comfort of the works racing triples, and much of the credit for the smooth ride was down to Arthur Jakeman's painstaking assembly of front forks and other chassis components.

Jakeman can still remember the day that Doug Hele got the news that it would be factory policy to race triples at Daytona. 'It was all-out from that day on,' he told the author. At that time, at the end of the 1969 season, Jakeman was already one of Meriden's most experienced race mechanics. He had worked under Doug Hele on twins prepared for Daytona, and when Percy Tait campaigned a 500 on British and European circuits, Jakeman and his Experimental Department colleague, Jack Shemans, were his regular mechanics. All three made their weekend expeditions on an unofficial basis, in unpaid free time.

Jakeman had joined Triumph at sixteen, working in the Service Department for two years before doing his compulsory national service from 1948–50. Returning to Meriden, he was employed on road machine production, assembling Triumph sprung-hub assemblies, and then telescopic forks, until his wish to be transferred to Experimental was eventually granted in 1964. He took a drop in earnings, but found the work much more interesting.

Better recompense came with the official 1970 campaign, but the hours were long and irregular. Jakeman was one of the core of technicians who assembled the team triples, his speciality being cycle parts preparation and fabrications. He recalled:

When I was working on ignition coil mounting brackets for the triples Doug Hele kept saying 'no, that won't work'. I had to make loads before he was satisfied.

> None of it would have been possible without Doug. Whenever we hit a problem, he would always seem to come up with the answer after sleeping on it.

One of Jakeman's abiding memories of the first year with triples at Daytona is of hearing them on full song in practice:

> We were using standard points then, and they were playing up – that was our main problem that year. We went into town to hunt round local dealers for spare points,

and I'll never forget hearing the noise of our bikes carrying from the Speedway. They sounded absolutely gorgeous!

Jakeman was specifically allocated to Hailwood's BSA along with engine man Herb Neas, a German-American who worked at BSA's Nutley, New Jersey, headquarters. Jakeman rated Neas as a brilliant mechanic, and found he could get on well with most of the Stateside personnel: 'The American riders were friendly and co-operative. They had their own mechanics who were generally good blokes. Politics went on, but that seemed to be more at management level.'

British mechanics carried out servicing procedures on US riders' mounts but left setting up, tyre choice, jetting and general preparation to their own staff.

In the UK-based team, a format developed where each race mechanic was paired with a particular rider, caring for one North-framed machine and one production mount. Jakeman became Ray Pickrell's spanner man for a string of successes in 1971 and 1972.

'Ray was so easy to work for,' Jakeman recalled. 'He often said "leave it all the way it is Arthur, it's perfect"'. He found all the team riders easy going and helpful:

> Paul Smart was good from a mechanic's point of view, too. Malcolm Uphill was a treasure, he often did all his own adjustments on the proddie bikes. Of the Americans, I thought Gary Nixon and Dave Aldana were the most down-to-earth. And Percy well, he was one of us!

Since the official racing ended, Arthur has always been in demand to fettle triples. He prepared Tait's machine for his final outing in a Lap of Honour at the TT in 1979, when the impudent Tait overtook the MVs of former world champions Phil Read and John Surtees. Tait's 'parading' lap at over 90mph

included clocking 139mph (224 km/h) at a speed trap.

Bert Hopwood is rarely mentioned in the triples racing story, but Jakeman found him sympathetic, even in 1972, when official blessing had been withdrawn from the activity:

> He made sure that both Steve Brown and I had trestles to work on engines away from the factory, and when Ray won the TT as a privateer that year, we got a telephone call from Hopwood. I liked him.

## Jack Shemans – Test House Dweller

'We were always striving to find a quarter of a horsepower from somewhere. Sometimes I would be locked away in the test house for months on end,' Jack Shemans recalled. Like Jakeman, Shemans brought 500cc twins experience to bear on triple race development.

Shemans had joined the Meriden workforce shortly after leaving the army in 1947. He graduated from sprung-hub assembly to the engine bench, and was then taken on by the Experimental Department, where he became the chief testbed operator.

His was a vital job, testing every aspect of engine development on the dynamometer, and keeping track of those things that worked well, as well as those that didn't. Apart from assembling race engines, one of his major contributions to the triples' evolution was setting up the Amal Concentric carburettors used from 1971. He explained:

> The GPs we used before had to have separate throttle cables, which made them heavy to operate, and difficult to keep in tune. The linked-throttle Concentrics on the road bikes worked well, and their built-in float chambers made them less complex to set up than GPs, so it was a matter of trying to get the same horsepower from Concentrics.

*Jack Shemans sets up a triple engine for bench testing. The intake trumpets seen on the Concentric carburettors were perfected by him.*

The track carburettor had a carefully shaped intake trumpet, and Shemans set about making an efficient stack suitable for the Concentric, which has small auxiliary air intakes on a step set into the bottom of the main intake. The inefficient short stock bellmouths threaded over the whole intake area, including the small holes.

His trumpets were made to attach to the body of the carburettor so that the intake stack would be fully concentric with the main carburettor, Venturi, keeping the small openings entirely separate outside the trumpet. For light operation of the throttle slides, he removed the normal body top caps and replaced them with items made from two layers of pressed sheet metal that could, if required, sandwich a layer of weatherproofing rubber. Three short cables linked the slides with the arms of the operating beam set above the instruments. The completed set-up made the machines sweeter running and easier to ride, at the cost of only one horsepower compared with the GPs.

Another Shemans trademark had appeared on factory racers at Daytona in 1970. On arrival in Florida, none of the machines would run. Handlebar-mounted ignition cut-out buttons, compulsory under AMA rules, had been fitted by Lucas.

'They were wired so that the ignition was permanently earthed,' Shemans recalled. He took the cut-outs off, and rigged up his own, using short lengths of junior hacksaw blades.

> The earthing wire was threaded through a hole at one end, which was taped to the 'bar so as to be insulated from it. To cut the engine, the rider simply pressed the other end of the blade against the handlebar. It was crude but effective.

The system worked so well, it was left in place on several bikes. Working on machines at meetings made a welcome change from weekdays in the noisy test house, and Shemans said the Isle of Man TT wins he contributed to stand out in his memory.

Along with Jakeman, he won several hundred dollars in mechanics' prizes at Daytona in 1971. They took the booty back to share with colleagues who hadn't been lucky enough to make the trip, a gesture that says much about the team's spirit.

## Fred Swift – Miracle Worker

Super-quick stripdowns were a Fred Swift speciality. When Percy Tait had an exploratory outing on a production racing T150 in mid-1969 at Brands Hatch, it was found in practice that his gearing was far too high for him to stay with the pack of twins. Fred changed the gearbox sprocket in the hour available before the race, an extraordinary achievement given the complexity of this particular operation on the triple.

At Daytona in 1970, he actually rebuilt David Aldana's engine on the morning of the race. The Californian's BSA holed a piston in the final morning's practice session, and Swift rebuilt the top end with a new barrel while the metal was still almost too hot to touch. He took the precaution of easing alloy off the new pistons' skirts to ensure maximum clearances and jetting up the carburation. The bottom end was left intact:

'We just swilled it out with petrol and hoped for the best,' Swift told the author. He also remembers changing clutch plates between races on Scarborough's Oliver's Mount circuit, where three hairpin bends per lap put stress on transmissions. The racers' clutches normally required little maintenance.

No mean rider himself, Swift partnered Dennis Greenfield to win the 1960 Thruxton 500-miler on a Norton when both men were employed there. When Norton's Birmingham factory closed he joined Triumph, but frustrated at being stuck on production line work, he moved to Royal Enfield in Redditch to work on the company's 250cc GP5 racer.

Swift finally landed an Experimental post at Triumph, fettling works-racing Bonnevilles, including John Hartle's 1967 TT winner, before becoming embroiled in preparing and occasionally test riding the North-framed triples.

Swift became Paul Smart's regular mechanic, and the two men have remained good friends. He missed Daytona in 1971, having been on the earlier South African expedition with Les Williams. Swift remembers that in Florida in 1970 a long swinging arm was tried on Mike Hailwood's BSA but the former champion said he couldn't detect any difference in handling. 'But his lap times were worse, so we knew it was not an improvement. Hailwood was so consistent that you could learn as much from checking his times as by talking to him. Nixon was very similar,' Swift recalled.

Like other Meriden men, Swift is sceptical about how effective American development work on the triples was: 'At the match races, Dick Mann asked me to put one of our cylinder heads on his bike, because his had

been gas flowed in America and he didn't think it was as fast as our engines.'

Swift moved on to Kitts Green after the Meriden closure, to get involved in NVT's rotary engine project for seventeen years, until being made redundant by Norton's Shenstone factory in 1990. He then joined Toga exhausts, the company where replacement ray gun silencers for the Trident and Rocket 3 are made.

Summing up the triples, he says: 'They were mechanically sound but the ignition was too finicky. And I think the engine should have been made with a horizontal split.'

## John Woodward – Crashing In

Apprenticed at BSA, John Woodward left Armoury Road because he could not get a post in the Experimental Department, which was not considered a 'skilled area'.

He wrote to Doug Hele at Triumph asking for a job, explaining that he prepared his own Nortons for racing. He did not receive an offer at first, so he took a post at Velocette. In due course, however, Hele contacted Woodward and he was employed at Meriden's Experimental Department.

'Staff who raced their own machines did not usually work on factory racing bikes, because Hele thought there was a conflict of interest,' Woodward told the author. When he crashed his own production Bonneville and broke a hip he was in hospital for several months and gave up racing. On return to work, he found himself in the thick of preparations for the 1970 Daytona meeting:

One of my jobs was making up carburettor assemblies, with three GPs and a single matchbox float chamber. The carb bodies had to be altered to fit the North frames, and I'll always remember taking a hacksaw to a bench full of new Amal GPs!

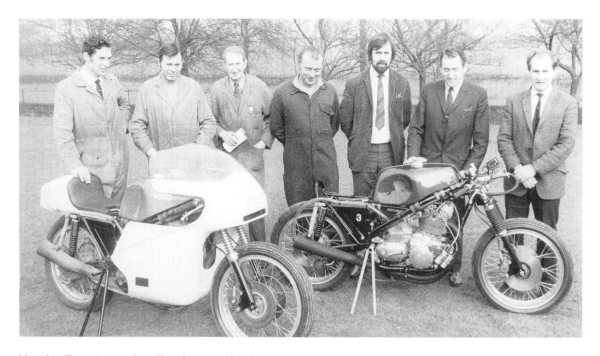

*Meriden Experimental staff with two unfinished works racers early in 1971. From left: Bill Fannon, Arthur Jakeman, Jack Shemans, Fred Swift, Norman Hyde, Doug Hele and Les Williams.*

For the 1971 season, Woodward was assigned to latest Triumph team member Tony Jefferies, building bikes for him from available parts. He spannered for the Yorkshire rider at the TT, where Jefferies won the F750 race on the squish-engined machine.

Later in the year, Jefferies' Triumph was lent to Gary Nixon to ride in the Brands Hatch Race of the South. A stripped timing pinion lost him valuable practice time, and the American rider had to settle for fifth place.

'Even though he was fed up, after the race Gary gave me a roll of notes. I counted them later and it was £50. I thought he was a great rider, with a lot of guts.' The Jefferies machine was then shipped to America, following the Ontario Claiming Rule episode.

Woodward left Triumph to work in the motor industry, ultimately at Land Rover, but he told the author that his Meriden job was the best he ever had:

> I was working with the cream of the industry, and Doug Hele was the best bloke I ever worked for. Although he was practically at board level then, he would value everyone's opinion. If you thought something was no good you could tell him – although you would have to be able to prove it!

The regular mechanic-rider pairings for 1971 were:

Steve Brown and John Cooper
Fred Swift and Paul Smart
John Woodward and Tony Jefferies
Bill Fannon and Percy Tait

## WINDING DOWN THE RACE TEAM

Amazingly, despite the gloomy outlook for the BSA Group, the triples did return for a limited campaign in 1972. But the days of largesse were over, and the previous year's machines had to be wheeled out again. The company did not make a formal announcement that it was withdrawing from road racing until September, but internal policy changed much earlier.

The last official international works outing in January 1972 saw another clash with the MV Agusta triple at the Pietermaritzburg South African TT, with a spectacular outcome. Pickrell and Smart were contending with Agostini and his MV when all three

*In the Daytona paddock 1972. Gene Romero (left) and Dick Mann (right) with respected Champion spark plug technician Bobby Strahlman.*

fell at the 60mph (97km/h) Quarry Corner on an oil slick. Pickrell, wearing a full-face helmet for the first time, had to be flown home after breaking a collarbone, an ankle and a bone in his back. Smart escaped with cuts and bruises.

The meeting was used to evaluate a new larger-bore exhaust system, designed with another Daytona campaign in mind. Although it gave useful power on the dynamometer, this did not translate into faster laps, and it was scrapped.

After the African outing, UK riders were given custody of 1971 factory machines and they had to make their own entries, but their regular factory mechanics were made available when necessary, and some of their expenses were covered.

At Daytona, it was left to the diminished American-funded teams to uphold the triples' prestige, with principal team riders Romero for Triumph and Mann for BSA, on machines that had been stripped and rebuilt at Duarte with numerous changes.

By now they had US-made versions of the North frame, made by the southern Californian fabrication company Wenco Industries, using drawings supplied by Meriden. Duarte boss Pete Colman told the author in 1996 that new chassis, closely modelled on North's but with altered head angles and said to be several pounds lighter, were necessary for the triples to remain competitive. New frames also allowed for the complete interchangeability of components between team machines, which Duarte technicians liked. Dick Mann approved of his triple's new frame. He told the author that it handled better than the British made chassis it replaced.

'I understood that the plan was to build a batch of twenty-five or so replica frames for private riders to use,' he recalled, but a much smaller number was actually built. The most obvious visible feature of the 1972 frames is that the swinging arm gussets are

*Artist Bill Bennett's cutaway drawing of John Cooper's BSA shortly after it was acquired by the Bee Bee Bros' private racing team.*

not fully boxed-in, as on the Hele-North version.

The triples had a poor year in Florida. Mann was afflicted by ignition gremlins that were to haunt his BSA all season, and a flat tyre dropped Romero well down the field. The best triple result was by Triumph veteran Eddie Mulder, who finished sixth on an ex-factory 1970 machine. Former BSA teamster Don Emde finally got the Daytona win he'd wanted so badly, aboard his 350cc Yamaha TR3 twin. Smart, who had opted to base himself in the USA for 1972 and ride team Hansen Kawasakis, started on pole but his two-stroke failed after its warm-up lap.

## New-Look Match Races

Norton had arrived on the Formula 750 scene, with major financial backing from the John Player tobacco giant. There had been speculation late in 1971 that the money might have gone to BSA, but accepting sponsorship was against factory policy. As it happened, the Nortons hastily developed for Daytona had not performed well in the

event. However, the new arrangements offered the chance for Player to sponsor the 1972 Anglo-American match races, and naturally Norton was included.

As a result, Percy Tait had to relinquish his captain's title, as well as his team place. The new skipper was Player Norton rider and reigning 250cc world champion Phil Read, who headed a team consisting of fellow Norton riders Tony Rutter and Peter Williams, plus Cooper, Jefferies and Pickrell, all on their 'retained' triples. BSA-mounted team captain Dick Mann was the only triple rider in the US contingent, which included three Suzukis and a token Norton provided by the Gus Kuhn dealer team for Emde.

Californian rider Calvin 'Cal' Rayborn was the sensation of the series, aboard a non-works iron-barrelled, four-speed Harley XR750 owned by Walt Falk, and prepared by the rider. Rayborn, who was to be killed racing in New Zealand in 1973, was considered by many to be the world's best road racer at that time, and he won three of the six matches. Britain managed to win overall, mainly thanks to Pickrell, who won the other three on his BSA – which was now a Triumph.

The machine still had its 1971 engine with tilted cylinders, but was now painted in blue and white with Triumph decals in line with company policy. The cosmetic work was done by Pickrell's usual mechanic Arthur Jakeman, who as a Meriden employee, had always found it odd to be tending BSA-badged machines.

Italy acknowledged the rise of Formula 750 racing by staging international events, the most prestigious in 1972 being a 200-miler (320km) at the 3.12-mile (5km) Imola circuit. In front of an enthusiastic crowd of 70,000, Smart, who had flown in from the US, won on a factory Ducati, followed by Bruno Spaggiari on another locally made ohc V-twin. Italian Walter Villa, on an ex-works Triumph triple entered by importer Bepi Koelliker, was third, ahead of Phil Read's Player Norton. Percy Tait had a lucky escape when the magnesium alloy rear hub on his Triumph began to disintegrate, bringing him to a halt.

Pickrell, who had persuaded Bert Hopwood to lend him regular mechanic Arthur Jakeman for the event, was the best privateer, finishing fifth, ahead of Jefferies.

## Still in the TT Limelight

At the TT, Pickrell kept Triumph in the Formula 750 limelight. His machine was tended by Arthur Jakeman, who took annual leave from Meriden to attend. Pickrell hoisted the class lap record to 105.68mph (170.04km/h) to win the race, lengthened to five laps (189 miles/304km) for 1972. Jefferies was second on the Triumph he had been supplied with when his original was despatched to Bob Bailey. It was spannered by his own non-factory mechanic, John Whittaker. Jack Findlay, on a TR750 Suzuki two-stroke triple, had to be content with third. John Cooper rode for the Player Norton team, but retired with gearbox failure along with JPN team mates Read and Peter Williams.

Cooper reverted to his Steve Brown-tended BSA for UK meetings and won the

*Aiming his F750 Triumph, formerly a BSA, through White Gates, Ramsey, Ray Pickrell heads for a TT win in 1972.*

*Fresh air gets under both tyres as Tony Jefferies bounces through the bottom of Bray Hill in the 1972 F750 TT*

*MCN* Superbike series on it. Semi-works triples took the first three places in the F750 race at the Silverstone International, led by Tait, who was second to Finnish sensation Jaarno Saarinen on his Yamaha in the main 1,000cc race.

## Mallory Park

At the Mallory Race of the Year, however, Agostini got his revenge by winning, beating Smart's Kawasaki and Cooper's triple on his 500cc MV. Williams' Norton proved a match for the triples, finishing third and relegating Pickrell and Tait to fourth and fifth respectively.

Disaster struck in the *MCN* Superbike race at Mallory, when a gear broke up in Pickrell's gearbox, locking the rear wheel. He was thrown off at Devil's Elbow, the 80mph (128km/h) left-hander leading on to the finish straight. Unable to avoid the fallen bike, Jefferies hit it, and his Triumph flew through the air to land with all its 380lb (170kg) weight on top of Pickrell, smashing

his pelvis and crushing an ankle. Tait was also brought down in the fracas, but escaped with a dislocated shoulder. The accident spelled the end of Pickrell's road racing career, and fans rallied to show their appreciation by voting him *MCN*'s Man of the Year at the season's end.

## Ontario and Daytona – 1972–3

Arthur Jakeman recalled that after the crash, Doug Hele asked him to rebuild the engine for US rider Gary Scott to use at Ontario. Scott had been signed to ride with Romero, and was scoring well in the Grand National rounds, including a third on a triple at Loudon. He needed the fastest available engine, and Pickrell's squish motor, rebuilt with new cases because of damage from the broken gear, filled the bill.

Cooper returned to Ontario with mechanic Steve Brown, and managed to finish fifth, with Smart scooping the big-money first prize on a Seeley-framed Kawasaki. Scott, who now had a works squish engine

*Push off – I'm adjusting the points! Working on Romero's Triumph after it had acquired cast alloy wheels.*

and lightweight transmission, was thirteenth overall. John Hately rode his ex-Aldana 1970 BSA triple into tenth place.

Dick Mann's BSA became a Triumph thanks to a repaint for 1973, and the veteran who had ridden BSAs since the fifties finished fourth in the Daytona 200, working up the field from a lowly grid position.

'From the point of view of precise riding and not making mistakes, I consider that was my best ride on the bike,' he recalled. The race was won by Saarinen on his 350cc Yamaha. Development continued on US machines: Scott's acquired an American-made North-style frame, and Morris cast magnesium alloy wheels. Later in the year, Gene Romero rode the best-placed British machine at Ontario, finishing eighth on his updated Triumph.

## Norton Fight Back

Intensive development of the John Player Nortons, much of it by Peter Williams, a clever engineer as well as a gifted rider, saw the 750cc twins defeat the triples on several occasions in 1973. JPNs with sheet metal monocoque chassis were first and second in the Formula 750 TT, relegating Tony Jefferies and his 1973 Triumph, built at the factory by his own mechanic, to third.

Tait was the top triple rider in the *MCN* Superbike series, ending the season in fifth place. The Superbike round at the Race of the Year meeting was marred by an accident at the hairpin early in the race, involving Tony Jefferies on his privately prepared Triumph, Player Norton teamster Dave Croxford, and Kuhn Norton rider Dave Potter. Jefferies received back injuries that left him permanently disabled.

The batch of Rob North frames that had been ordered for shipping to the USA arrived at Meriden during 1973, but they were too late. They were to be 'locked in' during the dispute following factory closure but most of them, believed to number twelve, ended up at Kitts Green.

In 1975, a big-engined factory racer was entered in a 1,000cc race at the Silverstone British Grand Prix, prepared by Les Williams at his home. Steve Brown, who assisted with the project, told the author that the engine, retrieved from storage at NVT Motorcycles Shenstone plant, was one of three prototype inclined-cylinder T180 units. With a long-stroke crank and standard bores, it had a capacity of 870cc and featured the roadgoing version of the lightweight clutch and primary drive developed for the abortive T180 roadster. Placed in the ex-Pickrell lowboy rolling chassis now owned by Williams, and enveloped by a prototype aluminium alloy fairing made for the factory by Don Woodward, it was painted yellow and white – matching Pickrell's helmet.

Despite being wheeled out so late, the 900 proved reasonably competitive. Croxford had a low-speed spill whilst awaiting the delayed start of the 1,000cc race, shifting one clip-on handlebar. Nevertheless he finished sixth in a top-class field, to the delight of many spectators. 'That was a really quick bike,' Croxford told the author. But as Doug Hele had predicted, the two-strokes were now invincible, especially as Yamaha were making the over-the-counter TZ700 four-cylinder racer in quantity.

## RIDERS REMEMBER

David Aldana, BSA factory rider (US) 1969–71:

> If you followed another rider on a triple, there'd be this high pitch shriek in harmony with your own engine. We couldn't hear ourselves think until the Tuesday after the race. We didn't think to wear earplugs in those days.

*Serious stuff: Gene Romero (left) talks to Triumph technician Pat Owens, while Pete Colman listens.*

John Cooper, BSA factory rider (UK) 1971, factory-supported 1972:

I told Peter Deverall of BSA: 'lend me the bike I had in the Match Races, and I'll win the Race of the Year. Because I know how to ride that bike.'

I think I revved mine to about 500rpm less than the others, and I always pulled a high gear. It was a very nice motorbike to ride, with plenty of torque and power from low down. I beat Ago at Mallory because I was prepared to stick my neck out more than him, but he really wanted to win, all the same.

Dave Croxford won 1971 Thruxton 500-miler with Tait:

Doug Hele was mystified as to why our proddie bike seemed to be as fast as the pukka racers, but there is such a thing as having too much power, especially at a track like Thruxton.

Don Emde, US BSA team rider 1971:

Those bikes were loud. I will always hold in my memory banks the sound of triples going around the Daytona bankings. To this day, I've not heard a more impressive sound from a motorcycle.

Mick Grant, won 1974 Production TT on Slippery Sam:

Les Williams fitted a quick-action twistgrip on Sam, so I could work the throttle with my hand in plaster, by moving it backwards and forwards. I used to test racers for *Motor Cycle News*, and I rode Percy Tait's at Snetterton. There was a bump that you could always feel going into Coram Curve, but on Percy's bike it completely disappeared. I rode Stan Shenton's Seeley Trident in the 1973 Transatlantic races, but I shortened

the wheelbase by about 15in when I crashed it at Gerards.

Bob Heath, BSA factory rider 1969–72:

The first time I rode a North-frame works BSA at Brands Hatch in 1971, Percy [Tait] said, 'don't fall off it, or you won't get another ride.' I think he was trying to put me off! Straight after that I went to the TT to ride the Meriden-built production Rocket 3. On the first lap of practice, I couldn't believe how heavy it felt at Quarterbridge. Back at the pits I asked why the huge petrol tank had been filled up to the neck. Steve Brown explained that they had a secret plan to do the race non-stop, and they wanted me to get used to riding with a full tank.

Tony Jefferies, UK Triumph team 1971, works supported,1972–3:

It felt like riding on a jet engine! [After winning his first Isle of Man TT, the 1971 F750 race].

Dick Mann, US Team BSA rider, 1970–3:

They were just great bikes, very nice to ride. Mine was good for about 155mph [250km/h] and very stable at that speed. You could ride it any style you wanted, and it would slide around nice on the pavement [tarmac]. A lot of people at the time thought that the 750s had more speed but worse handling than the 350 two-strokes. But the Yamahas were not so forgiving as the BSAs and Triumphs.

Gary Nixon, US Triumph rider, 1966–71:

It was definitely the best bike ever at the time, it handled real good. In 1971 I had a 750 done specially for me. I told Doug Hele I'd broken my leg and they built me a bike with the footrests lowered specially. But Gene [Romero] pinched the bitch off me!

**Ray Pickrell, UK factory team 1970–1, works supported 1972:**

All I did was aim them up the road! It was a great team to ride for. You would make a small complaint about a bike and it would be written down and put right by the next time you rode it. I once tried a really light-weight crank at Snetterton. It was terrific off the line, but otherwise it made the bike virtually unrideable.

**Gene Romero, Triumph works rider 1968–73:**

If I ever raced again, I'd want to do it with a guy like Doug Hele. I think the sun rises and sets on Doug. He was light years ahead of what was being done with the triple in the US: after all, that was *his* engine. The first year's bikes were excellent, very stable with great brakes, like being in a big comfy chair. Next year's lower machine felt lighter and could be tossed around easier, and it turned better.

The clutch was good, but it could sometimes be a problem getting off the start line.

# Surviving works machines

A number of factory racing triples have survived, and some are on public display in museums. A small number have remained in near original condition, but others have been modified, had engine changes or been cosmetically restored. The whereabouts of the following were known at the time of publication.

| *Bike* | *Owner/Location* |
| --- | --- |
| 1970 Aldana BSA | Willi's Motor Museum, Daytona Beach USA |
| 1970 Hailwood BSA | Pierre Sola, France |
| 1970 Triumph (believed ex-Nixon) | Jim Cotherman, USA |
| 1970 Rice Trackmaster BSA | Bill Milburn, USA |
| 1970 Rice Daytona BSA | converted for road use, USA |
| 1971 Triumph *Bol d'Or* winner | National Motorcycle Museum UK, owner Les Williams |
| 1971 Tait Triumph F750 | NMM, owner Mick Hemmings, UK |
| 1971 Romero Triumph F750 | Mark Earl, UK |
| 1971 Mann BSA (US frame) | Robert Iannucci USA |
| 1971 Jefferies Triumph F750 | Bob Bailey, USA |
| 1971 Smart Triumph F750 | Paul Smart |
| 1971 Cooper BSA F750 | NMM, UK |
| 1971 US-spec Triumph F750 | Mitch Klempf, USA |
| 1971 Pickrell/Hailwood BSA | Les Williams UK |
| 1972 Jefferies Triumph F750 | Mel Farrar UK |
| 1973 works-type BSA 870cc | Steve Brown, UK |
| 1970–5 Triumph production No2. | NMM, UK, Les Williams (Slippery Sam) |
| 1970 Triumph production No3 | NMM, UK |
| 1970 Steenson BSA production | anonymous, UK |
| 1970 Heath BSA production | Peter Bates, UK |
| 1976 George/Tait Triumph production | Mick Page, UK (Son of Sam) |

The only thing I could compare that noise with would be riding a double overhead cam Ford Indy Car.

Paul Smart, UK factory team 1970–1:

It really was one of the best times in my life. Riding for Triumph took me from being one of the crowd to being a works rider. It was the best machine available to anyone at the time, and they were great people to work with. The Ducati V-twin I rode at Imola in 1972 was ultimately faster than the triple, but not such a good package and not so much fun.

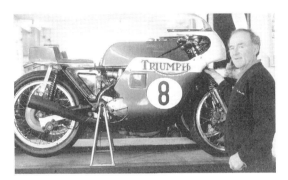

*Paul Smart in 1996 with his highly original 1971 Triumph, displayed at his shop in Paddock Wood, Kent.*

*A Triumph known to be substantially the 1971 Romero machine, seen in 1996. Restored with help from Les Williams, it is occasionally given UK track outings by owner Mark Earl.*

Malcolm Uphill, UK Triumph production class factory rider:

Compared to the Bonneville, the Trident was a high-speed armchair. It was very heavy, and you couldn't throw it about. But like anything done by Hele's team it was a nice job.

Uphill retired from racing after crashing heavily on a Suzuki in the 1970 Ulster GP.

*John Cooper on his team BSA in 1971. This machine is on display at the National Motorcycle Museum, Birmingham, along with other historic triple racers.*

*Recent photo of ex-Jim Rice BSA A75 Trackmaster flat-tracker built by Tom Cates for 1969. This machine is now owned by Texan dirt track historian Bill Milburn.*

161

# 7 Production and Dealer Team Racing

'Win on Sunday, sell on Monday,' is a slogan coined to justify racing, and the more a machine on the track resembles one available in the showroom, the more powerful the message. By 1970, the Trident and Rocket 3 were in need of a sales push, and with no replicas of the Daytona racers planned, both BSA and Triumph prepared works triples for production class road racing.

Early Triumph factory ventures with a production T150 in production class racing had not brought instant success. From a rider's point of view, the 650 twins were lighter and more nimble and they were fast, capable of speeds over 130mph (209km/h). But 750cc Norton Commando rivals with a 100cc advantage presented a threat. And, with Honda entering its CB750 four in races and more Superbikes in the pipeline from

*Percy Tait aboard the first factory production Trident at Brands Hatch in August 1969. Silencers like those on Bonneville racers are fitted. Doug Hele did not consider the machine to be a serious racing project.*

other makers, there was little choice but to pitch the street triples into battle.

Although it is debatable whether they ultimately boosted sales, the 'proddie' triples' track performances improved drastically for 1970. And over the following five years one Trident in particular – the second-built works production machine nicknamed Slippery Sam – achieved legendary status by notching up an extraordinary run of successes against the best that Germany, Italy and Japan could put up against it, especially in Isle of Man TT events.

As was described in Chapter 5, there were exploratory outings with a Meriden-prepared production class Trident during the summer of 1969. Despite the useful power available from the 750cc three-cylinder engine, many snags had to be ironed out to make the big machine as rider-friendly as the Bonnevilles, which had enjoyed continuous attention to details since the mid-sixties.

Les Williams, whose name became inextricably linked with Slippery Sam, recalled that riders were initially reluctant to transfer from the familiar twins to the heavier triples: 'The production Trident we ran in 1969 was heavy and the cornering clearance was limited because the engine timing cover was always touching down on left-handers.'

Production racing rules said that any special parts had to be homologated by the manufacturer, and had to be available for purchase as catalogue extras. In reality, few people apart from a handful of favoured dealer teams with good factory contacts ever prised special proddie racing parts out of BSA or Triumph.

Extras fitted to proddie triples in 1970 included a Screen and Plastic dolphin fairing of similar shape to the Umberslade Daytona type, the S & P seat used on racing T120s, clip-on handlebars, Fontana 250mm front drum brakes to replace the marginal standard items and alloy tanks. But stan-

dard road frames were used from the outset and the standard ray gun silencers had to be left in place, although they were raised to improve cornering clearance, and the front pipes were tucked up to the frame for the same purpose.

In early production outings with a Trident, cigar-shaped silencers like those used on the racing Bonnevilles had been tried, but it was found that, for all its styling faults, the ray gun was very efficient. There were experiments with stripping the internals from the big cans, but it was found that the best power figures were obtained by leaving the reverse-flow system in place.

According to Doug Hele, Meriden-prepared 1970 proddie Tridents were producing well over 70bhp, being essentially like the Daytona engines internally, although their TH6 inlet camshafts were retarded by a few degrees to compensate for increased back pressure created by the silencers. As dictated by the rules, carburation was by the standard 27mm Amal Concentrics, minus the air filter.

Two Rocket 3 Production racers were prepared in BSA's Competition Department at Small Heath for 1970. Parts like Fontana brakes were obtained via Meriden, but five-speed gear clusters and racing cams were not so forthcoming.

'There had been a decree that "special parts" could only be issued at Meriden,' Brian Martin, head of BSA's Competition Shop at the time, told the author. Tuning was confined to normal procedures such as removing air filters, fitting 10.5:1 pistons, valve gear lightening and careful cylinder head preparation.

Bob Heath, a twenty-year-old BSA employee, had been part of the small crew that collected parts to build the racing Rocket 3s, along with another staffer, side-car racer Mick Boddice. Heath had his first outing on one at the King of Brands meeting in April 1970, and led the production event until the last lap, when he was overtaken by Brian Kemp's Curley Norton. After taking the flag to finish second, Heath grounded the machine heeling it into the right-hand Paddock Bend, and fell off.

## THE 1970 SEASON

One of the works BSAs was the most successful triple in the season's first major production machine event, the Thruxton 500-mile race. Ridden by experienced BSA A65 twin racer Pat Mahoney and rising Irish star Brian Steenson, a Rocket 3 finished third overall, behind a 750cc Norton

*Les Williams with a replica North-framed racer he completed for a friend in 1995.*

Commando and a 500cc Suzuki two-stroke twin. At one stage the BSA was leading the wet race, when a broken condenser in the ignition circuitry forced it to make a long pit stop.

Triumph entered Percy Tait and Malcolm Uphill at Thruxton but their Trident was forced to retire because of valve gear failure when lying in fifth place after 80 laps. An inlet valve's tip had worn where it contacted the rockers – a recurring fault on early racing triples – and one of the valve's inner springs had broken.

Les Williams' post-race notes include the comments 'performance poorish' and 'handling poor'. Because of anxiety about 'digging in' the team had inserted extension plates between the tops of the rear suspension units and the rear subframe to raise the rear end by more than an inch.

The works proddie Triumph's engine was rebuilt for the next outing in the production race at the North West 200, run over a superlatively fast public roads circuit in Northern Ireland.

Before travelling to the event Tait tested the overhauled machine at MIRA, recording a top speed of 131.2mph (211.1km/h) with the fairing, similar in shape to the Umberslade streamlining on the Daytona racers, in place.

Tait's Trident finished second in the North West production race, behind Malcolm Uphill. The Welsh team rider had requested that he stick with his T120 Bonneville twin, presented to him by the factory after his '69 win. He set a fastest lap of 107.87mph (173.56km/h), and Tait's best circuit was only a quarter of a second slower. But if the T150 had been a really competitive tool, its extra horsepower should have allowed it to outpace the 650 on a circuit noted for its long straight sections. Steenson was lying third on his Rocket 3 until he retired.

Using reject machines off the everyday production line as raw material, two more

## Bob Heath – from shop floor to Slippery Sam

When he worked on Rocket 3 engine assembly at BSA in 1968, Walsall man Bob Heath was sometimes given boring work. On one occasion, he had to ease metal off clutch shock absorber wheels with an oilstone until they would fit their shafts. Poor sales of the triple later meant that Heath was among those made redundant in mid-1969, and he found a new job at Lucas.

Weeks later, Steve Brown called at his house, and invited him to join the team working on racing machines at Armoury Road. Heath became the regular rider of a 500cc single based on a BSA roadster, and was involved in gathering components up to build the two Small Heath racing Rocket 3s for 1970.

The North-framed triple also used by John Cooper was lent to Heath for some meetings in 1971, and he campaigned the Meriden-built production BSA with good results. When BSA abandoned road racing altogether, he moved onto Yamaha two-strokes with continuing success. In 1974, Heath partnered Percy Tait on Slippery Sam to finish fourth in the Thruxton Endurance GP.

Heath set up a business making helmet visors, and his name became known to all UK motorcyclists as a result. In the 1990s he made a comeback in classic racing, aboard 350 and 500cc replica Seeley singles, on which he has seldom been beaten.

factory Tridents were prepared for the Isle of Man TT production race in June. They carried orange and white fairings, and not the blue and white racing colours Triumphs wore. Uphill, who had been the hero of the 1969 proddie TT, lapping at 100mph (160km/h) on his Bonnie, agreed to ride a Trident although he had told the press back in May that he expected to ride his T120, and win on it. His team mates were to be Paul Smart and budding world champion Rod Gould, who had been a regular Triumph teamster on Bonnevilles.

For BSA, Heath was joined by Steenson. Small Heath's Competitions Shop had still not been able to get its hands on TH6 cams, and it was forced to install second hand close-ratio four-speed gearboxes. Steenson's bike was fitted with internals borrowed from the BSA twin sidecar outfit raced by BSA employee Peter Brown. Triumphs were still having grounding troubles, as Williams recalled:

Riders were grinding the primary chain covers away at the chain adjuster boss. To stop them wearing through and leaking oil we made protector plates. They were cut from the bumper of a wrecked Fiat car lying near our garage.

The slightly built Gould was unhappy with his Trident and asked to be released to concentrate on his open class two-strokes. His ride was taken over by Tom Dickie, 1966 Senior Manx Grand Prix winner and one of BSA's riders in the disastrous 1968 Daytona outing on 500cc twins.

The 1970 750 class production TT was one of the most thrilling ever to be run over the Mountain Course. Uphill beat Peter Williams and his 750cc Norton Commando twin by only 1.6 seconds after 188.65 miles (303.54km). On the last lap, Williams had led over much of the mountain section of the course. But Uphill, in great pain from a practice foot injury, swept past the Norton, which had started to misfire as it ran low on fuel, through the 100mph (160km/h) Hilberry right-hander.

The Trident had also slowed towards the end of the race, and was found to have lost about 20bhp through retarded ignition. The cause proved to be an unhardened part in the special contact-breaker points drive coupling. The modification had been fitted with the intention of improving reliability by overcoming the inaccurate timing bogey that had arisen with standard points drives at Daytona.

Smart, who shot through *Motor Cycle*'s slightly downhill speed trap at 140.60mph (226.23km/h), had looked a likely winner until he was forced out with front tyre deflation, believed to have been caused by a faulty valve. Dickie brought his Triumph triple home in fourth, after clocking the speed trap figure of 133.3mph (214.5km/h) the same as Bob Heath, fifth on his Rocket 3, and frustrated at having only four ratios in his gearbox.

*First TT win by a triple: Uphill urges his slowing Trident out of the Governor's Bridge dip in the 1970 750 production event.*

Steenson, who had taken the lead while Uphill was refuelling, had to retire, reporting gearbox failure. Heavily scraped exhaust pipes and a tattered lower fairing testified to the Irishman's heroic ride on the near-standard Rocket 3. Later in the week, TT racing was robbed of a future star when Steenson was killed after crashing a 500cc Seeley on the mountain section in the open Senior race.

Two Honda 750s, said to be very standard, were in the 1970 production TT race but they were no threat to the British machinery on the island's tortuous and bumpy circuit. Tommy Robb finished eighth on his, ahead of John Cooper on a second CB750 four.

At the Hutchinson 100 meeting at Brands Hatch in August, the production event was a three-cornered battle between BSA, Norton and Triumph. Smart won from Charlie Sanby, of the Gus Kuhn Norton dealer team, but triples followed them in, ridden by Tait, Ray Pickrell and fastest man in practice, Heath, now on equal terms with a Quaife five-speed box. Uphill fell off on spilt oil when lying fourth.

## The *Bol d'Or*

As part of the BSA Group's strategy in countering Honda, it had been decided to contest the *Bol d'Or*, a long established 24-hour marathon held at that time on the banked Montlhéry circuit near Paris. An international event for standard production machines, its importance was growing at the time, thanks to an upsurge in motorcycle sales in France.

In 1969, the winning French two-rider team had been mounted on officially backed Honda 750 fours. For 1970, BSA and Triumph factory machines were to be sent for an assault on the *Bol* in collaboration with the Group's Paris-based French distributor, CGCIM, a branch of the Peugeot organization, and ex-racer Georges Monneret.

'We were pretty green about the event, in fact we didn't have a clue,' Les Williams told the author. 'We took three bikes – they were very ugly looking, with twin headlights tacked on to the fairings.' They were the factory's production class racers with half-fairings and added lighting. He added:

We hadn't braced the fairing brackets, and during practice they cracked on the bike Paul Smart was sharing with Tom Dickie. The fairing dropped down and brought Paul off in a big way. He didn't like the cir-

cuit, and thought that would mean he wouldn't have to race, but we worked all night and rebuilt the bike. A French car racer with a body repair business lent us his workshop.

Despite its looks, the rebuilt Triumph did well, considering the problems. Smart and Dickie won by nine laps covering a total of 469, a distance of 1,838 miles (2,957km) at an average of 70.50mph (113.43km/h). Triumph beat not only the dismayed Honda équipe but the official Italian Laverda con-

*Ugly but a winner. Paul Smart during one of his stints on the successful rapidly modified production Trident he shared with Tom Dickie in the 1970 Bol d'Or at Montlhéry.*

tingent. An unfaired privately entered Honda ridden by Peter Darvill and Oliver Chevalier was second, and the best official Honda finished fourth.

Percy Tait and Steve Jolly could only manage fifth on an oil-smothered machine, which had dropped from a top-six placing to seventieth place during one long pit stop. Tait told the author:

> The problem was wet sumping, which had started happening after we changed from 25-50 multigrade oil to an R-grade racing oil. The engine wasn't scavenging properly and oil belched out everywhere – it had even collected in the channels on the rear wheel rim.
>
> The bike was sliding all over the place. We nearly packed up at one point, but the French importer told us that if we finished in the first six, we'd get money. So we went out and finished fifth!

Tait subsequently referred to this particular production Trident, the second to be built, as 'Slippery' and his nickname among Meriden colleagues had always been Sam the Transport Man. The two names came together and very soon the machine was universally known as Slippery Sam.

A third factory Triumph triple, ridden by French rider pairing Jean-Claude Costeux and Georges Passe, finished eighth after having a broken first gear and a burnt-out clutch replaced, along with two throttle cables, by Tait's regular mechanic Bill Fannon during the race.

BSA fielded its own specially prepared Rocket 3 ridden by Don Jones and Graham Saunders, a team who had contested earlier rounds of the European *Coupe d' Endurance* series on a 650cc BSA A65 twin. They were well placed in the first half dozen before missing a fuel stop through bungled pit signals and then crashed trying to catch up. After lengthy repairs in the pits they pulled back to finish in the first twenty. Even so,

## Magnifique!

Veteran racer, record breaker and *bon viveur,* Parisian Georges Monneret used the ex-Brian Steenson Rocket 3 production racer fitted with its usual dolphin fairing to break French records at the banked Monthléry track near Paris. On 26 September 1970, Monneret, then sixty-two, broke two records

Wearing an old-fashioned 'pudding basin' helmet, and using Dunlop K81 road tyres, Monneret maintained 188.877km/h (117.366mph) to cover the 10km (6 mile) distance from a standing start, and covered a flying-start 10km at 201.906km/h (125.462mph).

In February 1971, Monneret set further short-distance French records on a Rocket 3, again at Monthléry. They were a standing start 400m (¼ mile) in 12.70 seconds at 113.385km/h (70.45mph) and a standing start kilometre in 24.70 seconds, a speed of 145.748km/h (90.57mph).

Monneret helped French BSA-Triumph importer CGCIM to organise successful forays in France's *Bol d'Or* 24-hour road race, and obtained triples to use as official machines for the Tour de France cycle race.

they did better than other British visitors. Nortons entered by both the factory and Gus Kuhn Motors, two Dresda Autos entries and a pair of 750cc Royal Enfield twins, were all among the non-finishers.

Even allowing for the problems encountered, the gruelling *Bol d'Or* proved how little attention the three-cylinder engines needed over high racing mileages, especially in comparison with 650cc twins. Les Williams recalled that following the Monthléry marathon, the first-built ex-Uphill production Trident ridden by the French team, which had probably done 2,400 miles

(3,860km) of practice and racing, needed only a top-end overhaul, in addition to routine wearing component replacements such as brake linings, tyres and chains.

Fitted with a half-fairing, it was then given to team newcomer Ray Pickrell for the Race of the South meeting at Brands Hatch. He rode it in the main race, as there were no North-framed machines to spare for him, and took second place in the production race.

## HIGH TIMES – 1971

By the 1971 season, Triumph's production class machines had been reframed with a special chassis. Although ostensibly similar in appearance to the standard Trident chassis, the new tubework had been subtly changed. Arthur Jakeman told the author:

It was made using standard frame parts. But by altering the length of some tubes

and raising the swinging arm mounting slightly, we were able to raise the engine and the frame bottom rails, to be 1⅜in higher off the road than the standard frame.

He recalled piecing a prototype together to Hele's specification on the Experimental Department's precision surface table.

Increased ground clearance so gained allowed riders to corner at speed safely without the constant hazard of grounding the engine. The rule-bending chassis, known as the 'short' frame, was tested by the factory during 1970 and to satisfy homologation rules, forty were meant to be made. Many fewer were actually completed, but at least eleven were either or sold or 'loaned' to dealers and leading T150-mounted competitors in production class racing.

BSA and Triumph proddie machines played their full part in making 1971 the Year of the Triples. As the BSA Competi-

---

## The road North

In his book, *Whatever Happened to the British Motorcycle Industry*, Bert Hopwood states his belief that triples' sales could have vastly improved if a street version of the North-framed factory road racer had been marketed.

Hopwood himself started negotiations with frame builder Rob North with a view to quantity production. North told the author that he was offered a choice between a one-off payment or royalties on sales, but no deal transpired.

Bill Fannon, of the Meriden's Experimental Department and later NVT's development centre at Kitts Green, was involved in an interesting project at the same time that the T160 was being prototyped. 'Design staff had said we couldn't possibly use the North frame for a roadster, because the shape of the fuel tank it needed would make the bike unsellable,' Fannon told the author.

He made an experimental duplex Trident frame with North-style tubes running direct from the steering head to the swinging arm supports. However, to avoid having the taboo wedge-shaped fuel tank, he arranged the top tubes close together to pass through the tank's tunnel, splaying out below the tank.

'But the irony is, that if you look at today's motorcycles, they all have tanks shaped like the North racers!' Fannon said.

tions Department was concentrating on motocross, a third works Rocket 3 was built at Meriden for Ray Pickrell, using the high-clearance frame.

In May's Thruxton 500-miler (800km) triples made up for the previous year's disappointments by dominating the race. After more than five hours lying in second place, Percy Tait and Dave Croxford took the lead when Peter Williams crashed his Norton only 20 miles (32km) short of the finish. Their Trident won, ahead of the Meriden-built Rocket 3 ridden by Heath and Triumph staffer John Barton. Croxford and Barton had been enlisted as factory riders because the factory team was also committed to the 200-mile (320km) Formula 750 race run concurrently at the same meeting. Barton worked alongside Norman Hyde in Experimental Design, and built his own racing chassis for a Triumph triple.

Ray Pickrell's victory in the 1971 750cc Production TT was the first Isle of Man win for Slippery Sam, and the first time the four-

*Wearing Percy Tait's visored helmet, Ray Pickrell keeps Slippery Sam ahead of Peter Williams' Norton at Creg-ny-Baa in the 1971 production TT.*

lap event had been completed at an average of over 100mph (160km/h). Pickrell borrowed Percy Tait's visor-equipped helmet for the race, because his goggles had been affected by flies in the F750 race a few days earlier. Sam was now equipped with a Bonneville-style fairing, as well as the high-clearance frame.

Bob Heath brought his Meriden-built BSA home third.

The production race at the international Silverstone meeting in 1971 was a convincing triples whitewash, with Pickrell winning on the Meriden-built number three Rocket 3, with Paul Smart and Percy Tait second and third on their Tridents.

## SAM TESTED TO THE LIMIT

Scaling down of factory support for racing came close to curtailing Sam's TT career in 1972. Pickrell had asked Les Williams if he could race the Trident again, but the official factory's response was that no production machines would be available.

*Winner first time out on a Trident. Dave Croxford partnered Percy Tait to victory in the 1971 Thruxton 500-mile (800km) race. Half-fairings made pit maintenance easier in long races.*

Shortly before the TT Doug Hele did, however, agree that Williams could take Sam, then semi-dismantled and in storage, to his home.

Pickrell was entered in the production event on one of Stan Shenton's Boyer Team Tridents. However, Williams and colleagues worked long hours to make the factory bike raceworthy before Williams took his annual holiday at the TT. When on the Isle of Man, he had finally persuaded Hele to agree to Pickrell having a factory production ride. The condition was that it had to win.

On the Wednesday of TT practice week, Fred Swift rigged up a speedometer for legality (production racers were road registered), and rode Sam from the factory to the Isle of Man boat terminal at Liverpool. 'It was so fast, I got there well before I expected!' Swift told the author.

When Sam arrived on the island on Thursday morning, Pickrell had to use what precious little remaining practice time there was to qualify if he was to ride it in the race.

'I nearly flung it away,' Pickrell told the author. 'It slid sideways and I had such a tank-slapper it broke the steering lock-stops. Luckily everything came straight again.' Eventually he decided to correct the handling himself by borrowing a C-spanner from a spectator to adjust the Girling rear suspension units. Friday was spent on Sam's suspension and steering damping before Pickrell turned in the fastest practice lap in his class at 89.70mph (144.32km/h) in a wet and misty session. He recalled:

In the race we were undergeared by miles. I was so worried about breaking a con-rod, I rode with my knees sticking out to create some load. I had a good lead when I got a signal at the Gooseneck on the last lap. It said 1 minute, 1 second, but I read it as 11 seconds. I went like a loon from then – if I had crashed and not won, I think Les would have got the sack!

Pickrell recalled that he had felt bad about rejecting Shenton's bike, but ultimately opted in favour of the more familiar machine. Sam carried Boyer stickers as a gesture of goodwill. Shenton's Trident proved its capability by finishing third behind Peter Williams' works Norton Commando, ridden by Boyer Team regular David Nixon.

Pickrell really did fling Sam away in the Hutchinson 100 production race, but remounted to take third. He also won that year's Silverstone production event.

At the end of the 1972 season, Les Williams bought the machine from Triumph. To maintain its competitive edge, he made a lightweight frame. Although visually identical to the earlier high-clearance chassis, it was made from Reynolds 531 race frame tubing.

'Some frame sections had been supplied at one time by Reynolds and they were lying disused. I took then to the old chap in the frame repairs shop, and he brazed them together,' Williams recalled. He continued to enter it in the TT.

Tony Jefferies rode Sam in 1973, winning despite a hailstorm and streaming wet roads from John Williams on a Boyer Trident. Sam only just made it, for, as Jefferies admitted, Peter Williams had the race sewn up when his Norton's gearbox failed, a recurrent cause of Norton Commando retirements. Welshman Selwyn Griffiths competed on an ex-works Rocket 3, now Steve Brown's personal property, but was one of several riders who slid off in the treacherous conditions.

Percy Tait had the last of his many outings on the bike he had named, winning the 1973 Silverstone production race and hoisting the circuit's class record to 103.31mph (166.23km/h).

For 1974, the ceiling for the largest capacity TT production category was raised to 1,000cc, but Sam won again, piloted by Yorkshire's new TT maestro Mick Grant, enrolled by Sam's sponsor, Midlands racing Triumph dealer A Bennett & Son, who provided Williams with new spares.

'It was only when I met Mick Grant and shook his hand, that I realized he had his right wrist in plaster, from a racing accident. We had to modify the fairing slightly for the plaster,' Williams recalled. As disc front brakes were now standard Trident equipment, Les Williams had been able to convert his machine. It was allowed to compete with two discs, arranged by fitting a reversed left-side front fork slider on the right side. The added caliper was therefore set ahead of the slider. Sam beat BMW twins ridden by Germans Hans-Otto Butenuth and Helmut Dahne, who came second and third at the TT. And in the 1974 Thruxton Endurance race, Percy Tait and Bob Heath rode the Trident into third place against stiff opposition.

The ultimate reliability test for Sam was the ten-lap production TT introduced for 1975, with each machine to be ridden by two riders.

'People said I'd be crazy to try and win that,' Williams recalled. Sam was entered in the marathon at the request of NVT boss Dennis Poore, who realized that another Triumph win in the face of growing foreign competition would provide useful publicity.

'I spent a couple of weeks getting ready at the Norton racing HQ at Andover. I was very impressed with their set-up,' Williams told the author. In return for NVT backing, he had to agree to Sam being repainted in the John Player colours worn by Norton racers in the 1975 season. Instead of the Olympic Flame fuel tank, seat and mudguards, Sam was sprayed white with a red and black Player package-based design on the fairing.

For the long-distance TT, most people had their money on the 900cc BMW R90S ridden by Dahne and Werner Dieringer to win the 1,000cc category, but the German twin only lasted four laps. Ridden by Scottish TT specialist Alex George and Player Norton teamster Dave Croxford, Slippery Sam was put

## The favoured few

A notebook kept by Les Williams detailed special racing parts for triples released to the favoured few. They were mostly dealers, although some individuals were on the list, and components supplied to the BSA Competition Department at Small Heath are also listed. In some cases an added note in red ink says: 'charged for'.

The following received short T150 production racing frames between 1970 and 1972:

A Bennett & Son, dealer, Nuneaton (2)
Boyer of Bromley, dealer (3)
Charlies Motorcycles, Bristol, dealer (1)
Neil Coombes, individual (1)
Elite Motors, London, dealer (1)
Hughes, London, dealer (3)

A squish head, barrel and pistons were supplied to Bennett at the end of 1972, and Boyer received a set of three squish pistons. Items also listed were a small number of fairings and Fontana brakes.

Amongst other works hardware the Koelliker team in Milan were sent Bendix points, Daytona-type fuel and oil tanks, a *Bol d'Or* wiring harness and 'deep tread' Dunlop K81 tyres. The latter were an endurance racing aid only available to the well-connected. One pair of Koelliker cams were sold to Bennett by Meriden early in 1973.

on ultra-high gearing to score an incredible fifth victory, averaging 99.60mph (160.26km/h) for the 340miles (547km), including stops for fuel and rider changes. Sam's best lap was the ninth, when George nudged over the 8,000rpm ceiling agreed for the long event and set a new production record at 102.82mph (165.44km/h). Although Sam had been reframed for 1971,

*We did it! Co-riders Dave Croxford (left) and Alex George with Sam's owner, Les Williams, after their 1975 TT win.*

*Slippery Sam with fairing removed after the 1975 TT. A six-volt battery was used to save weight.*

and had had one major engine overhaul, his specifications were little changed over the years since the 1970 Production TT. In its final form, the Trident's weight was down to 405lb (182kg) dry, thanks partly to a small six-volt battery, and produced a useful 75bhp at 8,500rpm with ray gun silencers. Although excess weight was trimmed from the silencers' internals, the standard reverse-flow system was left in place for optimum power.

Another change for the 1974 season had been a change of five-speed gearbox internals for the stronger Mk II version of the Quaife transmission, making Sam the only factory machine to be so equipped.

Production racing regulations ruled out machines over five years old, and Sam was finally deemed obsolete. The legendary machine's last race was in a production race at Silverstone in mid-1975, when Percy Tait finished second, behind Tony Smith's Nor-

# Anatomy of a ray gun

Despite all the ridicule heaped on the Ogle-designed ray gun silencer, it proved itself as an efficient exhaust device, particularly for production class racing. Many were those who thought that stripping its guts out would boost engine performance while maintaining the appearance of street legality. But they inevitably found that Rocket 3s and Tridents ran better with the internals intact.

The secret lay not in the external form, but in the 'reverse-flow' plumbing, which could have been installed in a silencer of any shape, provided it had generous internal volume.

The system is believed to have been pioneered by Velocette in the fishtail silencers the Birmingham factory started using on its standard machines in pre-war years. Doug Hele adopted it during his period at Norton, having been introduced to the system by former Velocette employee Fred Swift, when he joined Norton's Experimental Department. Hele used reverse flow as a method of extracting maximum power from Norton's 650cc Manxman and 650SS twins, while muffling sound to an acceptable level. Hele told the author:

> When I went to Meriden, Triumph were using the Resonator silencer. But that seemed to leave a hole in the middle of the power curve. With a reverse-flow silencer and a small diameter pipe, we gained mid-range power around 4,000rpm.

This type of silencer was used on Triumph's Saint, the 650cc twin specially tuned for police use, and inside a large cigar-shaped muffler fitted to triple prototypes prior to the arrival of the ray gun.

Inside the ray gun, the exhaust gas is carried along a tube of the same diameter as the exhaust pipe. At its extreme end it is closed, but gas is able to flow out through louvres cut in the tube. They are arranged to deflect it in the reverse direction to flow forwards inside the silencer, before it finds its way out of the three tail pipes.

American legislation imposed ever-tighter noise restrictions on imported road machines during the seventies, so even if the ray gun had not been so reviled for its appearance, its days were numbered.

Not surprisingly, the factory race team experimented with 'empty' ray guns, both on dynamometer test and on the track. In July of 1970, works rider Malcolm Uphill carried out tests by trying ray guns with and without internals on a production racing T150 at Wiltshire's Castle Combe circuit. His verdict was that for the best results the standard internals should be retained, which they were on factory-entered production machines.

*Ray gun cut open to reveal its secret. The rear end of the internal tube is blanked off, forcing gas to disperse in the silencer.*

# Slippery Sam's Isle of Man production TT record

| Year | distance | rider | result | av. speed (mph) |
|------|----------|-------|--------|-----------------|
| 1970 | 5 laps (188.65 miles) | Tom Dickie | 4th | 94.14 |
| 1971 | 4 laps (151.09 miles) | Ray Pickrell | 1st | 100.07 |
| 1972 | 4 laps (151.09 miles) | Ray Pickrell | 1st | 100.00 |
| 1973 | 4 laps (151.09 miles) | Tony Jefferies | 1st | 95.62 |
| 1974 | 4 laps (151.09 miles) | Mick Grant | 1st | 99.72 |
| 1975 | 10 laps (377.3 miles) | Dave Croxford/ Alex George | 1st | 99.60 |

*Machine specifications*

| | |
|---|---|
| Engine | standard T150, with lightened crankshaft (standard crank from 1974), 11.5:1 pistons, S & W valve springs, racing valve seats, lightened timing gear, TH6 camshafts |
| Output | 74bhp @ 8,500rpm |
| Carburation | 3 x 27mm Amal Concentrics with intake trumpets |
| Ignition | 3 x 12volt coils, Bendix cb points with quill drive |
| Exhaust | standard 1969 T150, raised for ground clearance |
| Electrical | Lucas alternator, 12 volt battery (later 6v) |
| Transmission | Quaife close-ratio 5-speed gearbox (Mk II from 1974) |
| Frame | Standard 1970, from 1971 factory 'short' frame with increased cornering clearance, lightweight materials for 1973 |
| Wheels | 19in, alloy rims, Dunlop TT100 tyres 1970 and 1975, otherwise Dunlop racing tyres |
| Brakes | front: 250mm Fontana drum (from 1974, 9.5in Lockheed twin discs); rear: Triumph 7in drum |
| Suspension | front: Triumph telescopic fork, selectively assembled; rear: Girling 110lb spring/damper units |
| Fairing | Screen & Plastic |
| Seat | S & P, later P & P Seating |
| Weight | ready to race: 410lb (184.5kg) in final form |

ton, but ahead of Pete Davies' 1,000cc Laverda triple.

An eligible replacement was created out of an electric start Trident T160, which racing team fitter Steve Brown had bought from Kitts Green and converted for racing in collaboration with Les Williams. With high hopes, they entered it for the 10-lap 1976 Production TT, to be ridden by Tait and Alex George. Not surprisingly it was immediately dubbed Son of Sam.

However, on the first lap, a rider in close company with Tait ran wide at Ballig, forcing the Triumph into a stone wall. Although Tait did not actually fall off, he sustained serious injuries and had to be rushed to Nobles Hospital by helicopter. The accident marked the end of his amazingly long competitive career.

A 250cc Yamaha took advantage of handicapping to be overall winner of the 1976 race, the last production race held at the TT until the mid-1980s.

## MARSHAL LORE

Providing machines for Travelling Marshals at the Isle of Man TT and Manx Grand Prix races has always been a prestigious job for any manufacturer. To this day, the big makers compete to have their products chosen.

The Marshals' job is vital for the safe running of the Isle of Man's unique events, held on 37.733 miles (60.712km) of closed-off roads normally used by everyday traffic. The mobile officials inspect the course before racing, circulate during practice sessions, and in the event of an incident during racing can attend within minutes or even seconds.

If anything, their role was more critical in the past, before race organizers could rely on comprehensive radio communications. In the event of serious injury, a helicopter was used.

Riders must be highly skilled, and they are often drawn from the ranks of ex-TT racers. It goes without saying that their machines must be impeccably reliable. But they must also be swift enough to travel on the circuit during racing or practice without distracting or baulking competitors.

Triumph Tridents and a BSA Rocket 3 were used by the Isle of Man Travelling Marshals between 1969 and 1976. They were the responsibility of Ron Barrett, who also prepared press test Tridents. The triples were built and tested at Meriden and Barrett looked after them when on the Isle of Man. He told the author:

> The only non-standard parts we used were S & W valve springs, and Fontana front brakes until disc-braked bikes were used, although the standard front brake was used in 1969 and 1970.
>
> A great deal of care was taken in building the engines. Every rod and piston was the same weight, and valve timing had to be spot on, turning cam followers round if necessary to get exactly 150 thou lift at top dead centre on each overlap. The bores were honed to their top limit and checked for evenness.

Work was done on the primary drives to get everything properly aligned, which it often wasn't as the bikes came off the line. Sometimes shafts were as much as 29 thou out of true with bearings, and Barrett added extra locating dowels to casings. Four-speed close-ratio gearbox internals were used, except for the Trident of one Marshal, who preferred a standard five-speeder for its quicker change.

Barrett opened up the main crankcase oilways, bearing in mind that a machine might stand cold at one of the Marshal's six stations at The Bungalow, 1,300ft (400m) above sea level, before being started and run hard immediately. To simplify cold starts, he fitted a tickler extension lever, also found on standard T160s, to the centre carburettor.

On the Isle of Man, Barrett would work his way round the fleet of machines, which were often kept at marshals' homes, servicing the triples with a points and tappet clearance check between morning and evening practice duties. It is a tribute to his work that mechanical troubles were almost unknown.

Alan 'Kipper' Killip, a native Manxman who became chief Travelling Marshal in 1971, testifies to the safety and reliability of the triples:

> Ron was such a perfectionist: if you ever missed a gear, he'd know by looking at the ignition points. My bike never failed to start, never leaked oil and never ran out of brakes.
>
> I remember mine used to show 125mph [200km/h] along Sulby Straight (a flat and bumpy section). It used to ground, at Brandywell and Sarah's Cottage (tight bends), but I can never remember it stepping out once. I was happy with standard 'bars on mine: it was a beautiful thing to throw around, it gave you fantastic confidence.

Other Travelling Marshals who regularly rode triples were Peter Crebbin, Chief Marshal before Killip, local former racers Randall Cowell, Jack Harding, Mike Kelly, Roger Sutcliffe, retired sidecar racer Des Evans, and ex-TT rider Albert Moule.

The four unfaired Tridents were updated over the years, and changed their colours. Cowell's Rocket 3, CUE762J, was white, the trim it had worn when Barrett commandeered it at Small Heath. Believed to have been for overseas police use, it had been dropped and slightly damaged in its shipping container. When NVT took over, the A75 was rebadged as a Triumph but kept its inclined BSA engine.

Norton Commandos were also used in NVT days, but Barrett said that keeping them in one piece took all his time, making him neglect his beloved triples.

'I think the best of the lot was UUE14G, which started as Peter Crebbin's bike and then became Des Evans's,' Barrett told the author. 'When it was borrowed for testing prototype racing ignitions at Snetterton, Percy [Tait] was timed at 135mph [217km/h]

*Alan Killip pauses on his Trident in the TT Paddock in 1971. For the first time that year the Marshals' machines had Fontana front brakes.*

*Des Evans heels his disc-braked Trident into Braddan Bridge.*

# Ron Barrett – Mr Reliability

Better pay lured Ron Barrett from the Velocette factory in Hall Green, Birmingham to Triumph at Meriden in 1967. At the Velo plant, he had been engaged in building the company's ohv single-cylinder engines, acquiring a high level of skill on precision work such as crankshaft building and valve seat installation.

Working under his elder brother Alan, a foreman in the Meriden Experimental Department, Barrett had direct involvement with the P2 triple prototypes. He remembered vividly seeing the tailpipe of a Burgess silencer glowing cherry red when a P2 engine was running on static test, and how in early road testing the 750's power could wreak havoc on tyres.

'Testers – the main two on that bike were Percy Tait and Tony Lomax – used to come in and the treads were so hot that your hand would stick to the rubber,' Barrett told the author. Dunlop developed its K81 road tyre specifically to cope with the triples.

After the Trident's launch Barrett was assigned to preparing machines for press and publicity purposes, using his precise assembly skills to present fast and reliable machines that were ostensibly standard but more carefully put together than was possible with normal production procedures. He went to Germany with the *Motorrad* test Trident and tended the superlative Isle of Man TT Marshals' official machines for several years.

He gave every cylinder head individual attention, checking for a frequent casting fault that made the central exhaust port too small. When work started on the 750 racers, Barrett had the task of fitting their shrunk-in austenitic valve seats.

'Heads were heated in the oven and seats popped in with a mandrel. I knew that job well, as I had done it at Velocette,' he recalled. He also reamed the racers' phosphor-bronze valve guides when warm to obtain a combination of minimal clearance and accuracy: 'The valves on a lot of standard bikes tended to be recessed in the head, but on racers we made sure the heads protruded slightly into the combustion chamber to get more flow at small openings.'

One of Barrett's amusing recollections gives insight into how little was known about the racers in some quarters of the production shop floor. 'I was visiting Small Heath to collect parts just after Daytona in 1971. One of the BSA blokes said to me: "So *we* won, then". He just would not believe that Dick Mann's BSA had been done at Meriden.'

After a stint at Norton Villiers International's development centre at Kitts Green, Barrett joined Devimead to work on needle-roller bottom-end conversions and 750cc kits for BSA twins. But he continued to work on triples, latterly preparing machines for Pete Elmore and David Mead to ride in historic competition.

*Ron Barrett in 1996.*

on it.' That machine, along with UUE15G, had been used since 1969, when the Tridents were aquamarine. They acquired Fontana 250mm front brakes, some of which came off North-framed racers, and tanks were changed to keep pace with standard trim alterations. In its final form, UUE14G had twin discs at the front.

A Manx group put in a bid for the Marshals' Tridents when they were sold by NVT in 1975, but the successful buyer was London Triumph dealer Bill Slocombe. He loaned them for marshalling, but from 1977, Honda supplied official machines, and have done since. Killip said he once had to call Ron in to carry out strictly unofficial rectification on a Honda CBX 1000, which handled badly 'straight out of the crate'.

In 1971 Mike Nicks road tested UUE14G for *Motor Cycle News*. He was, in his own words, besotted with the well-sorted Trident borrowed to ride on the Isle of Man and on the mainland. He loved its 120mph-in-third capability, the absence of vibration, and the sound of the crisply tuned engine. He wrote, 'most Superbikes … are built for some mythical American, who, we are led to believe, cruises Main St at 40mph all day. They have high 'bars, and footrests and stands that scrape the tarmac.'

Nicks suggested, justifiably, that if BSA would only make triples like the Barrett specials for sale, Britain would soon reign supreme in the escalating Superbikes war.

## DEALER TEAMS AND PRIVATEERS

Roadster triples were being prepared for road racing by dealer teams well before the official factory campaign with 750s got off the ground.

*Four Tridents and a Norton Commando lent by new owner Slocombes of Neasden in 1976, photographed at the TT start area. Marshals are, from left, Des Evans, Albert Moule, George Short, Jack Harding and Alan Killip. Ron Barrett stands behind.*

Pre-launch machines had been supplied to a small number of UK BSA and Triumph agents for evaluation, and at least two of these triples purchased from the factory were soon converted into production class racers.

One was a Trident owned by Hughes, a dealer with shops in Wallington, Surrey and Tooting, South London. Proprietor Stan Brand enjoyed a good relationship with Meriden, and had in the past been able to obtain Thruxton Bonnevilles, factory-modified production class twins made in small batches.

Immediately after the UK release of 750 triples, a Hughes Trident competed in the Thruxton 500-mile race in May of 1969, ridden to seventh place overall by Rex Avery and Colin Dixon. Hughes claimed in advertising that it was the first triple on UK race tracks, saying it was 'straight out of the showroom'. Martin Carney rode the lone triple in that year's 750cc production TT, taking the Hughes T150 with a standard front brake into seventh place at 93mph (150km/h).

The first race win by a Trident in the UK was notched by another Hughes rider, Ray Knight, in a production class race at a Southern 67 Club Thruxton meeting in June 1969. His victory was in doubt because of controversy over the T150's factory-approved fairing, which had a headlamp unit behind the front racing number, but no transparent panel for it to shine through. In the end the win was allowed. Knight later rode his own high-framed Trident for four seasons.

## Boyer of Bromley

Another dealer to plunge into sport early with a T150 racer was Boyer of Bromley in Kent's London suburbs. Through the late sixties, proprietor Stan Shenton had sponsored two riders, Peter Butler and David Nixon, on Triumph twins, mainly in produc-

*Boyer team rider Peter Butler on the Boyer Trident in open-class form, with Fontana front brake and straight-through three-into-one exhaust system.*

tion racing and with outstanding success at club and national level. Their engines were tuned under the auspices of Bob Gayler, owner of the Ashford company Piper Cams. Nixon was also a proficient precision engineer, employed as Piper's workshop foreman.

Boyer marketed an electronic ignition conversion devised by Ernie Bransden, a college lecturer who had met Shenton at Piper. After much persuasion, the Triumph factory sanctioned it as legal for ACU production racing, although Meriden's own machines never raced with Boyer electronic ignition.

Shenton found it unsatisfactory that it was ultimately the manufacturers who deemed which parts were homologated. Shenton had been in the loop where Thruxton Bonnevilles and T120 tuning parts from Triumph were concerned, and the Boyer Team had beaten the factory riders in winning the Southampton Club's 500-mile race in 1968, when it had been run at Brands Hatch. To add insult to injury, Butler and Nixon were riding a 500cc Daytona twin against works Bonnevilles. 'They liked to see us taking part, but they always seemed a bit wary of us,' is how Shenton described his relationship with the factory after that.

Boyer received a pre-launch UK Trident. Shenton told the author:

> Samples went out to several dealers for mileage testing, with a schedule to cover so many thousands of miles a month. The problem with factory testers was that they were such good motorcyclists that if a bike got out of hand they would deal with it without thinking. They could miss things that ordinary owners might have a problem with.

Shenton personally covered high mileages on the T150 allotted to Boyer, and following the trials, it was decided to race-prepare the machine.

'Our 650 twins were beginning to lose out to the 750 Norton Commandos entered by my friend and racing rival Vincent Davey at Gus Kuhn Motors. The ACU had not homologated 750 conversions for Triumph twins,' Shenton explained.

The Trident took to the circuits in 1969 in near-standard form, but with electronic ignition. For the following season Shenton had the machine modified to take full advantage of homologation rules. A 250mm Fontana front brake and a five-gallon tank were fitted. Shenton told the author:

> My background was in insurance at Lloyds, so I was used to interpreting the wording of policies. Some parts of the ACU production rules were quite lax. For example, they said that original standard parts could be modified to 'suit riders' preferences'. That was meant to apply to things like handlebars, but we used the rule to grind the base circles off the standard cams and increase their lift. When people said that was cheating, we replied that our riders preferred them that way!

On its debut, the modified machine won the first round of a Shell-sponsored national production series at Snetterton in March 1970, ridden by Nixon, and went on to scoop the series. At the 1970 Thruxton 500-mile race the Butler/Nixon Boyer T150 was leading the field when it retired with a blown cylinder head gasket after two and a half hours.

When grand prix ace Phil Read told the press he was eager to ride a BSA or Triumph triple in the 1970 production TT, Shenton offered him the Trident. Read declined, complaining that the prize money for the race was very poor. He had a point: first prize in each production TT class was a paltry £50.

The Boyer team also fielded a standard-framed Trident with a three-into-one straight through exhaust system in open class 1,000cc and Superbike races. Unable to wrest North frames from BSA/Triumph, Shenton turned to Belvedere, Kent, constructor Colin Seeley to provide a full-race chassis. For the first version, it was made so that the engine could be removed and refitted readily, but the resulting chassis was too high.

With the accessibility stipulation waived, a Mk II version with lowered frame tubes made the Boyer Triumph F750 racer extremely compact. Dunstall disc brakes, with calipers cast integrally in the lower sliders, were fitted at the front, with a single disc at the rear.

Engine tuning, as on the Boyer Bonnevilles, was monitored on a dynamometer at Bromley College of Technology, where Bransden taught. Gayler was a keen exponent of gas-flowing who disagreed with Meriden's porting theories.

Crankshafts in Boyer triples were not lightened, but Nixon executed an oilway modification on them. Using a long, small-diameter drill bit, he bored additional oil passages to join up all of the crank's internal oilways so that oil from both centre mains

*Boyer team chief Stan Shenton with his 1972
F750 racer. Dunstall disc front brakes have
calipers cast integrally with the fork sliders.*

was pumped to all three big ends. Boyer
triples were modified in this way following
the lubrication troubles that had affected
both factory and Boyer engines at the 1971
Brands Hatch Anglo-US match meeting.
The modification is often made as a safety
precaution on latter-day historic racing
triples but was not featured on the works
racers, although they did have enlarged
main oilways in the left crankcase casting.

Seeley-framed Boyer Triumphs were
highly competitive in 1972 and 1973, and
like the Boyer production mounts they were
often close behind, and occasionally in front
of, factory machines.

'They were good. In fact, they must have
been too good, because the factory changed
its mind and said we could have North
frames after all,' Shenton joked about his
Tridents. Nixon had the distinction of winning the final event in the last race meeting

ever held at London's Crystal Palace circuit
on one in August 1972.

For production racing, Shenton obtained
short frames, although he says they were not
freely offered at first. 'In the end it was a
matter of them giving it to us to keep quiet
about the things we knew they were doing!'
says Shenton, who alleged that he once prod-
ded engine plates on a factory production
machine with a screwdriver to prove that
they were lightweight alloy painted black,
instead of standard steel items. Squish pistons were also prised from the factory, along
with unmachined cylinder head castings,
which could be modified to match them. Also,
when Shenton compiled an informative book
on tuning Triumph twins and triples, the factory helped with the project.

At the time of the Meriden closure, Shenton stepped in to take over rights to the
North chassis. 'I thought it was a super concept and I'd heard that Rob North wanted to
raise funds to set up in America. We bought
his stuff, including patterns for his alloy
wheels which we never used.'

Shenton aimed to adapt the North frame
to other Superbike engines and displayed a
chassis containing a Honda four engine at the
UK's winter Road Racing Show. But he was
not convinced of the package's merits and the
North Honda chassis was sold to racer Julian
Soper in 1974 and ridden on short circuits
with a 900cc engine, sponsored by Hadleigh
Custom, Soper's employer and a retailer of
Trident big-bore racing cylinder barrels.

When Boyer took over running the official
UK Kawasaki race team, initially with H2R
750 triples in 1974, the frames project was
sold in its entirety to Norman Miles, the
engineer who made components for the
Boyer Bransden electronic ignition kits.

Production Tridents, now with Dunstall
discs and, according to Shenton, sometimes
with squish heads, continued to be sponsored by Boyer. In the 1973 production TT,
Cheshire star John Williams, whom Les

*Busy scene at the Boyer workshops as machines are built following the acquisition of rights and jigs from Rob North late in 1973. Mechanics are former England speedway captain Lou Lancaster (left) and Vic Lane.*

*The North-framed Honda built by Boyer and later raced by Julian Soper, photographed as it was in 1996. This machine still competes in historic racing today.*

Williams had planned to put aboard Slippery Sam, rode a Fontana-braked Boyer T150. Not accustomed to kickstarting, he lost time on the first lap, but finished only 30 seconds behind Jefferies on the ex-works Trident, while Nixon brought the second Boyer triple home third. Butler had retired from the team that year. The Seeley-framed machine was ridden to eighteenth in the Imola 200 Formula 750 race in 1973.

In the 1974 1,000cc production TT, Nixon crashed his Trident at Laurel Bank and was killed. This so upset Shenton that he wanted to withdraw from road racing, but he was persuaded to persevere with the Kawasaki team, a very successful venture.

Dave Croxford's winning ride in the 1971 Thruxton 500-miler on a factory T150 prompted him to have a triple-powered machine built for himself. A chassis commissioned from Seeley was installed with a Rocket 3 engine for open-class 750–1,000cc racing in 1972. Croxford told the author it was reliable to the point where he took it for granted, resulting in a broken primary chain, but only after a hard season of successes.

## Other Dealers and Riders

Elite Motors sponsored rider Gary Green on a triple in endurance racing. The South London shop sold large numbers of Triumph roadsters and therefore was in a position to obtain highly sought-after factory parts, usually issued on the authority of the general sales department, rather than the racing shop.

Another prominent dealer team campaigning triples was A Bennett & Son, a Triumph specialist in Nuneaton and later Atherstone, Warwickshire. Bennett's main rider was Daryl Pendlebury, employed at Meriden as a production machine tester until the 1973 closure. He had been a front runner on production Bonnevilles, switching to Bennett triples in 1970. Despite his obvious talent, Pendlebury was never offered works machines to race. He told the author:

I would spend the whole of my dinner hour in Experimental pestering Les Williams for parts, but they were difficult to get. Especially cams, because they were expensive. If anyone was in a position to get them I was, and I couldn't. By the time we had got the Bennett North triple sorted, it was obsolete.

Bennett & Son did get two short Meriden frames for production Tridents, and the shop built two racers with frames obtained from Rob North, independently of the factory. Cams were specially made for the engines, based on American profiles. Other Bennett riders were Ernie Pitt, fifth in the 1973 production TT ahead of Pendlebury, and Steve Trasler, who later found fame beating Japanese fours on a Bonneville T140 in the *Bike* Magazine/Avon Production series.

Alistair 'Jock' Copland, employed as a tester at Meriden, raced non-works triples in the seventies, having already become an experienced campaigner on Manx Nortons. Hertfordshire rider Ken Buckmaster, who had been very friendly with Frank Baker, Doug Hele's predecessor in Meriden's Experimental Department, had teamed up with Hugh Robertson to ride a high-framed T150 in European endurance events. Its engine was prepared by Doug Cashmore, a Triumph employee. Copland shared the machine with Buckmaster to come fifteenth in the 1972 *Bol d'Or*, and with John Jackson to finish fourteenth in the following year's event. Copland bought one of North's last UK-built frames and built up a machine which he raced until he switched to Hondas in the late seventies.

Unable to find an ex-works machine, professional racer Ron Chandler had Arthur Jakeman build him a North-framed racer for 1973. Londoner Chandler won a two-leg 200-mile (320km) F750 race in Rouen, France on it in that year. Chandler had in fact nearly made it as a factory rider, being Triumph's reserve for the 1970 *Bol d'Or*.

Triumph 650cc twins had been a popular choice of engine for sidecar racing on British circuits, so it was no surprise that 750 Tridents were seized on by 'charioteers' for their power and torque. Although international grand prix sidecars were restricted to 500cc capacity, most UK national events allowed bigger engines. In 1968, a 750cc sidecar class was added to the traditional 500cc event in the Isle of Man TT programme, and British 750s were able to pit themselves against German competitors' ohc BMW Rennsport twins.

For two years in succession, 1971 and 1972, Essex rider-tuner Alan Sansum and his passenger Chris Emmins finished second to BMWs in the 750 event on their Quaife Trident, sponsored by RT Quaife Engineering, where Sansum was employed. A solo Quaife Triumph triple using Rickman Metisse cycle parts was also ridden on short circuits by seasoned racer Martyn Ashwood in 1972. During 1975, Emmins raced 'Super Sam', the ex-Pickrell machine with an 870cc engine fielded by Les Williams.

The ex-Heath 1970 factory production BSA was raced by Graham Saunders and then Pete Bates, an employee of West Midlands motorcycle component factory DMW/Metal Profiles. He finished thirteenth

## 1973 750cc production TT: best triples

The distance was 4 laps, 151.08 miles (243.09km).

| | | |
|---|---|---|
| Tony Jefferies | (T150) | 1st |
| John Williams | (T150) | 2nd |
| Dave Nixon | (T150) | 3rd |
| Ernie Pitt | (T150) | 5th |
| Daryl Pendlebury | (T150) | 6th |
| Roger Corbett | (T150) | 9th |
| Ken Huggett | (T150) | 10th |
| Alan Walsh | (T150) | 11th |
| David Jones | (T150) | 14th |

*At the Quaife Triumph équipe in 1972. Martyn Ashwood holds his Trident Metisse, Alan Sansum works on the front wheel of T150-powered sidecar outfit and Michael Quaife works in the background.*

*Three cylinders for three wheels. Alan Sansum and passenger Chris Emmins take the Quaife Triumph outfit though Parliament Square, Ramsey, in the 1972 750cc Sidecar TT.*

in the 1973 production TT, and shared the A75 with NVT employee Martin Russell in that year's European *Coupe d'Endurance* circus, sponsored by West London shop Reg Allen. The machine's best result was in the 24-hour race at Spa, Belgium, when the Rocket 3 was part of a non-factory BSA team that won the Princess Paola Cup manufacturer's trophy, along with a North-framed 750 ridden by an American/Belgian pairing, and a 500cc B50 Mead & Thompkinson single. Russell later raced his Rocket 3-powered Rustler BSA, which was fitted with his own frame featuring parallelogram rear suspen-

sion controlled by a single monoshock unit, and cast alloy wheels.

Overshadowed by Slippery Sam's success, the Welsh pairing of Selwyn Griffiths and David Williams finished third in the 1975 ten-lap production TT on a Trident.

## The Late 1970s

Triples hung on through the late seventies, being just competitive enough to figure in open-class Isle of Man racing and Continental endurance events. One of the most admired was the ex-Cooper BSA, owned by

# Rod Quaife – gearing up

Kentish engineer Rod Quaife's role in the triples story did not stop at providing the five-speed gearbox for racing and eventual production. Quaife's company made other special parts for the Meriden race team, sponsored its own riders on triples and developed after-market barrels for increasing cylinder capacity.

Toolmaker Rod Quaife had taken contract work making AJS, Matchless and Norton spares for the Associated Motor Cycles factory at Woolwich. This led to involvement with the AMC racing department, including the manufacture of transmission parts.

In 1966, Quaife responded to suggestions that there was a need for five-speed gearboxes to fit British racing singles. A cluster marketed by former Norton racer Harold Daniell had been briefly available a few years earlier, but manufacturing errors killed that project.

'We taught ourselves gear cutting,' Quaife told the author.

The result was a complete gearbox based on the AMC type, and John Cooper proved its worth by finishing ninth in the 1967 Junior TT on a Manx Norton with Quaife's transmission. Triumph dealer Geoff Monty, who raced Monard specials, urged Quaife to produce internal conversions for Meriden twins. Quaife recalled:

> When I started selling a five-speed Triumph and BSA box, I got a call from one of the top people in America, Pete Colman. He was really keen on the idea of five-speeds, and said he'd fix me an appointment at Meriden. That didn't go very well – they made me feel very small. Then I literally bumped into Bert Hopwood, and he had my cluster installed in a bike there and then for Percy Tait to test.

His cluster was adopted for factory racing 500s, 650s and ultimately the 750cc triples. Although Tait was brought off his 500 by a gearbox problem in practice for the 1969 TT, snags were overcome. In September 1970, BSA-Triumph bought the rights to use Quaife's five-speed design in production models, although RT Quaife Engineering Co. was still free to make and sell its own racing boxes.

'I think I got £5,000,' Quaife recalled. However, he became friendly with the Experimental Department staff, and rarely left Meriden without used Trident racing parts for his sponsored riders. Quaife attended Daytona in 1971 as a consultant, and worked so closely with the factory that a generous retainer fee was once suggested, but never received.

An A75/T150 cylinder barrel to accept oversize pistons was developed and collaboration with Norman Hyde in Meriden's design department saw work start on an intriguing project, the QH 500 racing engine. This was a short-stroke triple, with a horizontally split crankcase, on which a Quaife barrel and Trident head would be fitted. Eventually it was envisaged that a dohc head could be designed for it. A set of crankcase castings and a crankshaft were made by Quaife before the project was abandoned so that the company could concentrate on money-earning work. Drawings for the project, dated late in 1970, survive.

With the decline of the British motorcycle industry, Quaife also made close-ratio gears for popular Japanese machines and sponsored his son Michael on Yamahas. Then the company concentrated on car transmissions, RT Quaife's main business today. However, the factory near Sevenoaks in Kent still makes batches of motorcycle racing gearboxes, including five-speed clusters for triples. Used for Slippery Sam's last wins, the Quaife Mk II Triumph five-speeder conversion is stronger than the original.

'The Mk I Triumph box had a limited life in racing conditions. It did fail sometimes, and I got very upset if riders were hurt as a result,' Quaife told the author.

*Rod Quaife in 1996.*

David and Mike Hoskison, proprietors of Bee Bee Bros, a West Midlands-based scrap metals company and keen race entrants of privately owned machines. They had bought the machine in 1974.

Cooper's mechanic Steve Brown had played a part in the deal, and he continued to tend the 1971 works BSA for ten years. Other non-works North-framed BSA triples joined the équipe, including the ex-Ron Chandler machine, the ex-Gary Green and Dave Potter Triumph, and an ex-Alan Pacey bike.

Patriotic fans loved to see Bee Bee rider (and Bee Bee Bros truck driver during the week) Malcolm Lucas doing battle on Coop's old BSA. This was his TT record on Bee Bee triples:

1975 1,000cc
  5th, at 98.96mph (159.23km/h)   750 BSA
1976 1,000cc
  11th, 101.58mph (163.44km/h)   750 BSA
1977 1,000cc
  14th, 102.56mph (165.02km/h)   750 BSA
1978 Formula 1
  7th, 102.89mph (165.55km/h)    850 BSA

Bee Bee enlarged engines of some team machines to 830cc using exchange cylinder barrels from Hadleigh Custom. Bee Bee rider Alistair Frame carried on into the eighties with good TT placings and many short-circuit wins.

Lancashire enthusiast Phil Smithies acquired the machine Tony Jefferies had assembled with factory assistance for 1973, and it proved competitive in the Formula 1 TT ridden by Irishman Sammy McClements and Alex George, who was the fastest man round the Mountain Course on a British machine, until Norton Rotaries arrived in the late Eighties.

## European Events

On European tracks the 750cc Robertson Triple was a familiar sight at major long-distance races. Owned by Jock Robertson, Hugh Robertson's father, the machine's regular rider was Dutchman Jan Strijbis, easily identifiable at the time because he kept wearing a 'pudding basin' helmet even when full-face types were universal. In the early eighties, Roberston fielded a 980cc triple,

*Dutch rider Jan Strijbis aboard the Robertson Triple endurance racer. A small lamp to illuminate the front number plate at night is just visible above the front mudguard.*

*Stylish riding by Italian Renato Galtrucco on a Trident with Fontana front brake at Monza in 1970. He and co-rider Vanni Blegi finished second in a 500km (300 mile) race on the Triumph importer-entered T150.*

ridden in Europe by Bob Harrington and Bob Newby.

In Italy, the Milan-based Triumph importer launched a Trident racing team that was to benefit from factory assistance and become a semi-works team in the mid-seventies. Its first machine took second place in a 500km (310 mile) race at Monza in 1970, ridden by Vanni Blegi and Renato Galtrucco. It had led the field until running low on fuel in the closing laps. The pairing went on to win the event in the following year, when they also finished nineteenth in the *Bol d'Or* in France.

By 1972 the Italian Triumph concession had been taken over by Bepi Koelliker, who also sold Daimler and Jaguar cars in Milan. A wealthy and influential man, he often visited Meriden when on business in England. An official racing department was set up by Koelliker, with *Ingegnere* Rovelli as Senior Technician and Domenico Pettinari as Manager. Help received from Meriden included

supply of the first-built Triumph factory production machine, high-clearance T150 frames and sets of drawings. Pettinari told the author that he organized the construction of three North-pattern frames in Italy, and that the équipe produced its own racing cams for the triples, which proved very effective. Koelliker cams and pistons, developed by Rovelli with advice from Norman Hyde, actually gained factory approval.

Galtrucco and co-rider Giovanni Provenzano looked likely winners of the 1972 *Bol d'Or* at Le Mans until valve gear troubles slowed their North-framed Triumph. Walter Villa, who was to win two world 250cc titles for Harley-Davidson in 1974 and 1975, was teamed with Gianpiero Zubani on another Italian Triumph, but the fancied pair were set back by a first lap puncture and then gearbox trouble.

Other Koelliker Triumph team riders were Buscherini, Plinio Passetti, and Franco Bonera, the ex-cycling champion who went

*Dave Nixon on a Boyer Trident (58) up against Swiss Honda rider Gilbert Argo in the 1973 Imola 200-mile (320km) race.*

*Rusty Bradley on a Big D Trident road racer in 1970. Modifications include alloy fuel tank, racing seat and double-sided drum front brake.*

on to join the MV Agusta grand prix team for 1974. The team raced in F750 and endurance races at Italian circuits with considerable success, and factory mechanics, including Arthur Jakeman, were 'lent' to the équipe on occasion.

## Stateside Triples

In America, the most prolific triples dealer entrant was a Triumph specialist, Big D Cycle of Dallas Texas. The shop set about preparing Tridents soon after they arrived in the United States in an effort to encourage sales, relying on the expertise of resident Triumph wizard Jack Wilson. His credentials were second to none, for he was the tuner of the engine of Johnny Allen's 214mph (344km/h) 650cc Bonneville record breaker of 1956, and of countless other racing and record-breaking Triumphs. Big D's best known riders were Rusty Bradley, Virgil Davenport and Jon Minnono, who rode street and open-class Tridents in races in the western US, and had an early success when he teamed up with Davenport to win a 12-hour race sports road machines at Riverside, Cali-

fornia in 1969. Illinois-based Team C & D were victorious with a Trident in a 24-hour endurance race at Nelson Ledges, Ohio, in 1970. Jim Cotherman, a proprietor of C & D, who later claimed a works racer and received one in 1972 was one of the riding team.

Tuner and record breaker Don Vesco built a 750cc Triumph Metisse for sponsored rider Jerry Howerton to compete on in the 1970 Amateur race at Daytona in 1970. Vesco tuned the 350cc Yamaha on which Kel Carruthers threatened works triples in 1971, and which finished second to John Cooper at Ontario in that year.

After the 1974 season, when hard times had spread to the US-based works race shop, some hardware could be bought by those who turned up with ready cash. One was Minnesota BSA and Triumph dealer Mitch Klempf. Frustrated that he could not do a deal on the telephone, he drove a van 2,000 miles to Southern California.

'I knocked on the door, went in and did a deal. We bought boxes and boxes of stuff,' Klempf told the author. All the team machines he saw were dismantled, but he gathered together parts with a view to

## The RGM alternative

In 1972, Luton, Bedfordshire, specialist racing parts shop RGM marketed its own version of the triple, with a BSA or Triumph engine installed in a Metisse chassis made by Rickman Bros. John Judge, the proprietor of RGM, had previously produced sidecar racing chassis and was a distributor for Rickman products.

'I had an agreement with Rickman that if I did all the ground work on the project, they would make frames and I would have sole rights to sell them,' Judge told the author.

He estimates that he sold between thirty and fifty Rickman triples, either as complete machines, or basic frame kits. Although closely based on Rickman's nickel-plated frame in Reynolds 531 tube made for the Triumph 650 twin, the chassis was adapted for triples, mainly by having the bottom rails more widely spaced. Judge got most of his new engines from London dealer Hughes.

'The upright Triumph fitted easier, so we tended to discourage customers from having BSAs,' Judge recalled. Machines were sold in road and track form, with alloy fuel tanks made by Don Woodward, RGM's works-based exhaust system and fairings. AP Lockheed disc brake systems were used, the front 10in item being mounted on the sturdy Metisse front fork with 38mm stanchions. Weight of a kit, minus engine, was claimed to be 192lb (86.5kg), and the machine's wheelbase was 56in (1,422mm).

RGM triples were available for several years, and sold all over the world.

*Stock-framed Trident with high-level three-into-one exhaust being run minus its fairing during the 1970 Daytona meeting.*

*RGM's first Rickman Trident in track trim, supplied to UK road racer Tony Smith.*

assembling a complete lowboy machine, which included a fairing with Gary Scott's name on it, a seat marked Burritto, Gene Romero's nickname, and alloy disc rotors. Klempf raced the Triumph through the seventies, winning several Central Road Racing Association class championships.

The triple's success as a privateer's racer wasn't confined to Europe and North America: a 750cc Triumph Trident ridden by Trevor Discombe won New Zealand's production machine TT road race at Auckland in 1971.

# 8 Keeping the Faith

## TRIPLES TODAY

Those who rode, worked on, or just loved the triples were not going to let the story end just because production had terminated. A core of dedicated people have stuck fast with the Rocket 3 and Trident, ensuring that machines are kept running reliably and safely with full spares availability. Several specialist businesses grew up to cater for triple owners, some being run by, or employing, former factory staff.

### Mr Hyde's World of Triples

There can be few people with an interest in British motorcycles who have not heard of Norman Hyde. The former Triumph development engineer set up his business on Heathcote Industrial Estate near Warwick in 1976, and now presides over a worldwide empire, with appointed dealers in Australia, Canada, Germany, Holland, New Zealand and the USA.

Although Hyde also specializes in Triumph and Norton twins, his name has always been mainly associated with the triples with which he was deeply involved in his factory days. A key member of Doug Hele's experimental design staff, Hyde first became known to the motorcycling world through his exploits on Trident-powered dragsters and record-breaking projectiles. His machines used enlarged engines, and kits for increasing the triple's capacity are among the best-known Norman Hyde branded products.

Big-bore kits convert 750cc engines to either 850cc or 1,000cc for boosting power and torque. The 850 conversion incorporates a replacement barrel with 71mm bores, which accept standard-size Triumph Bonneville 8.25:1 pistons. A full 1,000cc is obtained by combining the big-bore barrel with a crankshaft modified by welding to lengthen the stroke from 70mm to 82mm. Heavy duty con rods are also supplied. Hyde's special cylinder barrels were developed out of his collaboration with Rod Quaife in the early seventies, when Quaife produced the first block specifically intended for oversize bores. The original pattern of Quaife barrel was also envisaged as part of the QH500 short-stroke triple project started by the two engineers in 1970 (see page 186).

High compression 10.5:1 kits are available for racing, and cylinder heads are tuned

*Kitted 1,000cc T160 engine with Hyde cylinder barrel, head, rocker box and clutch covers visible.*

*Hyde Harrier in racing form. A tuned T150 engine, bored and stroked to 1,000cc, is installed in a Harris tubular frame with Marzocchi front fork and disc brakes all round. Customers can select parts to build road or track versions with a variety of specifications.*

# Norman Hyde – high speed designer

After taking A-levels at Warwick School, Norman Hyde joined Avery, the weighing machine manufacturer, as an apprentice in 1964. After a year there, he switched to a three-year sandwich course with industrial experience gained by working in various departments at Triumph Enginering. 'As soon as my course was finished, I asked to be placed in Experimental,' he told the author.

As part of Hele's design team, Hyde was closely involved in design work on the racing triples, and then the development of the T160 roadster. During the period of the NVT development facility at Kitts Green, he participated in the T180 project as well as the Norton-based Trisolastic triple with rubber mounted engine.

Some records set by Hyde with his supercharged 830cc Trident 'Road Runner' sidecar outfit still stand, thanks to class rule changes made since by the governing body, the FIM.

Using a full fairing made for him from aluminium alloy by Don Woodward, Hyde ran the triple outfit at the RAF Fairford air base in September 1972, to set a world flying-start one kilometre record for 1,000cc sidecars at 260.39km/h (161.799mph). In the same session, he also set a world figure for the standing-start kilometre at 169.130km/h (105.093mph). In the previous year, he had taken 750cc sidecar records, including a flying kilometre at 242.751km/h (150.838mph).

Hyde had started his straight-line career with a Triumph Tiger Cub single, and then moved on to twins. His first Trident dragster was a supercharged five-speed 750 running on methanol with nitromethane. Larger bores made it an 830, and then a 1,000cc engine was built using a long-throw crank.

After his 1972 successes, Hyde received sponsorship from Triumph in the form of engines to build a double-engined machine. It was conditional, however, on them remaining at the standard 750 size. Shell also provided funds, but its condition was that normal carburation be used. 'The set-up was like two works racing engines with six Amal GPs and two three-into-one pipes, but it never worked like it should,' Hyde told the author.

Before redundancy forced Hyde to curtail his straight-line activities to start a business, he built his ultimate Trident dragster with two blown 1,000cc T150 units and a two-speed Laycock transmission driven by the train of gears linking the engines. Called Dr Jekyll, this machine carried the top-hatted Dr Jekyll image used as the Norman Hyde logo ever since.

in line with factory racing practice. Other Hyde products include half-race and full-race cams, heavy-duty sintered iron clutch friction plates and belt primary drive conversions. Cycle parts include twin disc and 12in disc front brake conversions.

Hyde's first shot at marketing a complete updated triple was his 1,000cc Missile of 1983. But the much more handsome Hyde Harrier, first made in 1987, made a greater impression, backed up by race track successes. The author was the first journalist to ride a 1,000cc Harrier roadster early in 1988, and he found the torque of the big engine and the taut roadholding of the chassis a brilliant combination.

Aiming to offer road riders the equivalent of a Rob North-type Trident, Hyde commissioned a tubular chassis on similar lines from leading British frame maker Harris, and designed tanks, seat and a half fairing with twin headlamps. Customers can now buy a basic frame kit, or a full chassis kit with modern forks, brakes and tyres, to install their own power unit.

Hyde bought Toga, the Birmingham based manufacturer of exhaust systems and silencers to original patterns, in the early nineties. Toga produces a replica of the Rocket 3 and Trident ray gun silencer, as well as the later megaphone, cigar and 'black cap' types originally fitted to triples.

## The Spirit of Sam

Tucked away on a small industrial estate in Kenilworth, triples specialist company LP Williams is known throughout the world. The business was started by ex-factory man Les Williams in 1976, a year after his job at Kitts Green ceased to exist.

Williams' name was already familiar to triple fans because of the exploits of Slippery Sam (*see* Chapter 7). As well as buying Sam from NVT, Williams acquired most of the race shop hardware after various works

*Trident T160-based Slippery Sam replica built by Les Williams for Nottinghamshire customer Steve Rothera.*

machines had been dispersed. The idea for a self-employed business venture had come from Mike Jackson, NVT's sales chief: why not build and sell Slippery Sam replicas? Williams set up a home workshop to do just that, and over the next few years, thirty-three road legal machines were assembled to race shop standard, and sold to eager buyers as Slippery Sam Replicas. He also built TT Marshals replicas, based on the much-admired Tridents supplied for official high-speed duties at the Isle of Man Tourist Trophy races. Raw materials for most of the machines were sourced from surplus T160 machines returned to the UK from Saudi Arabia.

Williams also launched a spares outlet to serve the many riders still using triples on the road, and moved to the Kenilworth premises. As the business expanded, staff were engaged, including former Meriden colleagues Arthur Jakeman and former Experimental Department man Harry Woolridge. Anyone looking for expert repairs or a full rebuild saw LP Williams as a repository of triples lore, and business flooded in.

In 1984, Williams announced an exciting new project. He had designed an updated 750 based on the T160, following his idea of what the Trident would be if it had still been in production.

The Legend, as he named it, was originally intended to be assembled at the rate of ten a year, but orders poured in and the target was easily exceeded. More than fifty Legends were made by Williams for customers around the world between 1984 and 1992.

Using the T160 chassis and power unit, the Legend was sleekly styled, with a look not unlike the Italian Laverda triples of the time. Mike Ofield, who had carried out styling work for NVT in the past, helped create the restrained good looks. With flatter handlebars than the T160, the Legend also had its footrests shifted slightly rearwards, for comfortable high speed cruising. Using late Meriden Bonneville front fork components, the front end sported twin discs, with a single rotor at the rear. Legends were built with both spoked and cast wheels.

Although kept in basically standard tune, the engine received some factory-style head tweaking, and ignition points were dumped in favour of maintenance-free electronic ignition.

In the first press test, *Classic Bike's* Richard Simpson praised the Legend's classy looks and quality finish and commented on the light clutch action, and handling that inspired confidence. Critical of high fuel consumption and some tingly vibration at around 5,000rpm, he nevertheless rated the machine as excellent value for money and a worthy competitor for new products of the time. The earliest Legends were bargains at less than £3,000 to overseas customers, but prices inevitably had to rise. Assembly of Legends slowed in the early nineties, mainly because donor machines were getting more difficult to find, and replacement

*Classic for the connoisseur: a 750cc Triumph Legend by LP Williams.*

Renold duplex primary chains for the T160 had become unobtainable.

In 1992, Williams retired from full-time business and sold LP Williams to one of his customers, computer systems specialist Trevor Gleadall. Using his background to streamline stock-taking and ordering procedures, Gleadall has consolidated on the company's success and he has even produced more Legends, using a double-row primary chain conversion marketed by Norman Hyde. Other blends of chassis components can be used to create the Renegade, a restyled T160 with Italian Grimeca drum brakes, and one customer commissioned a version he named the Tornado, based on a Rocket 3 'donor' bike. Customers ordering special editions are now expected to provide the donor machine to be converted.

Gleadall is working towards full parts availability for all triples, including the manufacture of replicated parts if it makes commercial sense. However, understanding that the market is of limited size, he avoids replicating good-quality products available from other sources. Rebuilds to standard specification for road machines is the company's specialist area.

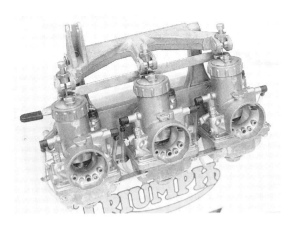

*The LP Williams Mikuni carburettor conversion. Customers provide an existing mounting beam for modification.*

Gleadall has introduced a Mikuni carburettor conversion, substituting a trio of the dependable Japanese instruments for the rapidly wearing Amal instruments. Coded VM26, the Mikunis have chokes opened out to 28.5mm on the engine side. The kit retains a modified version of the throttle operating beam.

Components used for Legend and Renegade conversions are also available separately, including German Magura handlebar controls and switchgear, Grimeca disc brake equipment, and shapely alloy fuel tanks made by Don Woodward.

## Preserving Prototypes

Bill Crosby, proprietor of West London Triumph shop Reg Allen, and one-time sponsor of an ex-works Rocket 3 in endurance racing, has restored two historic triple prototypes. He rebuilt one of at least two experimental overhead cam engines known to have survived, and installed it in a Rocket 3 chassis, as was done with Meriden's original road test version. Crosby also designed a new camshaft for a high-performance version he

was building into a Swiss Egli frame at the time of writing.

An even more ambitious project was undertaken by Crosby for the Trident & Rocket 3 Owners Club, after it bought the remains of a Meriden P1 protoptype engine in 1994. Allen has organized rebuilding of the power unit and installation in a 1965 Bonneville chassis, most of the work being done by Dave Whitfield. Although the geared primary drive components have been lost, the club succeeded in creating a rideable machine around the long-stroke unit.

## Performing a Service

John Anderson of Performance Motorcycles, formerly of Birmingham and later in rural Shropshire, has been a staunch triples specialist. He has been able to call on advice and services from factory man Ron Barrett and has produced latter-day replicas of TT Marshals machines for customers.

## Laurie, Scottish Showman

Alistair Laurie's lightweight roadgoing custom Trident special pulled crowds wherever it was parked at Isle of Man festivals in the mid-seventies. Scotsman Laurie built it around an engine that had been used by road racer Barry Scully. Because Scully had received unofficial factory help, the unit included a 1971 lightweight clutch. Laurie built a machine claimed to weigh only 300lb (135kg), using a North-style chassis made from Renold 531 tube, Foale alloy wheels and a Seeley front fork. The engine was enlarged to 870cc, and Laurie entered the 150mph (240km/h) machine in sprints and road races.

## RIDING A CLASSIC TRIPLE TODAY

BSA and Triumph triples are among the most usable of the classic British machines of the past. Their 120mph (193km/h) performance allows them to keep pace with modern traffic, and when properly assembled and thoughtfully maintained, they offer a high degree of reliability.

Understandably, buyers looking for an everyday mount usually look to the later T160 Trident model. Its advantages include disc braking all round and more modern electrical equipment, including direction indicators, which most all-weather riders see as an essential safety requirement.

Many owners like to keep well-preserved or restored classic machines in standard trim, and the availability of most parts for the triples, including original-pattern Dunlop TT100 tyres, makes this feasible. One change of specification forced on owners since the seventies, however, is petrol. The original triples were intended to run on leaded, premium grade fuel and it may be found necessary to vary slightly from the makers' carburettor settings for optimum performance on modern fuel.

Specialist triples restorers may also vary from other maker's settings in areas such as valve clearances in the light of their own experience.

Another desirable change, which is almost invisible, is the fitting of an after-market electronic ignition system. Its trigger unit mounts in the contact breaker cavity on the timing cover, necessitating a slightly bulkier cover over the points, but the main 'black box' control unit can be con-

*Waiting to go out on the track at the Cadwell Park Beezumph rally in 1995. The rider of machine 138 is Trident & Rocket 3 Owners Club archivist Richard Darby.*

# Trident & Rocket 3 Owners Club

Since being founded by Tim Smithells in 1978, the Trident and Rocket 3 Owners Club has developed into one of the UK's most energetic classic motorcycling organizations.

By 1996, the club had attracted more than a thousand members in Australia, Canada, mainland Europe, Iceland, New Zealand and the USA as well as in Britain. Since 1991, it has held a popular festival, the Beezumph Rally, at Lincolnshire's Cadwell Park racing circuit every year.

'The idea is a day to promote the use of any British motorcycles as well as for riding Tridents and Rocket 3s,' club Chairman and Beezumph organizer, Neil Payne, told the author in 1996.

The club purchased the remains of a Meriden P1 prototype engine in 1994, which has been rebuilt and reconstructed into a complete functioning motorcycle to display on the club's stand at classic motorcycle shows in Britain.

A bi-monthly publication, *Triple Echo,* is distributed to members and it often contains useful technical information and interesting triples history.

cealed. Better starting and an end to points adjustment are among the benefits.

The two main types are Boyer Bransden, descended from the type fitted on the original Boyer Team racing triples, and Lucas Rita. Boyer systems are compatible with the T160's six-volt coils if they are wired in series, but not the A75/T150's 12-volt coils, which should be changed. Rita (in short supply at the time of writing) can be bought ready tailored to either electrical system.

If deviation from standard appearance is not a problem, there are almost endless modifications that can be made for improved performance, reliability or safety. For example, changing the rear wheel's rim size from 19in to the more generally used 18in size will widen the choice of tyres that can be fitted, and the whole electrical system can be uprated by installing a high-output alternator.

## Modified for Mileage

An example of a classic triple mildly modified into a practical road machine for modern conditions is provided by the T160 of Tim Smithells. Proprietor of repair specialist Sussex Triples, he is a high-mileage rider, and founder of the Trident & Rocket 3 Owners Club. He had covered nearly 100,000 miles in all weathers on his own electric-start Trident in 1996.

Bought new in September 1976, his T160 is no show piece but practical alterations have made it ready for any journey.

For improved braking, he fitted twin front discs in the seventies, using a right-side fork slider. More recently the front brakes have been updated with Lockheed racing calipers and 9.5in disc rotors to suit them.

An 18in rear wheel carries an $18 \times 110$ Avon AM21 and the 19in front wheel carries a $19 \times 100/90$ tyre of the same make. 'The Avons give excellent handling. Even though I have raised anything that restricted cor-

nering clearance, it still scrapes down,' Smithells told the author. He likes the superlative grip of Avon's modern Super Venoms, but finds they wear with alarming speed.

Ray gun silencers, chosen to give better performance than the original T160 type, have been moved upwards in racer fashion, using linked adaptors between the pipes and silencers. A set of scruffy painted downpipes is used in winter months when corrosive salt lies on British roads, while a smart plated set is kept in storage. Smithells says he has found that some pattern-manufactured ray guns are of poor quality.

A pair of Fiamm horns mounted below the front direction indicators are highly visible, and purists have often remarked on their obtrusiveness. However, Smithells believes that horns must be loud and that they must face forward if they are to be effective warning devices in modern road conditions.

Also for safety, he fitted his headlamp with a Wipac 60/55watt quartz-halogen unit, and uprated the electrical system with a three-phase Lucas RM24 high-output alternator from Mistral Engineering. The T160 has been converted from points to electronic ignition, a change that the vast majority of triple owners will endorse. Once set accurately, the electronic system's spark should stay spot on without further attention. It also makes kick starting a sure-fire thing and increases the chance of firing up using the T160's starter motor, which is not very powerful. This machine runs on the Lucas Rita system.

A Mikuni carburettor conversion has been found to improve fuel economy with 50mpg (5l/100km) or better possible, although Smithells acknowledged that it is an expensive modification, costing about £350 in 1995. He found a minor drawback: when used from a dead cold start, the chokes have an 'all-or-nothing' action. With standard Amals, he advises his customers to expect

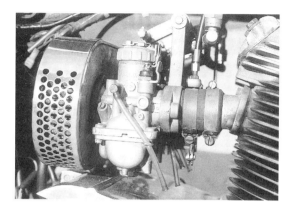

*Mikuni carburettors on Smithells' T160: expensive to buy, but more economical on fuel.*

40mpg (7l/100km) at best, and possibly below 35mpg (8l/100km) at worst.

A small addition considered by Smithells to be utterly essential is an engine oil pressure gauge. He likes to see 80–85psi indicated when cruising at 4,000rpm in mild weather, but acknowledges that engines built by the most reputable experts some-

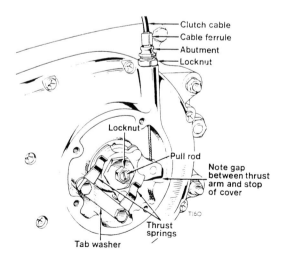

*Careful clutch adjustment and a high quality clutch cable are essential for reliable operation*

times run at 20psi less without coming to harm.

As with any motorcycle engine, regular oil changes are vital: a quick and simple tank-only draining at 1,500-mile (2,400km) intervals, and draining of the sump and changing of the cartridge filter every second change. Any quality 20–50 multigrade oil should be suitable, but proper warming-up of the engine before working it hard is strongly recommended. Smithells has found that that the triples' performance can lead owners to flog their engines unmercifully.

'A British twin will warn you by shaking itself to bits, but it is easy to wear out a triple by revving to 6,000rpm all the time,' he told the author, adding that he often sees

## Clean machine

Practicality and polish are combined in the 1973 Trident T150V restored for regular use by Tony Sanderson of Sheffield. He rebuilt the Triumph after it had been re-imported from America, fitting the home market fuel tank, the style of which he prefers to the export type.

The wheels have been rebuilt with modern Akront alloy rims using an 18in size at the rear, and fitted with Avon Roadrunner tyres. Double disc front brakes were added, using Grimeca calipers and a right-side slider supplied by LP Williams. Several Legend-style accessories from the same source have been fitted, including a two-piece handlebar carrying Magura controls and switchgear, and rear-set footrests.

Restoration of the engine, which had a holed crankcase, was carried out by former works technician Arthur Jakeman when he worked at LP Williams. Sanderson runs it on four-star fuel with shots of Redex upper cylinder lubricant.

'It cost me a lot of money, but I have no regrets,' Sanderson told the author.

*Left: Italian Grimeca brake calipers are readily available at reasonable cost.*

*Above: German Magura controls and switchgear on Legend-type handlebars.*

heavily worn big-end and main bearing shells inside customers' engines. Regular tappet clearance checks are advisable: on a standard engine the factory recommended settings are 0.006in on the inlet side and 0.008in on the exhaust side (cold).

There have been occasional piston shortages, although Hepolite make batches of standard items regularly. Some consumption of engine oil is inevitable with the triple engine, usually at the rate of 300–400 miles per pint (900–1,240km per litre).

The clutch cable must be of high quality and the operating mechanism should be well-adjusted. The gearbox needs only an annual oil change, and new selector return springs in the outer cover if their age is in doubt.

'Some classic British engines can be assembled clumsily and they will run. The triple isn't one of them. It cannot withstand an ignorant owner and the engine needs to be assembled by someone proficient,' Smithells warns.

## TEXAN TRIDENTS: BIGGER AND FASTER

Team Triumph Texas can boast the ultimate performance achievement by Triumph triple engines: a speed of 256.264mph (412.329km/h) officially recorded on Bonneville salt flats in 1992. It was set by a partially streamlined double-engined Trident prepared by TTT, a collaboration between Big D Cycle of Dallas and its proprietor, veteran tuner Jack Wilson, machine designer and constructor Ed Mabry, and crew chief David Wade.

Ridden by Jon Minnono, winner of many road races on Big D Tridents in the seventies, the twin-engined TTT machine was clocked at over 256mph (412km/h) over the last 132ft (40m) of a 3-mile (4.8km) run. A one-way speed of 250.63mph (403.33km/h) enabled the team to claim the Triumph as the world's fastest 'real' motorcycle, as all faster speeds at Bonneville were set by fully enclosed streamliners, with pilots seated

*Drive side of the turbocharged, fuel-injected TTT machine with fairings removed showing the fuel tank above the rear wheel. Trolley wheels are for ease of handling between runs.*

inside, rather than sitting astride the machine as Minonno did.

The six-cylinder Trident, with each engine bored and stroked to 1,028cc, ran in the 3,000cc capacity class on methanol fuel, pumped to the engine by a Hilborn fuel injector system. Power was further boosted by a single turbocharger. An estimated 400bhp was transmitted to the fat Goodyear rear tyre by a Harley-Davidson four-speed gearbox.

The machine had been developed from the earlier 1,740cc version with 870cc motors, which had its first Bonneville success in 1991, setting a 2,000cc class record at 221.51mph (356.41km/h). An earlier Team Triumph Texas triple with a single engine had set a record at 197mph (317km/h) in 1988.

## BACK ON TRACK – TRIPLES IN HISTORIC RACING

At the end of the seventies, a core of like-minded road racing enthusiasts decided to revive and race the best machines from the period before two-strokes dominated the sport at all levels. In Britain the movement was led by the Classic Racing Motorcycle Club, formed in 1979. In the years that followed, road racing for historic motorcycles became an explosive world-wide phenomenon. Machines and riders came out of retirement to join in, and specialists got busy manufacturing parts to keep them racing. Inevitably, parts supply reached the point where complete motorcycles could be replicated to period specifications, adding new

*Walsh racing at Three Sisters in 1993.*

machines to grids and attracting a new generation of riders.

For classic racing competitors aboard triples, the pressure may not have been as great as it was for the works BSA and Triumph riders of the early seventies, but competition was fierce and some great racing was the result. The noise was superb, too, but soon historic racers were brought into line with modern silencing standards, and the full-volume triple bellow was gone forever.

David and Mike Hoskison were among Britain's pioneers of classic racing, the Bee Bee équipe having never really faded away. But the most significant contribution to a three-cylinder racing revival came from Miles Engineering.

## Miles Ahead

Proprietor Norman Miles had been engaged to make components for Stan Shenton's Boyer team in the early seventies. Among other work, Miles manufactured trigger units for the Boyer ignition unit, a contract that was still keeping him busy in the mid-nineties.

When Shenton abandoned his plans for producing North chassis, he offered the ex-Rob North equipment to Miles, who bought it all. As well as frame-making jigs, the

## Alan Walsh – old faithful

The production Trident ridden by Alan Walsh in Classic Racing Motorcycle Club events is the machine he bought from London dealer Coburn & Hughes in 1970. It replaced an ageing Bonneville twin he had raced in production events. Walsh rode the Trident in several production and F750 TT races, his best result being sixth in the 1974 production race. Although the T150 was sold for £900 in the late seventies, he came across it again ten years later and bought it in dismantled condition for £1,100.

Still fitted with the high-clearance frame he obtained from the factory via Norman Hyde, the machine has been tuned for historic racing by sponsor Triple Cycles. Chassis modifications include post-1970 forks with modified internals and twin disc brakes. The rear wheel was changed from 19in size to 18in, for a wider tyre choice, and a Quaife/Triple Cycles five-speed gearbox is fitted.

'It is faster now than it was first time round, although this always was a good motor,' Walsh, a Lincolnshire-based service engineer, told the author. His T150 was timed through the TT speed trap at 133mph (214km/h) in the 1970s, and at 139mph (224km/h) in the 1995 Ulster GP 750cc Classic race, when Walsh finished second to Robert Holden's Miles-framed triple.

hardware included works exhaust pipe jigs and patterns for cast alloy wheel hubs once made by North.

It was taken to Miles Engineering's workshops in Twickenham, Middlesex. He then moved to neighbouring suburb Teddington, where series production of bare frames and complete ground-up replica racing triples commenced in 1977. Since then, more than 400 frames to the Rob North pattern have been made, showing how healthy the demand has been, especially for machines to be campaigned in historic racing.

At an early stage, Miles approached Dennis Poore of NVT in the hope of securing supplies of new T160 engines, but without success.

'He suggested I try Honda engines – I couldn't believe that,' Miles told the author. Demand for his products, to be built around existing power units, increased with the growth of interest in classic racing, and the shaky original tooling was put to one side and replaced with a more accurate set of jigs.

At times of peak demand in the late eighties, chassis were being made at the rate of fifty a year at Miles' factory. The frames are nickel-bronze brazed by Miles' skilled craftsman Mick Pearce, using lengths of T45 chrome-molybdenum tube. The sheet steel parts for fabricating brackets and swinging arm supports are now cut for Miles by an outside contractor, using an extremely precise laser technique.

Machines are built very closely to the 1971 works pattern, with 62-degree steering heads, but there are a few minor deviations from the original. A curved seat-stop tube on the rear subframe, which was moveable on factory bikes to tailor machines to individual riders, is now fixed. Most of today's racers like to sit well forward. For this reason

Miles has also slightly raised the screen-supporting 'ears' on his factory-pattern fairings, allowing riders to get close to the screen.

To suit the wide rear tyres now in use, machines are built with offset gearbox sprockets to move the chain line clear of the rear wheel. The Miles chassis are stamped with a serial number on the left swinging arm gusset, with the letters ME and a five-digit number.

Norman fondly calls his own BSA racer 'The Old Girl'. Built in 1981, she has been raced to numerous wins by John Cowie, Glen English (nephew of former Ogle designer Jim English) Hartley Kerner, and – over nine seasons – Tony Osborne.

As with many triples competing in historic racing, an engine bored to give an approximate capacity of 830cc is used in the 1,000cc or unlimited capacity classes. Miles uses a standard barrel casting, American Arias 11:1 pistons, Amal Concentric carburettors with choke bores opened to 33mm, and the Quaife Mk II-based five-speed gearbox marketed by Triple Cycles. In recent years, the outlet pipe of the Miles exhaust collector box has been enlarged from 1.5 to 2in.

'I can't remember how many races the Old Girl has won. But I've had a lot of enjoyment out of these things,' Miles told the author.

## Power from Peckett

Richard Peckett told the author:

> I first heard the noise of factory racing triples as I walked out of Crystal Palace railway station, on my way to a race meeting there in 1970. I made up my mind then to build something that sounded like that.

In those days, west Londoner Peckett was racing a Triumph/Norton hybrid twin, but he took to the track on his own Triumph

*Miles Engineering chassis prior to being painted.*

*Richard Peckett in his workshops in 1996.*

triple in 1972. Peckett's own chassis for it was built at Dresda Autos, where he worked for racer and constructor Dave Degens; Peckett's second chassis was built on his own jig. Resembling a North frame in the swinging-arm support area, it had the more traditional crossed-over tubing at the steering head.

Unable to get tuning parts from the factory, Peckett developed his own engine. Base circles were ground off the cams, a crankshaft was strengthened by Tuftriding and he made his own three-into-one exhaust system. In 1974 a useful boost was gained from American Webco camshafts.

From 1975 to 1979 he worked in conjunction with Peter McNab, and their P & M chassis gained a reputation for being among the world's best for taming powerful Honda and Kawasaki fours.

When that partnership ended, new business presented itself to Peckett in the form of owners wishing to make classic triples competitive for historic racing. In the mid-eighties Peckett dusted down his original Trident and returned it to competition. He then sold it to Phil Godfrey, who prepared it for Phil Davenport to race in CRMC events.

Still working under the P & M banner from his West London base, Peckett built his own T150 classic racer in 1988, and has been developing products to give triples improved performance ever since, often collaborating with Miles Engineering

By 1995, six P & M racing triples were in action and many more incorporated his products or tuning work. Peckett built himself a long-stroke 930cc engine, which indicated a power output of 100.4bhp at the gearbox sprocket on the dynamometer of London's Mistral Engineering.

Peckett parts for racers include Omega forged pistons, crankshafts lightened by 11lb (5kg), newly manufactured high-strength cylinder blocks, and oil-free belt primary drives. The latter use an elongated gearbox mainshaft to carry a multiplate clutch, which is part of the conversion.

P & M-built engines usually incorporate American Carrillo connecting rods, Megacycle camshafts and special valve springs based on the S & W type used by factory racers. Original spark plug apertures are blanked off and 10mm plugs used in relocated postions. Peckett has also used cylinder heads with two 8mm plugs per cylinder.

*Peckett belt primary drive, including racing clutch.*

*Peckett copy of works squish head.*

Squish heads and pistons based on the works pattern have been developed, as have Tuftrided stainless steel valves with detachable hardened end-caps to eliminate the age-old problem of valve stem failure.

## Triple Cycles

East Londoner Phil Pick bought a triple for road riding when he was employed afloat as a maritime engineer in 1976. He then built a racing Trident, and became so embroiled in Triumph twin and triple engines that he came ashore to set up his own specialist business, Triple Cycles, in Ilford, Essex.

Pick specializes in engine work for road and track, and runs a busy specialist spares business conducted mainly by mail order. Through preparing and sponsoring racing machines he developed his own ideas for increased performance and reliability. In collaboration with P & M, Triple Cycles has produced a high-capacity oil pump to improve the lubrication and cooling of triple engines.

A Triple Cycles five-speed close-ratio conversion, manufactured to Pick's specifications at RT Quaife Engineering, allows a set of ratios suitable for racing to be arranged in a post-1972 triple gearbox.

Triple Cycles sponsored Steve Veasey, one of the main contenders in the titanic CRMC triples battles of the late eighties, on a 750cc Miles-framed Trident, and more latterly, evergreen racer Alan Walsh on his production class T150.

## Rebuilds by Rustler

Martin Russell, a Small Heath employee from 1967 to 1974, is proprietor of Rustler Racing, appropriately accommodated in the the former NVT development shop on Mackadown Lane in Kitts Green, Birmingham. He rebuilds triple engines for both road and

*Triple Cycles' high capacity oil pump.*

*Triple Cycles' 750 Triumph at Brands Hatch with Steve Veasey aboard.*

track, and carries out 'short' T150 frame conversions to make chassis with increased ground clearance, similar to the factory's production racing dodge. Russell explained:

> The works frames retain the 'correct' geometry of a road bike, with the gearbox sprocket, rear sprocket and swinging arm pivot in line when the rear suspension is at half travel, but I alter it slightly.
>
> On the North chassis, the pivot is set slightly above the line, which lessens the effect of chain torque during acceleration and helps prevent the rear 'squatting'. I use similar geometry when I convert the standard frame.

## John Sims

Since buying a Miles Trident in 1980, John Sims estimates that he has built a total of twenty racing triples both for Miles Engineering and his own riders. A former racing car chassis constructor, Sims set up Trident Engineering in north-west London, where he works on road and race triples.

Alex George, who co-rode Slippery Sam with Dave Croxford in the 1975 TT and campaigned a North-framed triple through the late seventies, made his historic racing comeback on a Sims Triumph, with a run of wins in 1992 that included winning the CRMC F750 championship and the Classic TT Unlimited race, in which another Sims-built Trident, ridden by Asa Moyce, finished second. Trident Engineering products include a lightened racing crankshaft and a belt primary drive conversion, which includes a Mick Hemmings clutch.

## Big Banger

One of the most successful triple équipes in international historic racing has been that of South London businessman Alf Mountford. The first North-framed racer he acquired was the Triumph-badged BSA

*Tank-off view of a Sims racer with belt primary drive and relocated spark plugs. Hoses and deflector keep the area around carburettors cool.*

*Alex George on John Sims' 750 Triumph in the CRMC Unlimited Race of the Year at Snetterton in 1991.*

*Lightweight crankshaft by Trident Engineering.*

Percy Tait used after he relinquished his 1971 works machine. Mountford then bought a Triumph built by the Boyer Team from Norman Miles, and built a third machine with a Miles chassis.

Mountford's best-known rider is Leicestershire's Colin Breeze, who has notched up dozens of wins in major events, including Vintage Daytona, historic F750 racing at Monza and Paul Ricard in France, and the CRMC Race of the Year. Breeze usually rides the 'Big-'Un', a BSA with a long-stroke engine said to produce phenomenal power at relatively low revs. Its capacity has varied between 890cc and 1,000cc. The machine has magnesium-bodied Amal Concentric carburettors made for NVT in the mid-seventies and a belt primary transmission developed for triples by Mountford's other rider, Bob Hirst, in 1985.

## Colin Aldridge

A lifelong racing fan, Colin Aldridge has always been fascinated by the BSA and Triumph triples since seeing – and hearing them – in the match races.

He bought a Miles chassis to build a 750cc Triumph in 1988; this was later englarged to 830cc and joined by a 750cc BSA version. Among numerous other successes, his machines notched an outstanding record in Classic TT and Southern 100 races at the Billown circuit on the Isle of Man, where Aldridge now lives.

Manx rider Kenny Harrison switched from modern raceware to win seven races at Billown, telling Aldridge that the triple's handling was superior to that of his Honda RC30. Other riders used to modern machinery who have enjoyed racing Aldridge's machines include Glen English, Mark Farmer and Ray Swann. However, Aldridge decided to withdraw from sponsorship after Farmer was killed on a modern machine in practice for the 1995 TT races.

## Ian Rowell

When New Zealand race ace Robert Holden won the 1996 Formula 750 race at Daytona, some people jumped to the conclusion that his Miles-framed Triumph triple might be a 850, but post-race measurement confirmed that it was a mere 750. The machine was built by Ian Rowell, of Surrey, England, using an engine thought to have a works pedigree.

Rowell's triple now runs with a lightened crankshaft, a Peckett gas-flowed head, 33mm-bore Amal Concentrics and a belt primary drive to a gearbox with Triple Cycles internals. Its claimed output is 84bhp at the rear wheel. In the 1994 Unlimited Classic race at the Ulster Grand Prix, Holden beat another top triples competitor, Dave Pither, aboard the 850cc Miles Trident he rides for sponsor Geoff Thompson. In 1995, the New Zealander flew through a speed trap at Ulster's Dundrod public roads circuit at 152mph (245km/h). UK rider Micky Cook campaigns the machine in UK club racing and won the 1992 CRMC Race of the Year. Holden was killed practising for the 1996 TT on a modern machine.

## Italian Renaissance

Italy's thriving *Super Tre* team has built up a fleet of ten machines with Miles chassis, which compete in historic F750 races in Italy and France and also at Vintage Daytona.

The man behind the squad of BSAs and Triumphs is Milan-based Domenico Pettinari. He began working on Triumphs in 1960 and was part of the works-supported Koelliker team in the 1970s. In the winter of 1990–1 he teamed up with former Koelliker rider, Vanni Blegi, to build a triple racer using a Miles chassis. Blegi partnered former Koelliker rider and twice 250cc world champion, Walter Villa, in Monza's international 100-mile (160km) historic F750 race.

*Numero Tre-sponsored riders in 1993: Giovanni Provenzano (left) and Vanni Blegi. Both rode for the Italian importer's Triumph team in the seventies.*

*Miles-framed triple racers lined up at Team Tre headquarters in Milan.*

More machines were built, and other seventies' triples racers Gianfranco Bonera and Giovanni Provenzano joined the team – then called Triple Team – to score several successes at Maggione and Vallelunga. Former world champion Phil Read also had guest rides with the équipe in 1991 and 1992.

Sponsorship was provided by Italian Hinckley Triumph importer *Numero Tre* from 1993, since when former MV Agusta and Koelliker team rider Bonera has notched up a string of wins, twice winning the Italian class championship on one of Pettinari's Miles triples. For 1996 the team complement was six T150s, three A75s and one T160, all in the Miles chassis.

## Statesiders

Rob North has remained active in America, and by 1996 he estimated having made a total of more than ninety frames, including some for non-triple engines. As well as taking commissions to build fresh frames, North restores existing machines for owners. He favours TIG welding rather than brazing nowadays, but otherwise his product is to the original formula and may take a year from order to delivery.

One of the best known triples to compete with success in American Historic Racing Motorcycle Association events has a non-North frame. It is the ex-Dick Mann BSA preserved by Team Obsolete, the New York-based équipe run by Robert Iannucci, a pioneer of historic racing in the United States. Like other works machines originally based at Duarte, it was reframed with a lightweight North-pattern Wenco chassis for 1973. That year also saw the repaint to Triumph colours, which may explain why the BSA now carries a TRX prefixed engine number, as applied to Triumph Hurricane roadsters with inclined BSA-type engines. Such a code would have maintained its AMA legality as a Triumph. Now back in BSA colours, the machine has many victories to its credit, mainly in the hands of TO riders John Cronshaw and Dave Roper. Mann reacquainted himself with the machine to track test it for *Classic Racer* magazine in 1986, calling the BSA the best-handling bike he had ever ridden.

# 9   A New Breed of Triumph Triples

The Triumph name was reborn when John Bloor, a successful but publicity-shy Midlands house builder and lifelong Triumph admirer, moved in to buy the marque in 1983. The result was to be a new Triumph triple for the nineties.

When the Meriden Co-operative faced final close-down, Bloor purchased Triumph manufacturing rights, all patents and the trademarks. He recruited a team of designers and engineers, a few of them ex-Meriden personnel, and launched an ambitious – and risky – multi-million pound project. Commercially viable new motorcycles would be designed, and a plant created in which to manufacture them in volume.

Bloor's substantial financial resources, both from his own private companies and development grants, meant that he was able to make the large investment required – estimated at £65 million – over several years before seeing a return.

The whole operation was veiled in secrecy. Previous attempts to create a credible post-Trident British Superbike, notably the misguided NVT Cosworth Challenge scheme

and the Hesketh debacle of the seventies, had been highly publicized with the aim of raising the the type of capital that Bloor already possessed. Expectations had been raised but not fulfilled, causing disappointment and cynicism. Norton Motors at Shenstone persevered with the Meriden-born Wankel engine as the basis of an eighties Superbike, but the company had dubious finances and the design stood little chance of meeting emissions approval in overseas markets.

## CLEAN BREAK

Bloor was determined not to go down in history as yet another Glorious British Failure, and he made a clean break with the old industry. He did, however, start out with a Meriden project, the dohc eight-valve 900cc Diana twin, which had been displayed at Britain's annual Motor Cycle Show in 1982. That engine, designed by Brian Jones in collaboration with Sussex engine company Weslake, was put to one side as soon as Bloor had decided that something better would be needed.

Work started on new power units, and a modular approach, not unlike the system advocated by Bert Hopwood since the fifties, was adopted. The new range of transverse multi-cylinder Triumph engines would all have the same 76mm cylinder bore size, and the liquid-cooled units would be manufactured in two basic configurations, with three

*Hinckley Triumph logo.*

208

## David Green – a life of Triumphs

David Green participated in the design of both generations of Triumph triples. As senior draughtsman at Meriden, he drew up plans for the Trident T150 in the mid-sixties with pencil and paper. Twenty years later, he found himself shaping three-cylinder machines for John Bloor, this time using computer-aided design techniques.

Green had started at Triumph Engineering as the drawing office tea-boy in 1944, and his love of the marque prompted him to stay firmly at his post after the 1973 closure and occupation. When redundancy finally came in the eighties he imagined that at the age of fifty-five his career in the motorcycle industry was at an end.

But within weeks Green was invited to meet John Bloor, and asked if he would join his newly formed team. 'I was overawed by the confidence Bloor showed in us before he ever had a product to sell,' Green told the author. He was given help and encouragement to learn computer design, and became a senior member of the Hinckley staff.

When he retired from Triumph in the summer of 1995, David Green was one of a very few people of his generation who could claim to have been employed by the same British motorcycle maker all his working life.

*David Green in 1995.*

on a new factory on a ten-acre site in an industrial zone on the northern outskirts of Hinckley, a Leicestershire town close to several important road routes. As he was bringing employment to the area, Bloor received assistance from local authorities. Fitting inside the new plant got under way in 1986, and the most modern manufacturing equipment was installed.

## NEW TRIPLES REVEALED

Despite the high level of secrecy, unauthorized pictures of one of the new Triumph engines were leaked in the January 1990 issue of *Classic Bike* magazine. The author had been responsible for this, and a stern phone call from Hinckley left him in no doubt that he was out of favour with the reborn Triumph company!

New Triumphs were finally revealed to the public at Germany's Cologne Show in the autumn of 1990 and the range of six machines included four triples. The basic unfaired threes in 750 and 900cc form carried the Trident name, whilst the faired triples also had traditional Meriden names: Trophy for the tourer and Daytona for the sportster.

and four transverse cylinders. Crankshafts giving strokes of 55mm or 65mm would be used, making it possible to build triples of 748cc or 885cc, and fours of 998cc and 1,180cc using many common components. Four-valve combustion chambers, envisaged by Hopwood and Hele decades earlier and universally employed on Japanese multis since the late seventies, were specified.

While a small design team toiled at an industrial unit near Coventry, work began

## Alistair Copland – testing times

Another industry man who had two working lives with British triples is Alistair 'Jock' Copland. He originally joined Meriden's Service Department on leaving the army in 1958 and became a road tester.

He raced Manx Nortons at weekends and in the sixties became a regular competitor in the Manx Grand Prix, but was not an official Meriden racer. 'I was never invited. The nearest I got to a works ride was aboard John Woodward's Bonneville, which was almost a factory bike,' Copland told the author. His first competitive outing on a T150 came about via Ken Buckmaster, the Hertfordshire racer with contacts at Triumph who campaigned Bonnevilles, and then a short-framed Trident.

When Meriden closed in 1973 Copland found other work in engineering, and bought one of the final batch of Rob North frames delivered to Meriden in 1973 and later taken to Kitts Green. He built an endurance racer with a virtually standard engine and campaigned it around Europe for several years.

Copland was working at the Sussex-based Weslake company during its collaboration with the Meriden Co-operative on the Diana project, and from there he went to work for Bloor. He was one of several experienced riders who put many miles on Hinckley machines before production commenced.

'Hinckley is very different from Meriden,' recalled Copland, who runs the brake test facility in Triumph's design and development department.

Perhaps unable to grasp that such wholly modern engines had come from a British factory, some people seized on an enduring rumour that the machines had been produced in collaboration with Kawasaki. This groundless theory may have started because Triumph chose to place the dohc's chain drive on the right hand side of the cylinder block, creating a shape reminiscent of the Japanese company's products since the eighties.

Various items, including the connecting rods, disc brake systems, instrumentation and electronics *were* sourced in Japan, however, while forgings for crankshafts and camshafts came from Germany. Those patriotic Britons who frowned on this policy did not explain where large quantities of such parts could be reliably obtained in the UK. After all, the demise of the old motorcycle industry in Britain had been accompanied by the disappearance of the specialist contractors who once supported it.

In fact, it had been Bloor's aim to work steadily towards using an ever-increasing number of British made components, and by 1996 Hinckley could claim that in-house products made up 40 per cent of its machines, an extremely high proportion by the standards of modern car and motorcycle makers.

## BALANCING ACT

The Hinckley triple follows Meriden practice by having crankshafts with throws displaced at 120 degrees. Otherwise differences are legion. The crankcase is horizontally-split, and to ensure absolute smoothness, a balancer shaft running at engine speed is added ahead of the crankshaft and driven from it by gears. Unusually for a motorcycle engine, wet liners are a feature of the cylinder blocks. Primary drive is by helical gears to a wet multi-plate clutch and a six-speed gearbox, and the alternator is placed behind the cylinders along with a compact starter motor.

To the purist's eye, the liquid-cooled Hinckley engines cannot compete with the original triples on looks, but Triumph's products nevertheless succeed in being fully in tune with nineties' fashion.

The chassis is surprisingly old fashioned in concept. Although up-to-date single-shock rear suspension with a cast-alloy swinging-arm has been used, the main frame's large diameter tubular spine looks ominously like the old Umberslade Hall chassis adopted for the final Meriden Triumph twins for 1971. Running over the engine, rather than around it in the North style now favoured by many makers, it creates a high and rather ungainly profile. New frames announced for 1997 have addressed this problem, however.

But when production started rolling in 1991 and machines were issued for press testing in a market crowded with refined and all-powerful Superbikes, the Triumphs earned a high degree of approval. Not necessarily faster, better-handling or better-braked than the well-established opposition, they were neverthless good enough to be judged on an equal footing. That was the breakthrough Hinckley had made as a latter-day British maker. Its products could be evaluated objectively, without making pathetic allowances for valiant effort because of their country of origin. The Triumphs proved extremely satisfying machines to ride, with a degree of character lacking in some of their market rivals, and sales throughout Europe saw returns start to be made on the enormous outlay.

## NINETIES MODELS

The Trident proved deserving of the celebrated name, especially the long-stroke 900, with its immense mid-range pulling power. Variations on the triple theme came thick and fast through the nineties. The 900 Tiger, with the African desert-racer style much

*Trident, nineties-style. Triumph's basic unfaired 900cc triple.*

loved across mainland Europe, arrived for 1993 with wire wheels and a detuned engine. Then came a big change in company styling policy with the 900cc Thunderbird launched for 1995.

Previously, Triumph had appeared to have turned its back on tradition. A revised logo had been introduced, and some old-established Triumph dealers in Britain were dismayed to find that they would not be asked to sell Hinckley products. But concentration on launching into the potentially huge American market made some exploitation of Triumph's history inevitable. Triumph was aware that its reputation had endured from the old days across America, strictly in connection with the Meriden twins, many of which were still in use.

The USA has a sizeable constituency of Superbike admirers, but there is also a huge market for highway cruisers, following the pattern of US-built Harley-Davidsons and Hondas. These retro-styled, chromium covered machines built for steady 55mph (88km/h) touring and street cruising are sold by all major makers in the United States.

# Daytona 900/Speed Triple/Sprint/Trophy 900 (1996)

## Engine

| | |
|---|---|
| Type | liquid-cooled dohc transverse triple |
| Capacity | 885cc |
| Bore and stroke | 76 × 65mm |
| Compression ratio | 10.6:1 |
| Carburation | 3 × 36mm Mikuni CV flat-slide |
| Ignition | digital electronic |
| Claimed output | 98ps (96.6bhp) @ 9,000rpm |

## Transmission

| | |
|---|---|
| Primary drive | helical gears |
| Clutch | wet, multiplate |
| Gearbox | six-speed (Speed Triple five-speed) |
| Final drive | chain |

## Electrical

Alternator, 12 volt battery

## Cycle parts

| | |
|---|---|
| Frame | tubular spine, with engine as stressed member |

## Suspension

| | |
|---|---|
| Front | telescopic fork with triple rate springs (dual rate on Trophy) Adjustable pre-load and damping (except Trophy) |
| Rear | alloy swinging arm, single adjustable spring/damper unit |

## Wheels and tyres

| | |
|---|---|
| Front | three-spoked alloy, 120/70 × 17in |
| Rear | three-spoked alloy, 180/55 × 17in |

## Brakes

| | |
|---|---|
| Front | 2 × 310mm floating discs, 2 × 4-piston calipers |
| Rear | 1 × 255mm disc, 1 × 2-piston caliper |

## Dimensions

*Daytona*

| | |
|---|---|
| Seat height | 31in (790mm) |
| Wheelbase | 58.6in (1,490mm) |
| Dry weight | 470lb (213kg) |

*Speed Triple*

| | |
|---|---|
| Dry weight | 461lb (209kg) |

*Sprint*

| | |
|---|---|
| Seat height | 30.7in (780mm) |
| Dry weight | 474lb (215kg) |

*Trophy 900*

| | |
|---|---|
| Dry weight | 485lb (220kg) |

# Adventurer/Thunderbird (1996)

## Engine

| | |
|---|---|
| Capacity | 885cc |
| Bore and stroke | 76 × 65mm |
| Compression ratio | 10:1 |
| Carburation | 3 × 36mm Mikuni CV flat-slide |
| Ignition | digital electronic |
| Claimed output | 70ps (69bhp) @ 8,000rpm |

## Transmission

| | |
|---|---|
| Gearbox | five-speed |

## Suspension

| | |
|---|---|
| Front | telescopic fork, triple rate springs |
| Rear | Monoshock adjustable for pre-load |

## Wheels and tyres

| | |
|---|---|
| Front | 36-spoked alloy rim, 110/80 × 18in |
| Rear: | 40-spoked alloy rim, 160/80 × 16in or 150/80 × 16in |

## Brakes

| | |
|---|---|
| Front | 320mm disc |
| Rear | 285mm disc |

## Dimensions

| | |
|---|---|
| Seat height | 29.5in (750mm) |
| Wheelbase | 61in (1,550mm) |
| Dry weight | 496lb (225kg) |

By blending the style of the heavy cruiser with old Triumph trademarks, including a rounded fuel tank complete with Meriden's legendary grille badge of 1957–66, Hinckley came up with the ideal machine to complement its other machines on launch in America.

The theme was continued with the Adventurer triple of 1996, with megaphone-style silencers and late sixties-style Meriden tank badges. For the highway cruising set, a pillion passenger's backrest is available as an accessory.

Admirers of the original triples, however, saw the Sprint all-rounder, the sporty Speed Triple of 1994 and the later Super III as more worthy descendants of Hele's speed machines of the seventies.

To promote the Speed Triple, Triumph has backed a UK road race series for machines in standard tune with minor changes permitted to their cycle parts. Familar names from earlier triples history have been involved, including Boyer Racing. Past Masters races for famous motorcycling names have also been staged at the Mallory Park circuit in

*Useful and rapid all-rounder, the half-faired 900cc Sprint.*

# Tiger (1996)

## Engine

As Trident except:

| | |
|---|---|
| Claimed Output | 85ps (84bhp) @ 8,000rpm |

## Transmission

As Trident

## Suspension

| | |
|---|---|
| Front | telescopic fork |
| Rear | single spring/damper unit with adjustable pre-load and damping |

## Wheels and tyres

| | |
|---|---|
| Front | 36-spoked alloy rim, 110/80 × 19in |
| Rear | 40-spoked rim, 140/80 × 17in |

## Brakes

| | |
|---|---|
| Front | 2 × 276mm floating discs, 2 × 2-piston calipers |
| Rear | 1 × 255mm disc, 1 × 2 piston caliper |

*Start of a Past Masters race for Speed Triples at Mallory Park in 1995, with Phil Read (1) quick off the mark. Former Meriden triple racers are John Cooper (8) and Dave Aldana (7).*

*New generation Speed Triple for 1997, with alloy frame. Centre of gravity is lower and fuel-injected 885cc engine produces a claimed 108bhp.*

collaboration with the same dealer-entrants. Those who have participated include former works BSA triple racers John Cooper and David Aldana.

By 1996 it was clear that Triumph's triple was a favourite with customers. Three-cylinder machines had accounted for a convincing 90 per cent of Hinckley's sales. The Daytona triples have outsold Daytona fours by a ratio of more than three to one, and the older Trophy triples bettered their four-cylinder counterparts by four to one. Hinckley's sales chief, Bruno Tagliaferri, told the author:

Our engineers tell us that it is a challenge to get a three to work as well as a four, but we are absolutely committed to triples.

The three-cylinder engine is our trademark, in the way that Ducati has its V-twin and Honda has its four. Nowadays a manufacturer must offer something that is highly individual to compete with the Japanese.

## Trident 750/900 (1996)

### Engine

| | |
|---|---|
| Capacity | 749cc/885cc |
| Bore and stroke | 76 × 55m/76 × 65mm |
| Compression ratio | 11:1/10.6:1 |
| Carburation | 3 × 36mm Mikuni CV flat-slide |
| Ignition | digital electronic |
| Claimed output | 90ps (88.7bhp) @ 10,000rpm |
| | 98ps (96.6bhp) @ 9,000rpm |

### Transmission

| | |
|---|---|
| Primary drive | helical gears |
| Clutch | wet, multiplate |
| Gearbox | six-speed |
| Final drive | chain |

### Suspension

| | |
|---|---|
| Front | telescopic fork, triple rate springs |
| Rear | alloy swinging arm, single spring/damper unit with adjustable pre-load (and on 900) rebound damping |

### Wheels and tyres

| | |
|---|---|
| Front | alloy six-spoke, 120/70 × 17in |
| Rear | alloy six-spoke, 160/60 × 18in |

### Brakes

| | |
|---|---|
| Front | 2 × 296mm floating discs, 2 × 2-piston calipers |
| Rear | 1 × 255mm disc, 1 × 2-piston caliper |

### Dimensions

| | |
|---|---|
| Seat height | 30.5in (775mm) |
| Wheelbase | 59.4in (1,509mm) |
| Dry weight | 467lb (212kg) |

## Super III (1996)

As Daytona 900 except for:

### Engine

| | |
|---|---|
| Compression ratio | 12:1 |
| Claimed output | 115ps (113.4bhp) @ 9,500rpm |

### Wheels and tyres

Sport compound tyres

### Brakes

| | |
|---|---|
| Front | 2 × 310mm floating discs, 2 × 6 piston calipers |
| Dry weight | 465lb (211kg) |

One of the main claims Hinckley has made for its products is that they are durable and finished with the worst British weather and corrosive road salt in mind. So it looks certain that there will be Triumph triples on the roads for many years to come. And despite silencing regulations, a hint of that unique sound is still there.

# Appendix

## DIRECTORY OF CLUBS AND SERVICES

The following list of addresses is provided for owners and potential owners of BSA and Triumph triples. The addresses were correct when this book went to press, but are subject to change, especially in the case of voluntary club officials. Fuller, up-to-date details of specialist clubs and services can be found in the leading classic motorcycling magazines.

### Trident and Rocket 3 Owners Club

H. J. Allen
Secretary
50 Sylmond Gardens
Rushden
Northamptonshire NN10 9EJ

### BSA Owners Club

PO Box 4
Hythe
Southampton PO45 5ZB

### Triumph Owners Motorcycle Club

Mrs E. Page
101 Great Knightleys
Basildon
Essex SS15 5AN
(stamped addressed envelopes should accompany postal communications to club officials)

### Triumph International Owners Club (USA)

PO Box 6676
Holliston
Massachusetts
USA

### Classic Racing Motorcycle Club (CRMC)

Tim Jefferson
33 Healey Avenue
High Wycombe
Buckinghamshire HP13 7JP

### International Historic Racing Organisation (IHRO)

Smithy Cottage
Liverpool Road
Bickerstaffe
Lancashire L39 0EF

### American Historic Motorcycle Racing Association (AHMRA)

PO Box 882
Wausau
Wisconsin 54402-0882
USA

# SPECIALIST TRADERS

**Reg Allen**
37–41 Grosvenor Road
Hanwell
London W7 1HP
Tel/fax: 0181 567 1974

**Norman Hyde**
Rigby Close
Heathcote
Warwick CV34 6TL
Tel: 01926 497375
Fax: 01926 400807

**Miles Engineering**
Unit 4
Princes Works
Princes Road
Teddington
Middlesex
Tel: 0181 943 2022

**P & M Motorcycles**
8 Setstar Industrial Estate
Transport Avenue
Brentford
Middlesex TW8 9HF
Tel: 0181 847 4807

**Performance Motorcycles**
Chapels Cottage
Leysters
Nr Leominster
Hereford
Tel: 01568 750658

**Carl Rosner Motorcycles**
Sanderstead Station Approach
Sanderstead Road
South Croydon CR2 0PL
Tel: 0181 657 0121
Fax: 0181 651 0596

**Rustler Racing**
Mackadown Lane
Kitts Green
Birmingham B33 0LQ
Tel: 0121 784 8266

**Sussex Triples**
12 Walters Cottages
Wadhurst
East Sussex TN5 6BG
Tel: 01892 783434

**Trident Engineering**
343A Rayners Lane
Harrow
Middlesex
Tel: 0181 868 1476

**Triple Cycles**
228 Henley Road
Ilford
Essex IG1 2TW
Tel/fax: 0181 478 4807

**LP Williams**
(also incorporates JR Technical
Publications)
Common Lane Industrial Estate
Common Lane
Kenilworth
Warwickshire CV8 2EL
Tel/fax: 01926 854948

## USA

**Big D Cycles**
3600 West Davis
Dallas
Texas 75211
Tel: 214 339 2285

**Collier's Cycles**
7401 Charlotte Pike
Nashville
Tennessee 37209

Tel: 615 353 1919

**Dave Quinn Motorcycles Inc.**
335 Lichfield Turnpike
Bethany
Connecticut 06524-3505

Tel: 203 393 2651
Fax: 203 393 1725

**Klempf's Motorcycle Repair**
204 20th Street SW
Rochester
Minnesota 55902

Tel: 507 288 8393

**Rob North**
Unit B
1747 Broadway
Chula Vista
California 91911

Tel: 619 474 6424

**Rabers European Parts**
1984 Stone Avenue
San Jose
California 95125

Tel: 408 998 4495

**Triple Specialities**
137 East Fremont
Tempe
Arizona 85282

Tel: 602 897 7761

Other classic BSA and Triumph parts, repair and restoration specialists also cater for Rocket 3 and Trident.

**Triumph Motorcycles Ltd**
Jacknell Road
Dodwells Bridge Industrial Estate
Hinckley
Leicestershire LE10 3BS

Tel: 01455 251 700
Fax: 01455 251 367

# Index